LANGUAGE A

Dorothy S. Stri
Donna E. Alvermann and
ADVISORY BOARD: Richard Allingto
Anne Haas Dyson, Carole Edelsky, Mary J.

MW01071146

Teens Choosing to Read: Fostering Social,
Emotional, and Intellectual Growth Through Books
GAY IVEY & PETER JOHNSTON

Critical Encounters in Secondary English:
Teaching Literary Theory to Adolescents,
4th Edition
DEBORAH APPLEMAN

Reading With Purpose: Selecting and Using
Children's Literature for Inquiry and Engagement
ERIKA THULIN DAWES, KATIE EGAN CUNNINGHAM,
GRACE ENRIQUEZ, & MARY ANN CAPPIELLO

Black Immigrant Literacies: Intersections of Race,
Language, and Culture in the Classroom
PATRIANN SMITH

Core Practices for Teaching Multilingual Students:
Humanizing Pedagogies for Equity
MEGAN MADIGAN PEERCY, JOHANNA M. TIGERT, &
DAISY E. FREDRICKS

Bringing Sports Culture to the English Classroom:
An Interest-Driven Approach to Literacy
Instruction
LUKE RODESILER

Culturally Sustaining Literacy Pedagogies:
Honoring Students' Heritages, Literacies, and
Languages
SUSAN CHAMBERS CANTRELL, DORIS WALKER-DALHOUSE,
& ALTHIER M. LAZAR, EDS.

Curating a Literacy Life:
Student-Centered Learning With Digital Media
WILLIAM KIST

Understanding the Transnational Lives and
Literacies of Immigrant Children
JUNGMIN KWON

The Administration and Supervision of Literacy
Programs, 6th Edition
SHELLEY B. WEPNER & DIANA J. QUATROCHE, EDS.

Writing the School House Blues: Literacy, Equity,
and Belonging in a Child's Early Schooling
ANNE HAAS DYSON

Playing With Language: Improving Elementary
Reading Through Metalinguistic Awareness
MARCY ZIPKE

Restorative Literacies:
Creating a Community of Care in Schools
DEBORAH L. WOLTER

Compose Our World: Project-Based Learning in
Secondary English Language Arts
ALISON G. BOARDMAN, ANTERO GARCIA, BRIDGET
DALTON, & JOSEPH L. POLMAN

Digitally Supported Disciplinary Literacy for
Diverse K–5 Classrooms
JAMIE COLWELL, AMY HUTCHISON,
& LINDSAY WOODWARD

The Reading Turn-Around with Emergent
Bilinguals: A Five-Part Framework for Powerful
Teaching and Learning (Grades K–6)
AMANDA CLAUDIA WAGER, LANE W. CLARKE,
& GRACE ENRIQUEZ

Race, Justice, and Activism in Literacy Instruction
VALERIE KINLOCH, TANJA BURKHARD,
& CARLOTTA PENN, EDS.

Letting Go of Literary Whiteness:
Antiracist Literature Instruction for White Students
CARLIN BORSHEIM-BLACK
& SOPHIA TATIANA SARIGIANIDES

The Vulnerable Heart of Literacy:
Centering Trauma as Powerful Pedagogy
ELIZABETH DUTRO

Amplifying the Curriculum: Designing Quality
Learning Opportunities for English Learners
AÍDA WALQUI & GEORGE C. BUNCH, EDS.

Arts Integration in Diverse K–5 Classrooms:
Cultivating Literacy Skills and Conceptual
Understanding
LIANE BROUILLETTE

Translanguaging for Emergent Bilinguals: Inclusive
Teaching in the Linguistically Diverse Classroom
DANLING FU, XENIA HADJIOANNOU, & XIAODI ZHOU

Before Words: Wordless Picture Books and the
Development of Reading in Young Children
JUDITH T. LYSAKER

Seeing the Spectrum: Teaching English Language
Arts to Adolescents with Autism
ROBERT ROZEMA

A Think-Aloud Approach to Writing Assessment:
Analyzing Process and Product with Adolescent
Writers
SARAH W. BECK

"We've Been Doing It Your Way Long Enough":
Choosing the Culturally Relevant Classroom
JANICE BAINES, CARMEN TISDALE, & SUSI LONG

Summer Reading: Closing the Rich/Poor
Reading Achievement Gap, 2nd Edition
RICHARD L. ALLINGTON & ANNE MCGILL-FRANZEN, EDS.

Educating for Empathy:
Literacy Learning and Civic Engagement
NICOLE MIRRA

Preparing English Learners for College and Career:
Lessons from Successful High Schools
MARÍA SANTOS ET AL.

Reading the Rainbow: LGBTQ-Inclusive Literacy
Instruction in the Elementary Classroom
CAITLIN L. RYAN & JILL M. HERMANN-WILMARTH

Educating Emergent Bilinguals: Policies, Programs,
and Practices for English Learners, 2nd Edition
OFELIA GARCÍA & JO ANNE KLEIFGEN

continued

For volumes in the NCRLL Collection (edited by JoBeth Allen and Donna E. Alvermann) and the Practitioners
Bookshelf Series (edited by Celia Genishi and Donna E. Alvermann), as well as other titles in this series,
please visit www.tcpress.com

Language and Literacy Series, *continued*

Teens Choosing to Read

Fostering Social, Emotional, and Intellectual Growth Through Books

Gay Ivey
Peter Johnston

TEACHERS COLLEGE PRESS

TEACHERS COLLEGE | COLUMBIA UNIVERSITY
NEW YORK AND LONDON

Published by Teachers College Press,® 1234 Amsterdam Avenue, New York, NY 10027

Copyright © 2023 by Teachers College, Columbia University

Front cover silhouettes by Kirsty Pargeter / Freepik. Texture by Kseniya Lapteva / Unsplash.

All rights reserved. No part of this publication may be reproduced or transmitted in any form or by any means, electronic or mechanical, including photocopy, or any information storage and retrieval system, without permission from the publisher. For reprint permission and other subsidiary rights requests, please contact Teachers College Press, Rights Dept.: tcpressrights@tc.columbia.edu

The research for this book was partially funded by an International Literacy Association Elva Knight Research Grant to the authors. Some of the student, parent, and teacher quotes used in this book were previously published in the following articles and are requoted without individual references with the permission of the publishers:

Ivey, G., & Johnston, P. H. (2013). Engagement with young adult literature: Outcomes and processes. *Reading Research Quarterly*, 48(3), 255–275. https://doi.org/10.1002/rrq.46. Reprinted with permission of the International Literacy Association.

Ivey, G., & Johnston, P. H. (2015). Engaged reading as a collaborative, transformative practice. *Journal of Literacy Research*, 47(3), 297–327. https://doi.org/10.1177/1086296X15619731. Reprinted with permission of the Literacy Research Association/Sage.

Johnston, P., & Ivey, G. (2016). Classroom talk and individual differences in reading. In P. Afflerbach (Ed.), *Handbook of individual differences in reading: Text and context*. Routledge. Reprinted by permission of Taylor & Francis Group.

Ivey, G., & Johnston, P. H. (2017). Emerging adolescence in engaged reading communities. *Language Arts*, 94(3), 159–169. Reprinted with permission of the National Council of Teachers of English.

Ivey, G., & Johnston, P. H. (2018). Engaging disturbing books. *Journal of Adolescent and Adult Literacy*, 62(2), 143–150. https://doi.org/10.1002 /jaal.883. Reprinted with permission of the International Literacy Association.

Library of Congress Cataloging-in-Publication Data is available at loc.gov

ISBN 978-0-8077-6868-6 (paper)
ISBN 978-0-8077-6869-3 (hardcover)
ISBN 978-0-8077-8189-0 (ebook)

Printed on acid-free paper
Manufactured in the United States of America

Contents

PART III. NEGOTIATING LITERATURE, TEACHING, AND TEEN DEVELOPMENT

Acknowledgments

It's fair to say that this book started to take shape nearly 20 years ago, when Gay and an 8th-grade English language arts teacher, whom we call Mr. Simmons in the book, began conversations about what it might take for his students to want to read. Gay had been researching this problem, and what she was learning resonated with Mr. Simmons's informed hunches and his vast experiences teaching middle-schoolers.

But it was a group of students one year who helped set in motion the research we report here. In the spring that year Mr. Simmons—at the request of his supervisors and because of low student performance in his school—began using a portion of each class period to review test-taking strategies and released past test items in advance of the upcoming state reading assessment. He wasn't actually excited about this task, and he noticed that neither were students. But some, he noticed, seemed not just inattentive, but also distracted . . . by something that had them staring down at their laps. Upon closer inspection, he could see they were hiding books under their desks. They were reading! But these weren't just any books. They were books by best-selling young adult author Ellen Hopkins, who had recently been a guest speaker in a local community-wide book festival. These books, with realistic and heartbreaking portrayals of drug use, psychological problems, and difficult family relationships, were not to be found in the school library at that time, so it was clear the students had found them in other ways. Plus, these weren't students Mr. Simmons would expect to see reading, even when it was assigned. He knew Gay would be as intrigued by this scene as he was, so he invited her in. It was clear to both of them that if they wanted to understand more about what motivated students to read, the students themselves were pointing the way.

The rest is history. What followed were serious conversations with Mr. Simmons's other 8th-grade teaching colleagues about research, about what they wanted for students, and about what it would take to make it happen. They took a leap of faith and said, "Count us in!" To this day we are blown away by their trust and courage to go against the grain. We are endlessly grateful to them for allowing us into their classrooms and for the learning we experienced together over the years. They helped to change the lives of so many students, and they helped elevate our thinking about what it means to teach. We also thank the school administrators who listened respectfully to what we wanted to do and learn and who gave the green light for the teachers to go off-script in the interest of the students. And although we have not met her, we thank Ellen Hopkins, who writes books that engage and move young people, some in life-changing ways. We are so glad she visited the small community where we conducted this research and showed students that in books, they can find new perspectives on their lives and relationships.

As we studied and wrote about this work, we appreciated the support and feedback we received from our colleagues and graduate students at the University of North Carolina-Greensboro, the University at Albany, the University of Wisconsin–Madison, and James Madison University. We were also aided by funds provided to Gay through the University of Wisconsin–Madison when she served as the Tashia F. Morgridge Chair in Reading, a position generously endowed by John and Tashia Morgridge.

We are grateful to Teachers College Press, and in particular, to our editor, Emily Spangler, who nudged Gay for a book about this nearly a decade ago, who enthusiastically embraced the book when we finally wrote it, and who demonstrated the patience and critical feedback we needed to make it better.

Finally . . . we thank the remarkably articulate 8th-grade students whose voices carry this book. We are endlessly indebted to them (and their consenting parents) for showing us why young people—maybe all of us—should want to read in the first place. We are forever transformed by what they taught us.

We hope you are, too.

Part I

ENGAGING READING, A SOCIAL PHENOMENON

CHAPTER 1

Young Adults Reading Literature (or Not)

I didn't know that books were so interesting until I read one.

—Jeremy, 8th-grader

Adolescents have a lot on their plates. On top of academic pressures, they're busy separating themselves from their parents, deciding who they are, and sorting out their often-fraught social and emotional lives, not to mention their sexuality. (Indeed, some might prefer we not mention their sexuality.) When Julia Moeller and her colleagues asked nearly 22,000 teens how they felt while in school, three-quarters of the words they chose were negative, the top three being "tired," "bored," and "stressed."[1] Teens are so stressed that nearly a third of them have been diagnosed with an anxiety disorder.[2] In 2019, over a third of high school students reported experiencing persistent hopelessness or sadness, and about one in six young adults say they made a suicide plan in the past year. These figures are higher than 10 years earlier by 40% or more.[3] Additionally, more than one in five report being bullied.[4] Perhaps as a result, 8th-graders' drug use increased over 60% in the last 4 years, and by 12th grade, over 60% of teens have abused alcohol.[5] The indicators of teen development do not paint a rosy picture. But then, adolescent life is no bed of roses. Well, not the petals anyway.

You might think these serious issues would dominate conversations about school curricula and communications among school leaders, teachers, and parents and other caregivers. Some would say they have, if you consider the growing accounts of parents who complain to school boards about particular contemporary books and the supposed dangers they pose to their teens' well-being.[6] Never mind that in reality, students are more likely to be assigned traditional, unrelatable books that other adults believe are good for them—in many cases the same books their parents were required to read in school. All involved seem to sidestep the fact that most teens don't read anyway, particularly older teens and especially boys, which is reflected in a persistent gender achievement gap.[7]

But if we are concerned about the pressures of adolescence, it turns out that reading actually is a good place to start the conversation, one that we hope will be fueled by this book. Grounded in hundreds of interviews we conducted with young adults in one school who were extraordinarily engaged in reading (see Appendix A) due to their 8th-grade teachers' efforts, along with extensive additional research, we show that most can become enthusiastic readers and, in the process, circumvent many current adolescent afflictions; experience better family and peer relationships; and become more academically, socially, emotionally, and morally secure. We explain how and why this happens and how it relates to arguments over what students should and shouldn't read. As you will see, young people can be quite articulate about their reading experiences and their lives.

TEENS *CAN* BE ENTHUSIASTIC, ENGAGED READERS

Eighth-grader Marcus announced in class, "I got up early today to read. I woke up, got right in the shower, ate, so then I'd have time to read *Unwind* before I came to school. It's good. I've never done anything like that before." (All young adult books are listed in Appendix B.) Another student told us about reading *Identical*, a 592-page novel-in-verse with alternating narrators that requires readers to infer the complex psychological struggles of its main characters:

> It's like it was good throughout the whole book, and then when you got to the end it confused you, and then you had to go back and read it all over again. Like when I got to the end, I was like . . . what?! And I went back and reread it all, and I was like, whoa!

When 8th-graders, previously not readers, get up early in order to read, or voluntarily reread a long and confusing book, something is happening. Their teachers were not heroic "stand and deliver" types, who, as David Denby puts it, "grabbed [their] students by the throats and shook them into life."[8] Their teachers didn't set out to "teach" particular books. Their initial goal was simply to engage students with books, a goal that led to a cascade of changes in their teaching, which we will document throughout the book. The effects were startling. Students began reading inside and outside of school, at lunch, in math and civics classes. They began talking about their books with each other, with teachers, with parents, grandparents, and other family members. Norma, one of the students, remarked:

> I think it's changed a bunch of 8th-graders. I'll walk down the hallway, and kids will be stuck in their books. And it's amazing how four teachers, or six teachers

can change 250 kids. Just to read and like books. It's crazy because it happened all year long. . . . Yeah, everyone has gotten so much smarter. Like they're all . . . we always talk about books. And it's so crazy. Usually, you would just talk about things that happen outside of school and stuff, and I hear people walking down the hallways talking about books, and I'm like, . . . what has this class come to?

What indeed! As a 10th-grader reflecting on his 8th-grade experience, Miguel observed:

That was a good year for me. That's when my English was better, 'cause I actually read books. I got interested in books, and I read. I read when I had free time. When I was in math, I would start reading. I just liked reading. I don't know why. It just got into me . . . that's when my English was a lot better. I was using a lot bigger words. . . . When we talked about books, everybody was so passionate. They had, like, to argue, to debate, and it was just so . . . I don't know. It was really good. Our conversations were like, the best, 'cause it was about, like, real books, so it just, like, got to us. . . . Different points of view, you know? It was good.

Warming to his subject, he began smiling. Was it a good memory? "Yeah," he says. "It was awesome!" In his mind, returning to 8th grade, specific memories came flooding back:

So, I was in gym class, and maybe Wilson was in there, and we just talked about it. Why do you think she did this [in *The Secret Story of Sonia Rodriguez*]? And then we talked about, like, we just had our different opinions. . . . And then I would go ask, like, questions to Jamad, people that weren't in that class, and ask them about *Gym Candy*. How was that book? What do you think? . . . and I read the WHOLE THING! It was like a big book! I was like, I'm not gonna read that! No way!

These students' experiences buck the norm. American students' attitudes toward reading hit bottom around 8th grade.[9] Only 17% of 13-year-olds report reading daily, and 29% report reading never or hardly ever. Young adults in America are less engaged in reading than those in most other developed countries.[10] Why should we care? Academically, reading engagement improves academic achievement and reduces achievement gaps among groups of students.[11] Perhaps more important, students who are engaged in school have more friends, make better decisions and feel more in control of their lives. They tend to be happier, less lonely, and less likely to get pregnant, get in trouble with the law, or take drugs.[12] Engaged reading is not just about academics; it's a public health issue with serious consequences for teens' social, intellectual, emotional, and moral development.[13]

In that context, we asked Miguel whether his experience in English classes in the two years since leaving 8th grade had been similar. His smile disappeared:

> Honestly? No. My passion for reading has stopped. . . . I really miss that year, because that was the year I read. Now, I don't pick up a book and read. . . . Yeah. I just don't read. . . . I stopped the habit. . . . I just stopped. I completely stopped . . . I just—that was one of the best years. That's the year I read . . . and I use some advices, or like some people's point of view from the book and use it in life today.

The contrast in Miguel's facial expression as he reported these two experiences, from smiling and animated to wistful and dispirited, was striking. We suspect that offering parents a choice of which face they would prefer to see on their adolescent might provoke useful conversations about schooling. Indeed, parents noticed the transformations. Remarking on the change in her daughter, Riley's mother observed:

> Maturity. I'm seeing a confidence in Riley. [In the past] I think she has masked some insecurity. And I hate that . . . I see her as not always so self-absorbed. . . . Reaching out beyond herself to credit other people. Yes, seeing beyond herself, which is huge.

ENGAGING BOOKS

That good books can be transformative is not a new claim, but in this book, we'll document the breadth and depth of these transformations and explore how and why they occur (and why they don't). Notice, for example, that Miguel named specific books (from 2 years earlier). At the end of 8th grade, we asked about a third of the graduating class whether they had read anything that year that they either couldn't stop thinking about or that they absolutely had to talk to somebody about—qualities that we think define an engaging book. Although many students' lists overlapped, the 71 students named 159 distinct titles. [*I've got an idea. Let's make them all read the same book, at the same pace, and address the same discussion points! (see Chapter 13)*]

Critics might say, "Fine, but were they reading The Great Books?"— books such as those advocated by David Denby in *Lit Up: Twenty-Four Books That Can Change Lives.* Generally, no. Nonetheless, students were quite certain that the books they read changed their lives, and them, for the better. And they offered details. For example, Lindsay observed:

> I read a couple of books where people get bullied, and it changes my mind, 'cause in a couple of books I read, people commit suicide for it. And in *Hate*

List, that book is really good, and it changes my mind about how people feel about things. And even, like, a little comment can change someone's life. And, like, the other day, I saw people on Facebook picking on this one girl, like, saying nobody liked her because she was ugly and had no friends. And I kind of put a stop to it. I told them it was wrong and that people commit suicide for it all the time. So, it changed my way of seeing things. Normally I wouldn't have said anything to stop. But now, if I see anything, I stop it.

Lindsay's transformation is increasingly important given the Internet and the fact that young people's empathic concern for others has been falling, quite drastically.[14] Between 1979 and 2009, it fell by nearly half. Their propensity to imagine others' perspectives dropped by over a third.

Most parents would applaud Lindsay's moral agency, her recognition of language as a potential act of violence, and her courage in stepping up to defend another against bullying.

Paradoxically, some of those applauding her will likely object to her reading the book that led to her development because it references suicide. Indeed, we suspect that some adults would object to some of the books the students found meaningful because of issues of race, gender identity, sex, and such. Still others, while celebrating inclusivity in the books, might worry about whether characters were portrayed with cultural sensitivity, as has been the case recently with canonical works such as *Of Mice and Men* and *The Adventures of Huckleberry Finn*.[15]

The various objections to books—particularly those written for young adults—have provoked the recent eruption of book challenges, bannings, and all hell breaking loose at school board meetings.[16] PEN America reports that between July 2021 and June 2022 there were 2,532 cases of book bans, including 1,648 unique titles, and during the first half of 2022-23 school year, there were another 1,477 cases with 800 unique titles, an increase of 28% compared with the prior six school months.[17] This escalation from previous years is being stoked by about 300 parent and community groups, three-quarters of which have formed since 2021. The fact that more than 70% of parents oppose book banning suggests that those calling for censorship represent the minority.[18]

Many, ourselves included, think that just reading a good book changes us. But arguing about whether individual books are good or bad misses the point. Recall that Miguel didn't just name specific books that meant something *to him* (and not necessarily to everyone); he also named his conversations with his peers, which he remembered, in Technicolor, 2 years later: "When we talked about books, everybody was so passionate. They had, like, to argue, to debate. . . . Our conversations were, like, the best . . . it just, like, got to us. . . . Different points of view, you know?" For Miguel, the conversations with his peers, more than anything else, were transformative—"Different points of view, you know?" Though the books that engaged students were indeed important, we offer a more expansive story detailing the students' experiences with books and the associated complexities of their conversations, relationships, and development.

THE SUBTLETIES OF SUPPORTING TEEN DEVELOPMENT

Reading has particular significance during adolescence because of the expansive developmental changes during that period, and adolescents' observations can be revealing. Consider Paloma's wistful reflection from 10th grade on her 8th-grade English class:

> [We used to talk] like, in a way, it was for some people, I understand that they were going through some personal things. I mean every teenager does, whether it's big or small, or we just blow it out of proportion 'cause, you know that's just what we do, and so it's, like, throughout the book you could, in a way, always find yourself somewhere. And, um, like I was saying, like it's like a life lesson . . . because it's, like, you may not want to express what you're going through, but this book does it without you even having to say anything, and that's the cool part about urban fiction, because it's, like, today, and the way you talk, and you can just relate to a character and get attached, and you're like, "I should handle it this way," and it gives you different points of view, and so [in] that class you were just basically talking about yourself, but at the same time you weren't, and you just don't have to give it away like that . . . it was, like, a comfortable environment . . . 'cause we would always say, "What happened in the classroom stays in the classroom," and it literally did. And I just felt, like, instead of being students and teachers, we just became friends and like Ms. Tucker said, a family. 'Cause we just shared so much.

Paloma's observation suggests intimate connections among teens' reading; their social, emotional, and intellectual lives and development; and the qualities of classroom life. These are the connections we explore in this book through hundreds of interviews with students, parents, and teachers and many hours of classroom observations and recordings. We will show you why Miguel's, Norma's, Lindsay's, and Paloma's experiences with books offer a tool not only for surviving the complexities of adolescence but also for building more successful, happier, resilient, moral beings and, ultimately, a stronger democracy. Later, we will show you how their teachers helped them to become engaged in reading and, through their instruction, helped facilitate these transformations.

NOTES

1. Moeller et al. (2020).
2. National Institute of Mental Health (n.d.).
3. Centers for Disease Control and Prevention (n.d.).

4. Lebrun-Harris et al. (2019).

5. National Center for Drug Abuse Statistics (n.d.).

6. Natanson (2022); Zalusky (2022).

7. National Assessment of Educational Progress (2013).

8. Denby (2016).

9. Schaeffer (2021).

10. OECD (2011).

11. Guthrie et al. (2012); Valenzuela et al. (2015).

12. National Research Council (2003).

13. Ivey & Johnston (2013).

14. Konrath et al. (2011).

15. Pineda (2020).

16. Clark (2021); Grizzard (2021); Li (2010).

17. Friedman & Johnson (2022).

18. "Large Majorities of Voters Oppose Book Bans" (2022).

CHAPTER 2

Choosing to Read

Last year I didn't read at all. The only book I read is *The Outsiders* . . . but now I read whenever I can get the chance.

—8th-grader Max

We heard variations on Max's assertion from many of his classmates, for instance:

Back then I hated books. I never read. I tried to read one, but every time I tried to read through it, I never read it and just left it in my house. And then I had to write an essay about it or something, and I never knew what to write about. (English language learner)

I didn't read at all last year, in class, in school, or at home. Only what they forced me to read.

Being "forced" to read assigned books was tedious at best, according to students from across achievement levels, including those taking honors classes. At worst, students found ways to evade the reading. As Johnny put it, "I used to hate to read. I didn't read at all. I'd sit there and turn the pages when the teacher looked at me, and that was pretty much it." It wasn't simply that they weren't reading but also that they were building negative attitudes toward reading.

Aware of this and frustrated by efforts commonly used to entice students to read—from rewards, to grades, to giving a metaphorical song and dance about a book—the teachers looked to research for answers. They found their previous efforts lacked a fundamental principle: Students are motivated to read when they have interesting texts and a sense of autonomy or control over their reading lives.[1] Although there was more to learn, this principle led to some simple yet bold changes. They stopped assigning books, book reports, and projects, because no one book would be compelling to all students and because assignments take control of reading from students. With Gay's help, they added to each classroom 150 to 200 novels specifically written for young adults, books with positive reviews on Amazon.com and from respected sources such as *School Library Journal* and *Kirkus Reviews*, many receiving starred reviews. There were no more than three copies of any one novel, and sometimes only a single copy; scarcity of a popular book increased its value (Capitalism 101).

Teachers began the year reading evocative sections from the novels, inviting students to sign up for books that caught their interest. Following research on autonomy and on classroom talk, the teachers committed to not asking closed, "comprehension" questions.[2] Instead, they focused on provoking conversations with prompts, like, "What are you thinking?" and "Catch me up." Finally, they made sure the students had ample time to make their choices, ample time for sustained reading, and permission to talk about what they read whenever the urge hit them during that time. In practical terms this meant devoting roughly one-third of the hour-and-a-half class period to student reading, one-third to teachers reading to students a book drawn from the class collection, and one-third to student writing. Admittedly, the portion of the class devoted to student reading frequently spilled into the scheduled teacher read-aloud time, which also sometimes spilled over into the writing time. Most often, this was due to the students' desire to keep talking about the books, for example, when small groups of students having friendly disagreements about characters brought their unresolved issues to the larger group for consultation as reading time was supposed to end.

In later chapters, we'll detail the instruction teachers provided in these contexts, but perhaps already you think this a recipe for chaos—students all reading different books (and talking!) and not being held accountable for their reading! And yet they read like crazy, averaging 42 books each the first year. Students across achievement levels began reading, inside and outside of school, at lunch, in math class, on the bus, on car trips, sometimes straight through dinner, and later in bed. Many of the students had, in previous school years, been assigned to read every night for homework, but, at best, only some were compliant. The idea of "having" to read for a minimum amount of time became irrelevant, as Carson explained: "I set my timer for twenty minutes and when it goes off, I just keep reading for about an hour after that." They even read when they weren't supposed to. Tory admitted, "I usually read, like, all the time at night . . . if I hear [my parents] come upstairs, I'll, like, just put it under my covers, then they go away, and I'll start reading again."

And it was not just *that* they chose to read that was new. *How* they read was also new. In part, there was a different intensity, for example, "I was so trapped in that book that somebody had to shake me, shake me, and yell in my ears to get me out of it to get me to go to class." This intense engagement was new for most students, as Lacey observed, "*Before I Fall* is one of those, like, the first books I've ever truly gotten into, like one of those books where you could really picture yourself in that scene. Like you feel like you're with them."

These and many more changes in students' reading were radical shifts for most, making it possible for them to recognize and articulate both the changes and their source. Their accounts are revealing. Equally revealing are their explanations of their less promising reading histories prior and subsequent to 8th grade.

GOOD (MEANINGFUL) BOOKS

Does anyone really think it a good idea to read books they don't find personally meaningful? Pointing out the obvious, Candace observed, "I read a lot when I was little but not as much as this year, because last year, in 7th grade, we didn't have good books." Winnie concurred: "I read [now] a lot more than I used to in 6th and 7th grade 'cause I couldn't find any really good books. Then I came to 8th grade, and they had so many [good] books to choose from, it was like I was in heaven." Also reflecting on 7th grade, Addie pointed to what counts as a "good book": "The things we read about last year were not really satisfying because it didn't really relate to us at all." The reading material they referred to had been either short selections from dusty old anthologies the school had long ago invested in or whatever dated young adult novels the school already owned in class sets of 25 or so.

This assertion of the need for personal meaningfulness runs throughout our interviews. In 10th grade, no longer a reader, but keenly aware of what it means to be engaged rather than compliant, Michelle observed:

> Like, *The Odyssey*, we don't want to read that . . . we read part of *The Odyssey* together, but it was just . . . people weren't going to get into that. It's like, "let's just read it, get the facts, and get it over with."

Not merely wasted time, such experiences leave a permanent stain on the reading experience. A good book, Michelle argued, "Has to make you FEEL something. To make me wish for something more. Or you get so involved with it that I had to just, like, tell people."

Many students were clear that the social worlds of the books needed to reflect what they were encountering in the here and now. *In Ecstasy* was popular because it dealt with competition and comparisons between teen girls, self-image, and the lure of drugs. Amber exclaimed to a group of girls, recounting its realistic context, "They deal with school situations, like being called a slut. They deal with that." Addie agreed, "I feel if you're gonna write a book, you need to include like every setting your readers are gonna know about," to which Elisa reiterated, "At that age! At that age!" It's important to note that *In Ecstasy* and other books the girls preferred are not formulaic-type series books featuring stereotypical mean girls. In fact, some girls admitted to reading the latter prior to 8th grade but found them lacking once they were exposed to books with situations and characters that illuminate the complexity of humanity.

The lack of attention to personal meaningfulness before (and after) 8th grade was not constrained to school reading either. Parents made the same mistake. Kelly shared, "Like, sometimes my mom would go out and buy books for me, but she gets like boring books . . . and I don't really read most of them." Even when teachers and parents try to match books to students' presumed interests, they are often thwarted by the fact that personal meaningfulness takes many, often unique, forms in the sense that they are not necessarily shared with an abundance of peers, but instead shaped by specific connections or life circumstances. Jason, who had relatives in the military, found military books completely absorbing, particularly those involving snipers and the moral dilemmas faced in the line of duty. Having read *Marine Sniper*, he went out and bought his own copy to keep. Similarly, Roberto reflected on *The Secret Story of Sonia Rodriguez*:

> That was more of like a cultural book, 'cause it was going off of her Hispanic life that she had. And it . . . just attracted to me 'cause I'm Hispanic, and she was Hispanic . . . I like that book . . . because of the sympathy for her and her life. . . . It kind of angered me, especially with her uncle that tried to rape her.

Carmela, having lost her mother when she was 11, was drawn to *Far from You* in which a girl struggles with the grief of losing her mother to cancer. Carmela found the book not only a comfort but also an instrument for working through her unresolved grief. Dean's affinity for *Snitch*, which deals with gang culture in an urban setting, was harder to figure out since he lived in a rural area and was more familiar with farmland, hunting, and fishing than city streets. He explained to us, though, that he had seen his fair share of violence and drug-related activity even out in the country and that was precisely what had him glued to the pages.

Although these reasons for engagement are in some ways unique, they were also not uncommon. Roberto was not the only student of color who felt an affinity for characters reflecting their culture. Carmela was far from alone in her struggle with the loss of those close to her, whether to suicide, cancer, drugs, prison, or other means. Each found books that helped them come to grips with their experience. A student grieving over a friend's death found stories containing suicide, explaining that through the experience, "I got my anger out and stuff." Another read to understand the mind of an autistic sibling, another to explore the implications of teen pregnancy, another to understand the consequences of drug use. This is why the 71 students we interviewed at the end of the first year of the study named 159 titles that they couldn't stop thinking about or *had* to talk to someone about. But it isn't that they only read different books. All together they named 327 books. In other words, they named many of the same books.

It's important to note that although teachers (and parents) who know students and their interests can be quite influential in helping to identify personally meaningful books, in this context it was immersion in a community of peers talking about books that mattered most. The conversations, even just overhearing them, made it possible for students to get a sense of what each book offered—not just basic plotlines, but the dilemmas, emotional struggles, and decisions characters made, often not apparent from a published book review or a back-cover summary.

DISTURBING BOOKS

Riley's confession, a common theme, might seem less comforting:

> It's really hard for me to get hooked on books, especially last year. I didn't really read at all. But then, this year, I guess 'cause the material is more, I don't know, more disturbing, and unfortunately that's what gets me hooked. Like I'll stay with something like that.

"More disturbing" included matters of sexuality, teen pregnancy, suicide, sexual abuse, cutting, anorexia, drug use, race, and gang violence, issues that students viewed not only as disturbing but also as issues they were either already confronting or expected to confront in the near future. This personal relevance, the more "adult" nature of the material, and the fact that they could identify with the characters and the moral ambiguities produced significant engagement.

Of course, the thought of teenagers reading disturbing books is itself disturbing to some teachers and parents, so we will return to this tension in greater detail in subsequent chapters. In the meantime, the disturbingness of the books many students chose lay in their portrayal of the complexities of being human and acting responsibly in morally complex situations. Further, the descriptor "disturbing" was often accompanied by the term "intense," which was how one student described a book featuring a character who learns as a teen that she had been switched with another baby at birth, that the couple who raised her were not her biological parents:

> I like the books that are intense. Like I really love this book we got—*The Day Before* . . . [describes book] It makes me mad! . . . My sister was yelling at me because I was yelling at the book. She's like, "Why do you keep yelling at the book?"

This intensity reflects the reader's identification with a character who, in a morally complex situation, makes what readers recognize as bad choices.

A further complication is that adolescents' interests are changing as they move into adulthood, a point not missed by some of the students. As Addie observed, "You're at that age where you're questioning things, and by reading, you're learning things you wouldn't otherwise have the courage to ask." Recognizing that the books offered a tool for providing distance on their changing life problems, Paloma pointed out:

> There's all these conflicts and problems with the family and stuff, and so I feel really drawn to it then because it's like at this age you have so many problems with your parents that you think the whole world's against you, but it's not even that way. So, I felt like reading like, how everybody else got through it.

Moriah noted another shift in tastes. While she previously found *Harry Potter* exciting:

> Something about these books made me want to read more. For example, with *Harry Potter*, I can't really have the self-connection with that. These books are mostly realistic fiction. *Bittersweet*—she was talking about being an ice skater, and she was trying to like balance her priorities, and she wasn't sure how. And I guess I can sort of relate to that, 'cause sometimes I want more things than what I actually need.

These shifts for some to realistic fiction reflect both a shift in the interests of the adolescent reader and a shift in the function of reading from entertainment to self-construction, a complex topic we will return to as we unpack the nature of reading and adolescents' engagement.

Asserting that a good, personally meaningful book is key to engaging students in reading seems uncontroversial. However, it flies in the face of the standard practice of assigning everyone to read the same book. Students had more to say about this contrast.

AUTONOMY

Jana commented that, "Before this year, we kind of *had* to read books they assigned to us, so I pretended to read it, and I just wouldn't care about books at all." Those who spend time with adolescents (or 2-year-olds for that matter) will not be surprised by Jana's need for autonomy. A sense of autonomy is, after all, a human need.[3] It's our sense that we are choosing voluntarily, that we have some control over our lives. Indeed, Jana continued, "Now they give us a choice if we want to read it, where we get to pick the book that we read. I actually read it instead of pretending to read it."

Lack of choice in what to read had been compounded by other constraints on autonomy. For example, not only were they previously assigned books that everyone was to read and that "weren't that good" but those books also came with strict pacing requirements: "You had to read a certain amount of chapters every night. You couldn't go ahead. You couldn't read any less." And then there were the assignments. Honors student Daphne observed: "I don't want to write a paper on it. And that made the experience worse, too. I always think if I had read it on my own, it would have been better, but having all those assignments—paper after paper on it—then it was just not good." The assignments and the lack of meaningful choice undermined the entire reading experience. Tenth-grader, Michelle, another honors student, pointed out:

> For most kids, if you tell them to sit down and "read this, you have to read this," they're not gonna. They're just gonna be sitting there like, "How long is it gonna take for me to get this done so I can answer those questions and not have to, like, look at it anymore?" And it's not working, honestly.

Many of the students made it clear that these practices were unlikely to lead them to becoming committed readers. Besides, as Calista pointed out, "I've always been required to read the class book, and they kind of limit what you read."

TALK ABOUT BOOKS

When adults read a compelling book, we immediately want to talk about it. Students are no different. Moriah confessed:

> If I see someone else like reading the same book, I would just shoot up to them and start talking about the book, and like, "What do you think? Do you think she's going to do this?" . . . You have to let it out, like, I think so, 'cause you get so excited and then you just can't, like, keep it to yourself.

Also, like adults, the second response to reading a good book is to try to compel others to read it, both to share the experience, a common human need, and to deepen the conversation. This is no less the case with adolescents: "With my friends a lot, I'll be like, 'Did you read this?' And they'll be like, 'No,' and I start raging to them about it, and they're like 'What the heck?'

We should not be surprised by this new behavior or why it occurred. Trinity noted, "We never talked about our books last year, 'cause I was never hooked with any of the books that we did."[4] Michelle complained, "I never used to talk about books a lot . . . because . . . there was a certain book level you had to read and a certain type of book you had to read, and it was just really frustrating." Does anyone seek conversations about books they don't find personally meaningful? Perhaps, but only to gripe about the experience. But when adolescents find a book deeply engaging, they will talk about it, anywhere, any time, and to anyone. Ella remarked:

> We feel like such nerds because we always talk about books . . . if we just finish a book and we want our friends to read it, we'll be like, "You *have* to read this book!" . . . That usually happens at lunch, after school, on weekends and stuff. I feel like such a nerd because I always talk about books. But it's fun.

The conversations were sufficiently "fun" to overcome a potential "nerd" identity. They were enjoyable not just because they involved sharing a meaningful experience and a little of themselves. They were enjoyable because of the *intellectual* engagement. Different points of view were provoked by the complexities, moral ambiguities, and uncertainties in the books, prompting students to talk with each other, with parents, grandparents, teachers, and siblings. It was a compulsion to talk, as one student put it, "You can't *not* talk about it." For many, these conversations encouraged further reading to beget further conversations.

And students were forceful salespeople, as in, "You *have* to read this book!" and "Students, they would come to me and be like, 'Oh, girl, you need to read this.'" The sheer force of these episodes was fueled partly by the passionate need to share the intense experience of the book, partly by a need to talk about the moral uncertainties the book opened, and partly by the sense of social agency achieved by successfully persuading someone to read a book. When Ella and a classmate each tried to persuade a new arrival in their class to read particular books, the new arrival chose Ella's suggestion. Ella put this persuasive success in the same category as getting on the JV sports team. And the persuasiveness did not simply apply to peers, as Ella claimed:

> We talk about books a lot. Like this weekend, Rose and Avery came over my house, and we talked about books, and my mom like came in, . . . and she was like, "I didn't read books when I was younger." And I was like, "Yeah, I know." . . . but I got my mom to read some of *Hate List*!

When students desperately want to talk with a peer about a particular book but there is only one copy in circulation, there are really only two options. One is to find someone who has read it. The other is to convince someone to read it. Students generated strategies for finding others who had read the book. Slamming the book on a table, they would announce "I read this book in 2 days," at once advertising the book and the fact that they were open for conversations. Traveling between classes, they carried their book as visibly as possible, regardless of the class they were going to. Addie's comment about a book whose main character has been abducted and abused by an adult male captures much of this phenomenon—the choice of books, the intensity, and the attention to possible conversation partners:

> I've branched out with disturbing books. *Living Dead Girl,* I could not put down. I started it in Ms. Tucker's class and finished it an hour later. . . . In the end, I looked up and saw things clearer. It was a different feeling, one of gratitude and thankfulness that that wasn't my life. I was just like, Oh my gosh. . . . Oh my gosh. It does—haunts you. It haunts you for a long time. It's been 2 weeks and it's still on my mind. It gives you a new perspective. I remember opening my eyes and I was like, Whoa. My eyes are bigger. It was a different feeling. . . . *Living Dead Girl* is the first book I've read that changed my perspective on the world. That's a really powerful book. I read it, Ms. Tucker read it, Elise took it, Phoebe took it. Shea read it and she finished it the next day in Civics. I watched her finish the book.

Notice Addie's surveillance of her peers' reading. She has a mental catalogue of who reads which books, but, in this case, she also wants to see her peers' response to the impending ambiguous twist at the end of the book—the focus of their unavoidable conversation.

Teachers were also potential conversation partners, and it was not unusual for students to hound them to read particular books. One teacher showed us how Dennis had strategically placed notes on bookmarks throughout *Tyrell* before handing it over to her, urging her to slow down for these "best parts." These were also signals to debrief with him along the way.

This hunger to share personally meaningful experiences coupled with the limited availability of particular titles resulted in unexpected conversations and relationships, relationships that overcame social barriers:

> We've talked about *Love and Leftovers, Identical,* um *Bittersweet.* . . . It's like OK there's this thing where I like dress different from other people and then if . . . like I wear like band T's and everything and then the girl will wear like Aeropostale and the cheerleaders' clothes or whatever, and I found myself talking to them about books. Whoa! They're actually cool to talk to about, books and everything.

If you really want to talk about a book you're passionate about but the only one who has read it is the goth kid or cheerleader or jock who you would *never* otherwise talk to, the conversation wins out, expanding the complexity of the conversations and, conveniently, the value of the conversations for the participants and the value of the participants to each other. Though the benefits of interactions across these specific subgroups have not been the focus of research, the benefits of friendship relationships across racial and ethnic boundaries are associated with a reduced sense of vulnerability on the part of students, and because of the books, these relationships were common.[5] These interactions should also enable students to more accurately take others' perspectives, a foundational social skill.

To summarize, these young adults taught us that access to a range of interesting, personally meaningful books and a degree of autonomy invited engaged reading that was as social as it was intellectual. These adolescents began *choosing* to read and (consequently and reciprocally) *choosing* to talk, and their conversations with peers—even unlikely ones—spawned a cascade of social, personal, and intellectual changes we will explore in subsequent chapters. They also taught us that requiring everyone to read the same book and then insisting on assignments to assert accountability is probably not the best way to inspire young adults to read.

A side note: If you work with young people who don't care much for reading, you might be dying at this point to know the teachers' role in all of this. If you can't wait, you can certainly jump ahead to the third section of this book, starting with Chapter 10, where we detail the teachers' learning and the instructional interactions in these classrooms that supported engagement. We've structured the book to show first the consequences of engagement—consequences that were recognized by teachers as the teens became engaged in reading and that shaped the teaching you will read about in those later chapters.

NOTES

1. Guthrie & Humenick (2004). The effect sizes for interesting texts and choice of reading material, respectively, were 1.15 and .95
2. Nystrand et al. (1997); Stefanou et al. (2004).
3. Ryan & Deci (2000).
4. Ivey & Johnston (2015).
5. Graham et al. (2014).

CHAPTER 3

"Talk to Me": Cultivating Peer Relationships

> Like if I have a new book, then I'll sit at lunch—and I have a problem: I have to have my biggest book on the bottom, then my planner, then my reading book—and then a lot of times my friends are like, "Oh, what's this book about?" cause they've never seen it. Like *10 Things We Did* . . . nobody's ever seen that one before, so I got to tell a lot of people about it. And if I see a book that I've never seen before, I usually go over and ask about it, too. And then start a big discussion about books. One time, we were talking about books at lunch, I forgot to eat, 'cause we were just talking so much. . . . And I'm hungry. I like food.
>
> —8th-grader Ella

Like a duck hunter using decoys, Ella strategically arranges her books to generate conversations. The conversations lead to more books, which lead to more conversations. Initially, we viewed Ella's comment as a new reading strategy—a technique for harvesting leads on good books and soliciting conversations to expand comprehension and meaningfulness. We quickly realized that, for Ella, the stimulation and pleasure of the social engagement that follows are a central point of reading. She was strategically using the books to engage more often and more deeply with her peers, the books being the worm on the social hook. Of course, these motives are inseparable. To people who love to read, Ella's comments will come as no surprise.

In a culture that prizes competitive individualism, it's easy to forget that we are essentially and necessarily a social species. Our socialness gave us our evolutionary edge, so even our biological systems have evolved to support our social behavior. We are social to our neural, hormonal, cellular, and genetic core.[1] As Mary Helen Immordino-Yang and Linda Darling-Hammond point out, we "coregulate one another's physiology . . . which means that the quality of a person's relationships and social interactions shapes their development and health, both of the body and of the brain."[2]

Reading, like the species doing it, is fundamentally social. When students are fully engaged with narrative texts, they not only build relationships in conversations with each other but they also form relationships with the characters. For example, Lacey noted that when you're engaged with the characters, "you feel like you're with them, and you wish you could be there to help them." Darla observed, "This book, *Delirium*, has helped me a lot." Describing the book, she added, "It's like I'm helping her with her problems, as well as she's helping me." Similarly, our readers formed relationships with authors, recognizing them as community members and strategically trying to connect with them both imaginatively and on social media.

The adolescents' use of books to build social relationships is not merely a collateral benefit of engaged reading. Human beings have a fundamental need to form social relationships. We are born with not only a need for relationships but also a propensity to attend to the details of social interaction—the sounds, the gaze, the rhythms of movement—in order to acquire the social tools of survival. Children are dependent on safe, trusting relationships with parents or other caregivers for their development. This dependency shifts in adolescence. As teens begin to assert independence from their parents, peer relationships become increasingly important. They become more reliant on friends for support, and their need for social relatedness and belonging becomes stronger.[3] They are, in fact, most happy when talking with peers.[4] They also become more influenced by their friends, and it is within these relationships that they build identities.[5]

SUPPORTIVE PEER RELATIONSHIPS

The quantity and quality of friendship relationships become critical in adolescence.[6] Let's first think about the quantity—the network size:

> Like, I talk to all of my English class about books. I feel like my English class, we've grown a lot closer as friends. Like, we can all be friends. I have some friends in other classes. Sometimes we just sit and talk about books.

This was a standard commentary. Another observed:

> At the beginning of the year, you've known everybody, but you're not really friends with everybody. And, like, once we start doing this and everybody starts speaking out, and like everybody's having conversations with each other about it, it seems like you're friends with everybody.

Just having something interesting to share that you potentially have in common opens a relationship. As relationships develop, old boundaries dissolve: "Like, you're compatible with these people. Like, I never thought I'd be compatible with that person." Consequently, as another pointed out, "maybe it's due to reading, people are less in cliques and groups than we were last year." Indeed, the conversations even neutralized old animosities. Robbie observed, "I talk to, like, Terrence in my class, Hudson, and these different people. Me and Terrence are the only ones in my class who read *Prime Choice*."[7] Was Terrence his friend before this? "Terrence? Well, we've had our differences. I think we've bonded more. We really have." Political scientist Emily Kubin and her colleagues would not be surprised by Robbie's confession. They found that sharing personal experiences, as happens in these conversations, particularly experiences that involve harm, is an excellent way to bridge political divides.[8] The process elevates participants' respect for the other as a reasoning, moral being. Robbie continued: "'Cause, like the other day, I think it was Friday, I wrote, I was like, 'Man, me and my class is all like a family. We wouldn't do nothing to hurt each other'. Then I showed mainly everyone in the class, and they agreed the same thing."

In other words, the relational properties of the *learning community* changed in important positive ways. Remember, these are adolescents who normally face not only collective disengagement and alienation but often fairly deep clique divisions. Why does this matter? Students who feel accepted by their peers enjoy school more, find it more interesting, experience less anxiety, and have higher achievement expectations.[9] They also show greater commitment to their work. Their sense of relatedness makes them more positive toward themselves and toward others, which is reflected in more supportive, respectful, and helpful interactions even outside the normal group of friends.[10] What parent wouldn't want this for their teenager? What teen wouldn't want it for themselves? The students we talked with lived it, appreciated it, and recognized its source, sometimes sounding a bit puzzled by their good fortune.

The process is, in some ways, quite predictable, as Josie explained: "Even people who aren't my friends, like, when I've talked about a book that I've recommended, then they end up coming, like they'll talk to me about that book, and now they just talk regularly to me." And the social network expands:

> The more books I read, the more things I have in common with a lot more people and the more I talk. . . . If I read one book, then there's a certain amount of people that has read that book, and I talk to them about it. And then I read another book, there's so much more people that have read that book, too, and there's people that overlap over a bunch of books.

The tendrils of these expanded relationships persisted well into high school. Tenth-grader Paloma wistfully recalling her 8th-grade year observed:

> 'Cause we just shared so much, and even when we see each other today, like whether it's in Walmart or Food Lion looking all lazy, we'll just sit there and

talk and then like next thing you know it's like 30 minutes we've kind of got to leave, and it's like I just came for like a pencil, and we're just standing there like talking.

The positive relationships might not always have risen to the level of friendship, but many students cited an increased level of trust, and they recognized the source: "I don't know how to put it, but it's just that talk, you get to talk between each other, and that makes you feel you can trust that person more." Trust is key to developing deeper friendships, and the talk that produced it was thoroughly normalized, which Moriah recognized:

> [It] isn't a bad thing. It's a good thing, but people are getting too involved in the books, like it's really happening. We talk about it, like, it's actually school gossip and stuff. It's really cool like that. It's now, like, a daily conversation. In the morning, we'll be like, "I just finished this and this." That was the first thing I said to Tanya this morning. It's like an everyday conversation.

Has it changed her relationships with people? According to one student, "In English class, some of the people I didn't really know and wasn't comfortable with, like, in Spanish class and in English class, I've gotten really close to them because of the books we read."

CLOSE FRIENDSHIPS

In the students' comments, we hear not only an expansion of the number of friendships but also an increase in the closeness of the relationships, which, in itself, is a critical part of adolescent development. Researchers have found that close friendships provide emotional support during adolescence and the necessary sense of belonging and self-worth.[11] They predict both academic motivation and achievement[12] and offer safe spaces for validating and exploring identities.[13]

Building intimate friendships requires establishing not only an emotional bond but also levels of trust, loyalty, and commitment necessary for sharing personal thoughts, feelings, and experiences.[14] This "self-disclosure" is what increases the sense of intimacy. But anxiety about social evaluation also increases during adolescence, so there are real risks to sharing vulnerabilities and personal thoughts, feelings, and struggles.[15] This is where the books really help. They make it possible to start by sharing a common experience and disclosing surface-level thoughts and feelings, while exploring the relationship for the trust and commitment needed to share deeper personal experiences.

Recognizing this, Jana noted: "sometimes when you're in an awkward situation with someone you don't normally talk to, it's easier just to come out and talk to them about what you're reading and what they've read. It's like an icebreaker." While conversations might start with the books, they rarely ended there, as one observed:

> I've grown in friendships with people who have books I've also read and liked, and we've started talking about the books and we just talk about other things, too. The books will lead into conversations. So, I've made some new friends through books.

That the books were personally meaningful and often unsettling made this level of sharing not only more likely but almost inevitable. The conversations changed the relationships, making deeper self-disclosure possible: "'Cause, like, when we do talk about books, we get together, and, like, it helps our friendship, talking about stuff." Students began to realize that they were not alone. Monica observed:

> You think you're the only one going through the problems that you're going through, but then you realize that there's plenty of other people that have it worse than you, and they've been through that, so you can talk to them and it will make you feel better or get you through what you're going through.

It is the meaningfulness of the reading experience that sparked these deeper relationships, as Kevin put it: "One of my friends who did recommend like, one book, we really weren't that close before, but it turns out we both had an experience in that book, and we bonded over that." Or, more simply, Priscilla exclaimed, "I was like, "YES! Someone understands! So, I like talking to different people about books."

LEARNING RELATIONSHIPS

This sense of trust enabled, and was fueled by, bringing together students with different perspectives, helping those with unique interests find one another and build learning relationships. For example, in Chapter 2 we mentioned Jason's interest in the armed forces, particularly sniper stories. His seemingly unique interest might have been isolating. But carrying his book between classes, with its title clearly visible, he discovered Johnny:

> I knew Johnny last year, but not really knew him. I mean I knew who he was. He saw me carrying a book down the hallway, and he was, "Hey, do you mind if I read that?" I was like, "Are you sure? 'Cause it's pretty graphic." So, more and more we just kind of started talking a lot more and everything.

This quite naturally led to a supportive learning relationship:

> Johnny has helped me a lot, too. If I find a book I like, I really like it, I'll go
> to him and tell him about it, and he'll read it, and he'll give me feedback, and
> he'll be like, "Oh, and here's a book that I really enjoyed." He'll tell me, just
> vice versa.

This relationship persisted. We caught up with Jason 3 years later, his junior year of high school, when he was preparing for a career in the military. He had recently read a book about Navy SEAL Chris Kyle, which he described as "a real eye-opener" that made him believe that "one of the big things in the military is you always do the right thing, no matter who's watching." That particular book, he said, "really stuck with me for a couple of months," and he convinced Johnny, who was not only still his friend but also a fellow volunteer in the fire department and also planning to enlist, to read it. He recalled 8th grade as the time he became close with Johnny and that they formed a personal connection around shared reading interests.

It's common to organize education around the teacher as the expert delivering the nuances of classic texts—an asymmetrical relationship between an expert and a collection of novices. Although, as we shall see, teachers contributed a great deal of expertise, supportive, more symmetrical learning relationships, like that between Jason and Johnny, flourished. Rather than relationships between an expert and a novice, we saw these as pairs of expert novices, in which each partner contributed something to the learning relationship. Jemila offers another example:

> Like I talk to Paloma about what happens in the books. The books she hasn't
> read I give her a little bit of info about it. She can read it when she's done with
> her book. And some parts I have to get off my mind and talk through with her.
> And she helps me get through parts I'm stuck at. I'm either confused or it's bug-
> ging me. Like, then I'll go back to the book and I figure out what's happened,
> then I go back and tell her about it.

In these relationships, students felt comfortable seeking help from other students, knowing that they also contributed by offering their perspective.

The relationships also made it possible for students to be nudged by each other when they might have otherwise given up or passed on a particular book or genre. Gwen was, admittedly, prone to abandoning books, but was frequently prodded by her classmates, as she put it, "Everybody tells me to keep reading." She joked about Meleisha, in particular: "[She's] always on me. I need to push her off on other people. I need a break." Pretending to be appalled, she added: "Meleisha stuffed [a book] in my locker. She didn't ask me if I wanted to read it. She just assumed I wanted to read it . . . I figure I'll read it." While reading a different book, Gwen complained one day that "the author spends too much time on one day," but Meleisha reassured her, "I had a book . . . where it takes place over just like a few days. . . . The whole book is just a few days, and it had to be like that." That was all it took for Gwen to reverse course, responding, "There must be a reason . . . I should think about that before I give up this book."

The voices of Meleisha and Gwen's other classmates seemed to reverberate in her head when she lost steam in her reading, but she shared that *Identical* was "the first book where I told myself, 'I want to read that.'" Then she returned some favors. For instance, when Meleisha's engagement with *Identical* started to fizzle, she said it was Gwen who told her, "You gotta read it, keep going," warning her there would be "twists and turns" that she "wouldn't see coming." In another book, Meleisha was struggling with a first-person narrator's speech impediment, and it was Gwen who suggested that the author's reasons for writing the character's language that way might clear up if she kept reading, and thus, Meleisha persevered.

A side note: This dynamic was not restricted to the students, but extended to the relationships between students and their teachers. Students pestered their teachers to read certain books and supported their understandings—because teachers, like all readers, come across difficulty in their reading. Rashad convinced Ms. Tucker to read some of the books about gang life, including memoirs of former gang members, but she had lots of questions for him along the way about gang culture and discourse that was unfamiliar to her. Ms. Tucker would say after reading the particularly disturbing ones, "This book isn't finished with me," and Rashad explained to us that meant "She doesn't get it yet." And their conversations continued. Most importantly, they were using these opportunities to understand and know one another.

The prodding between peers, and between students and teachers, sometimes forceful and sometimes gentle but firm, might have been resented outside of close relationships. But trust created by mutual disclosures in conversations about books and knowing each other as people and readers made the nudging normal, expected, and even welcomed.

That these relationships were widespread reflects features we have already discussed, but also the fact that teachers actively connected conversation partners, as Yolanda explained:

Okay, me and Lindsay were not friends, and [the teacher] was like, "Tell Yolanda about *In Ecstasy*." She said that to Lindsay, and Lindsay came over and explained the book to me and I was like I really want to read it and that's how we became friends, through that book. That was really good.

The resulting friendships contribute to learning in another way. When students are working on solving difficult logic problems together, they are more successful when paired with friends than with acquaintances.[16] Not only that, but after collaborating, the friends also do better at solving problems by themselves, which is not the case with acquaintances. The reason is that friends more often build on and critique each other's logic and justify their own reasoning. These interactions are the source of their individual and collective learning.

WHEN POSITIVE RELATIONSHIPS ARE ABSENT

So far, we have described the benefits and sources of positive peer relationships. But consider this: About 40% of teenagers report that they do not have anyone to talk with and feel quite lonely, misunderstood, sad, and detached. Adolescents are particularly vulnerable to loneliness and social isolation, and they are lonelier than any other age group and growing lonelier.[17] Even if our only interest were academic development, students who don't feel accepted often drop out of school.[18] The emotional distress of peer rejection affects their academic achievement, their interest in school, and their sense of social competence.[19] Peer rejection even predicts attention problems, which, in turn, predict peer rejection in a self-reinforcing negative spiral.[20]

But the stakes are much higher than mere academic success. Researchers have found that loneliness is particularly insidious because it affects physiological and mental functioning, including how we process social threat and reward, the intentions we attribute to others in social interactions, and the associated emotions.[21] Adolescents are more sensitive to rejection, so they experience their social world as more threatening and anxiety-producing.[22] Loneliness and social isolation increase the risk of low self-esteem, depression, anxiety, social withdrawal, and attempts at suicide.[23] And suicide is now the second-leading cause of death among teens, having increased 56% between 2007 and 2017.[24] Loneliness also breeds depression, which increases the risk of self-injury, substance abuse, and sexual risk-taking.[25] According to the National Center for Health Statistics, 12.7% of American teenagers (ages 12 to 17) are prescribed medication for depression.[26] And these problems are not transitory. Poor peer relationships in adolescence are associated with depression; withdrawal; anxiety; and physical ailments such as obesity, alcoholism, high blood pressure, high cholesterol, and reduced immunity in adulthood.[27]

Bullying is another relational problem teens face. When students are being bullied and excluded, they can't focus on their academics. Worse, being bullied is associated with suicidal thoughts and actions and has long-term effects on mental health, including depression, anxiety, sadness, anger, and self-harm.[28] One in five adolescents experience bullying—for young women, it is closer to one in four, with cyber-bullying increasingly common. Currently, antibullying programs are somewhat effective in 7th grade and below, but from 8th grade on, they are so far ineffective.[29] But positive relationships can make a difference. When students feel socially accepted, as was the case for the students we interviewed, they are more likely to stand up for a student who is being bullied.[30] Further, it appears that when adolescents' needs for relatedness and autonomy are satisfied, as they were in the classrooms we documented, they are less likely to cyber-bully.[31] We will return to the reduction of bullying in subsequent chapters.

THE SOLUTION? ENGAGED READING

Adolescents' experience of loneliness depends on whether they feel accepted by their peers, the extent of their network of friendships, and the depth and intimacy of their close friendships.[32] Close friendships moderate the negative effects of peer rejection and provide a buffer against depression.[33] And, like the negative effects, the beneficial effects of those friendships persist well into middle age.[34] In other words, the relationships developed by the students in our study through book conversations offer the real possibility of diminishing adolescent loneliness, the rates of suicide and depression, and even medical bills in adulthood. In a meta-analysis of interventions to reduce loneliness, Christopher Masi and his colleagues found four successful strategies, two of which were increasing opportunities for social contact and enhancing social support.[35] Both are clearly evident in what we have so far described. We'll return to the other two strategies later.

Supportive peer relationships can be particularly important for some students. For example, the more lonely an adolescent, the more important positive peer relationships become.[36] Quiet students often do not experience themselves as part of a supportive peer group.[37] Adolescents with mental health disorders—by some estimates as many as one in five—are especially dependent on positive peer relationships.[38]

The students in this project had little difficulty building social relationships by opening conversations with others—conversations that build relationships effectively inoculate students against major threats to their mental and physical health and expand their ability to learn with and from each other. The 8th graders had a lot to say about how the book conversations affected their relationships by changing how they saw themselves and their peers. The following monologue from Hattie offers a reflection on how the process works.

> I think I've changed as a person, 'cause last year, I really didn't know much about others, and at times I think I've said some things to people last year that could have hurt them. This year, I understand how much pain people can go through, just what I should and shouldn't say. I've learned you have to be careful with how you speak to people, 'cause they could take you the wrong way,

even if you're joking. . . . I met this one girl, she was also pretty picked on in 6th grade. . . . She was in my math class. I really didn't like her that year. But this year, we're friends now, and I realize I didn't even talk to her that much in math class. The times I did, she did annoy me, but when I talked to her more, I started to think she's a really cool person. And I've done that with a lot of people now this year. . . . Friends of mine, I don't know how to describe it, but they seem like they're different. I don't know, maybe the same as me, more nicer, more understanding. I think reading is actually helping people come together, like I've said before. I think it's helping people change and understand what others think better. And even though there's still drama, . . . I think people are slowly starting to change. I'm pretty sure by the time we graduate high school and go on with our futures, that, I'm not saying we'll all like each other, but we'll all understand each other a lot more and be able to get along with each other.

A group of girls in conversation about *In Ecstasy* one day offered an example of this phenomenon. At one point their talk turned to how one might get to know others when, as Addie put it, "you can't see inside someone's soul." Addie, a very popular student, further problematized the issue when she suggested the real issue is with the self and that outward appearances could be deceiving. She said she could relate with "the little green monster inside," a character who lived in the shadow of her best friend, and she confessed, "I don't want to look like the sidekick." She attributed the need to be popular to feeling like "a nasty little ugly person" as a younger child and needing affirmation from others "to feel worthy." In the midst of this lengthy exchange, Riley asked, "Do you guys know if [the author] has any more books? . . . We need to get in touch with this woman." Shea's suggestion that "We should email the author a video [of the conversation]" suggests they not only understood the significance of the narrative as a tool but also their engagement around it with each other and possibly the author.

As the class period ended, the group talked about how their conversations around texts were becoming more productive and so should be more frequent. Notice the agency with which they take up their inquiry into their own and others' motives, relationships, and emotions. It's as if they recognize the value of the books and conversations for the expansion of their social-emotional development. They are not wrong, as we shall see in the next section of the book. But first, we should consider what happens as the books and conversations spill over into family life.

NOTES

1. Cacioppo et al. (2011); Immordino-Yang et al. (2019).
2. Immordino-Yang et al. (2019).
3. Pfeifer & Berkman (2018); Somerville (2013).

4. Csikszentmihalyi et al. (1977); Ragelienė (2016).

5. Ragelienė (2016); Xu et al. (2020).

6. Umberson & Montez (2010); Laursen & Hartl (2013); MacEvoy et al. (2011).7. Ivey & Johnston (2015, p. 17).

8. Kubin et al. (2021).

9. Solomon & Watson (1996).

10. Osterman (2000).

11. Parker et al. (1995).

12. Altermatt & Pomerantz (2003).

13. Buhrmester (1990); Call & Mortimer (2001).

14. Bauminger et al. (2008).

15. van den Bos et al. (2014).

16. Azmitia & Montgomery (1993).

17. Qualter et al. (2015). Although some of this has been attributed to teens' use of technology, that seems to have its effect through more familiar vehicles: feeling excluded and not accepted by peers or family, with accompanying lack of self-esteem, loneliness, and isolation.

18. Parker & Asher (1987).

19. Wentzel (1998).

20. Ji et al. (2019).

21. Goossens (2018).

22. Maes et al. (2019); Qualter et al. (2015).

23. Hall-Lande et al. (2007).

24. Curtin & Heron (2019).

25. Ribeiro et al. (2016).

26. National Center for Health Statistics (2016).

27. Landstedt et al. (2015); Hawkley & Cacioppo (2010).

28. Bonanno & Hymel (2013); Kaltiala-Heino & Fröjd (2011).

29. Yeager et al. (2015).

30. Pronk et al. (2020).

31. Fousiani et al. (2016).

32. Asher & Paquette (2003).

33. Furman & Rose (2015).

34. Marion et al. (2013).

35. Masi et al. (2011).

36. Roekel et al. (2014).

37. Jones & Gerig (1994).

38. Roach (2018).

CHAPTER 4

Re-seeing Family

> When I was with [my dad] for spring break we were just kind of like talking in the car on the way to his house and then I just started telling him about my book, and we just kind of talked about my book. That was *Gym Candy*. That's the one I was reading at the time.
>
> —8th grader Gunnar

If reading and conversation changed the 8th graders' relationships with peers, it changed relationships with family members at least as dramatically as new habits became visible at home and conversation partners (and fellow readers) were recruited from whoever was in the house. Why care about that? Because healthy relationships with family members, particularly parents, can help avert adolescents from some of the social and emotional landmines that exist on the paths to adulthood. Adolescence has long been considered a time of asserting one's own identity, separate from parents.[1] It's also expected that young adolescents will start to spend more time with their peers and less with family.[2] But healthy development and positive well-being during this time still depend on maintaining strong emotional bonds and a sense of operating from a secure base.[3] In fact, adolescents who report higher levels of parent attachment report more self-esteem and greater life satisfaction and are more likely to seek out parents in times of trouble than those who report insecure attachments.[4] They are less likely to engage in excessive alcohol consumption, drug use, and risky sexual behavior.[5] Females who feel secure attachment are less likely to get pregnant[6] or develop an eating disorder.[7] Conversely, low perceived attachment to parents is associated with behavioral problems and inattention,[8] as well as depression and anxiety,[9] feelings of resentment and alienation,[10] substance abuse, and suicide.

As adolescents find their own way, then, the emotional bonds they maintain with parents provide a safety net. We can't claim that the students' reading resulted necessarily in more time spent with their parents. But from what they said, the reading and conversations brought them closer to family members and even shifted, in positive ways, how they thought of family.

FAMILIES READING

We and the teachers first suspected that school reading had seeped into family dynamics when classroom books went missing for long periods of time. "My mom's reading it," became a frequent reason for delayed returns, particularly as other students were waiting for a book to be available. Gay was at the local high school one day when she spotted a 10th-grader she had known as an 8th-grader clutching a book she recognized—but one she wouldn't have expected the student to know, much less have in hand, because it was a new book not yet available to the buying public. Gay had picked up an advance reader copy (ARC) from a publisher's representative at a recent professional conference, but where in the world would this student have nabbed one? After the student gushed about the book for a minute or two ("Oh my God, you HAVE to read it!"), Gay managed to get to the bottom of things: This student got it from her mom (who read it), who got it from a co-worker (who read it), who got it from her own daughter (who read it), who was an 8th grader in one of the classrooms we were studying, who got it from . . . by golly, this was Gay's copy!

Some students told us that sharing books at home became a regular thing. Due to Ella's frequent raving about books, she said her stepmother "literally took down a list of all the books I was telling her about," adding that "she wants to read *In Ecstasy, Perfect Chemistry, Jumping Off Swings,* and *Twisted.*" Riley, who was not likely to pick up a book before 8th grade, exchanged books with her mother, who was taking classes to become a school librarian. During lunch dates, the two talked about books with Addie and her mother, who brought back new books for the girls from the well-stocked public library in a neighboring city where she worked.

Siblings were also drawn in. Ella made her young sister keen to read the books she talked about, but as a wise older sibling, she carefully screened what she would hand over, even though Ella considered her "mature for her age." Other students echoed this practice. Ella explained: "Some of the books I don't want [my sister] to read, cause some of them are a little old for her. . . . Like when she gets to 8th and 9th grade, I think I would let her read the *Crank* series." Likewise, Calista explained, "I've got a younger brother, so I can't really talk about some of the books, but I talk to my mom and my parents about my reading a lot."

Aisha's brother was in high school and hardly ever read, but started enjoying a book he noticed her reading and wondered, "Where are you getting these books from? . . . My school don't got none of them books." Reflecting on getting her brother to read, Aisha said, "I'll be like my teacher." Similarly, Wilson noticed that his younger siblings were "doing the thing where the teacher just gives them a book and they have to do a report." He planned to use the summer after 8th grade "[getting] my brothers and sisters reading, so they could start liking it, too." Recruiting readers was not constrained to immediate family, though. After hounding his dad to buy *Perfect Chemistry*, Thad convinced his cousin *and* his grandmother to read it! As we noted in Chapter 2, this effective persuasion offered students a strong sense of social agency.

Thad wasn't the only student to report pestering parents for help acquiring in-demand books they couldn't wait to read. It wasn't unusual for parents or grandparents to request booklists from teachers for holiday and birthday gift ideas. The process likely sustained a local chain bookstore and doubtless increased circulation rates at the local public library.

FAMILIES AND TALK

For some students, falling into conversations around books with family members was effortless, particularly when the family member was also an avid reader. Jemila explained, "My mom likes to read, too, and I give her ideas about books. Like I've told her about *Sold*, and she's, like, really shocked about what's happening." Kendall said she talked to her mom "all the time," so that it became routine for her mom to ask about the current book: "And I tell her, and she's like, 'What's that about?' And I tell her, and she's like, 'Oh, I might want to read that book!'"

Other students lured family to their books by recounting an intriguing episode or situation or reading a section aloud—some of the same strategies they used to instigate conversations about books with their peers. And just as in school, others used more passive-aggressive measures, such as Opal, who reported that she "got really mad" at *Love and Leftovers* and threw the book, alarming her father who was seated next to her on the sofa. Her effort paid off: "He asked me what was wrong, and I told him about it. He said that sounded like a really good book, and he said he was really glad I found something I like, even though it wasn't something I would normally read." Aisha, on the other hand, said her new habit of reading itself got her mother's and grandmother's attention: "Like they ask me 'cause they know I'm 'bout to tell 'em something. Like they'll just get mad 'cause I'll be sitting there reading and not talking to them."

The talk itself was an important tool for shaping how the 8th-graders related to their family members. Often, boys reported that the books provided a vehicle for connecting with their fathers. Moses reported, "I talk to my dad, when he's home, but he usually be at work all the time. I only see my dad in the morning and on weekends. I talk to him about *Homeboyz* and how it relate to my cousin." This vehicle for connection was particularly important in divorced families. Gunnar, whose father had been a successful quarterback in high school and now lives in a different state, reported, "I talked to him about [*Gym Candy*] when I was there at spring break. I was, like, reading instead of going to sleep, and he's like, 'What are you reading?' I'm like, 'I'm reading this book about football.' He's like, 'Oh.' So, we just talked about it every time I'd read a chapter. I'd tell him about it." Similarly, Zeb, an honors student, said the books helped to change how he interacted with his father: "My parents are divorced so I only see him on the weekends. So, we just talk about normal things. And once I started reading those books, I talked to him about that."

The strategy also worked for girls. For example, three years after 8th grade, reflecting on how she learned to use reading, Addie explained that she intentionally seeks out her father when she has questions about books: "It helps me . . . cause my dad's sometimes hard to talk to, 'cause he's just a very unemotional person, but um, it helps me to connect with him, almost, because it gives us something to talk about."

Conversations over books helped the adolescents see and be seen in new ways at home. Zeb found a book—part of a series he liked at school—sitting on his college-aged brother's shelf and convinced him to read and talk about that book with him. As a result, he observed, "I think about my brother more, because I figured he was just a guy that liked computer programming and stuff, but he actually likes books too." These conversations changed the relationships in many different ways. Zeb noted, "I think my dad, he's always wanted me to read more. I think he's kind of proud that I read more now." Aside from opening the door to greater intimacy and trust, some students reported that family members viewed them as more academically successful. Thad said his father seemed gratified that he was now reading and that his grades had improved. Likewise, Arturo shared, "Last year I hadn't read nothing, I had horrible grades, I was a bad student. And now I'm trying to proceed to college . . . [my family members] actually are proud."

The books mediated changes in family relationships, too, through the conversations they enabled. In some instances, the change was quite radical, as Dennis confessed:

> [Reading] gives me something to talk to my mom about. . . . I'll talk to her for an hour just about a book . . . and not have to worry about arguing with her. . . . That made me want to be around my mom even more. Because I didn't want to lose my mom, you know? . . . [Now] I actually listen. Because I used to not even care. My mom was telling me to go do stuff, and I'd just be like, "No, I'm not doing that." Or "Mom, you can do it yourself." And there was one point where I actually got mad at my mom and punched a hole through my door, and I cussed her out. And I regret that now.

It is important to note that Dennis was nearly obsessed with the book *Tyrell,* along with its sequel *Bronxwood*, throughout much of his 8th-grade year, recruiting as many people as he could to read and bringing up the book's main character in nearly every conversation about books with classmates and teachers. It is not trivial that the mother in that book consistently shocked and disappointed Dennis, frequently sacrificing the well-being of Tyrell and his younger brother to satisfy her own needs. It's easy to imagine Dennis comparing that mother to his own, more selfless mother and rethinking his relationship with her.

FAMILIES, MINDS, AND TRANSFORMATION

Dennis was not the only one to mention growing sensitivity toward the feelings of family members because of reading. Students' expanding empathy and propensity to contemplate their own minds and the minds of others had them reconsidering their dispositions toward family, even beyond parents (more on this in Chapter 5). Tiana reported that in the book she was reading, "there was this girl, and her mom was all rude to her, and it kind of made me feel, it kind of had me feeling real bad, 'cause I was rude to my aunt, and my situation could have been worse." Other students saw siblings in a new light. For example, Hattie reported:

> When I read *The Sky Is Everywhere*, I thought, what if I lost my brother? Usually, I make comments about me hating him and all, but in the end, we do love each other because we're family. And even though he gets on my nerves, I'm glad he's my brother. 'Cause he's helped me out a lot, especially with my computer. I think people need to cherish their relationships with their family more. Even though they may hate them and sometimes they have really good reasons to. But life's too short, and you never know what's going to happen.

These reflections extended to feelings of concern. For example, Calvin confided: "Like suicide books, in *Glimpse* how her sister tried to kill herself. I worry, sometimes, if my brother tries to."

A more common observation had to do with adolescents rethinking their parents' motives and roles in their lives. Books adults might consider disturbing often helped the teens to consider that advice from their own parents—which they previously viewed as out of touch or just plain irritating—might actually be coming from a place of love and concern. In other words, they started seeing their parents' side of things. Adolescents who understand others' emotions, which, as we shall see in the next chapter, is expanded by engaged reading of narrative texts and related conversations, have higher-quality relationships with their parents.[11]

The role of talk in this process, both with peers and family members, once again can't be overestimated. The parent characters in books sometimes bugged the students as much as their own. In a discussion we observed, several girls pounced on a stepmother character who searched the room of a stepdaughter who was behaving oddly. Addie asserted, "I don't like it when parents in books try to, like, control their kids," and Riley even went as far to say she "wanted to jump in the book and slap" the stepmom. At first, Elise joined the attack, but after listening to the pounding of her peers for a bit, she gently pushed back: "But part of me understands [the stepmom's] like worried." Addie quietly echoed, "the worry . . ." and Riley, cautiously, agreed, "yeah." When Amber responded, "I understand the worry part, but I mean . . ." Elise interrupted and wondered aloud: "If I found [a journal], I wouldn't read it, but I understand, like, going through it and making sure she's okay. Like if you're not going to talk to me . . ." Shea, who had been mainly silent, agreed, "It's, like, different." Elise reiterated: "It's, like, different. It's a point of view thing. Like if I was someone's stepmom, and I was worried 'cause they won't talk to me, they hate me, and something's going on, like, I would try and find something." Amber conceded, "It's perspective." The point was not, though, about which of the girls came to agree or disagree about the stepmother's invasion of privacy. It was the acknowledgement that people—in many cases parents—might have good reasons to make decisions that initially rattle them.

The combination of conversations and reading helped them see the bigger picture about themselves and family. In the context of an ongoing family conversation about his older brother's future, Akeem offered an example of both relational and self-change that included his whole family. According to Akeem, his brother "plays basketball, and he never used to like to read much" and that "a bunch of colleges call." Unfortunately, his brother's grades would be too low for a scholarship. Akeem lamented, "He started to try this year, but he tried too late." As part of the ongoing family conversation, Akeem shared *The Last Shot* and in particular, how a character in the book was in a situation similar to that of his brother. In April, he quoted to us a relevant line from the book, which he had finished 6 months earlier: "They say, 'I'm going to be the only Johnson to ever graduate and go to college'. . . . And he does get good grades. He said, 'I made my mom happy with me.' And then she said, 'You keep it up.'"

To suggest simply that Akeem experienced dialogic relationships with characters within books and separate dialogic relationships with family outside of the texts does not fully explain this phenomenon. More accurately, the lines between engagement within and outside of texts were blurred at best. Akeem consistently noticed and reflected on the consequences of characters' actions, linking them to his own life, his brother's life, and the voices of his parents. He put it this way: "All the things my parents tell me, happens. I know it's true, because I used to think they was just trying to scare me, and all that . . . but it happens in the books. It happened to my brother." In other words, he didn't believe what his parents said until he read it in a book.

In explaining the significance of a Michael Jordan biography, Akeem seamlessly fused his life, Jordan's life, and the voices of their fathers (and grandfather) in an attempt to make sense of his own experiences:

> My dad tells me, and his dad, he tells him, like "If you dress like a businessman, you'll be treated like a businessman." He said, "If you dress like a bum, you'll be treated like a bum." And then he's talking about like when you go to all these places you want to dress good. And my granddad says, and he says, "Use your manners," and all that.

The perspectives of characters in books and those of Akeem's family existed in tandem, and he used them as tools to construct his identity and to make decisions.

Akeem claimed to have changed not just as a reader in 8th grade but also as a person and in relationships with others, and he attributed these shifts to his engagement through and around textual narratives that resonated with him. He said he began to see his older brother as "a second dad" and explained, "I changed this year because I want to do good when my brother leaves the house." Then, echoing the words of the character from *The Last Shot*, he added, "When he leaves I want to do good; I want to go to college."

But we'd be remiss if we didn't provide examples of when reading and talk served a role for adolescents making sense of difficult or absent family relationships. In the midst of a conversation about a character pressured to take steroids to impress his father on the football field, a couple of boys admitted to each other that their own fathers were barely present. The book's narrative and the permission to talk about what was important allowed them to unload nagging worries and insecurities and realize they weren't alone. The same was true with students whose families were facing challenging times. Another boy, after reading an Ellen Hopkins book, asked for another because the troubles experienced by her characters helped put into perspective his family's different set of struggles—financial loss, including the recent loss of their home. Reading didn't change the circumstances, but knowing, as he put it, that "[e]very family has problems" helped him endure the stress. We suspect that regardless of the health of family relationships, there were many students for whom reading and related talk made the inevitable tribulations of family life more bearable.

DISTURBING BOOKS AND DIFFICULT TOPICS

It wasn't easy for all the students to bring up difficult topics from the books with their family members, nor was it easy for all parents to accept that the books weren't exactly *Alice in Wonderland*. Not surprisingly, there were stories of resistance regarding the most provocative books. For instance, venting over her parents' opposition to her reading choices, books she said they had not read, Ginny explained:

> I think most of the books I read have life lessons. Like *Crank*. When I read those [books by Ellen Hopkins], it's not telling you, "Hey, go out and do drugs and have sex and stuff." It's telling you about how bad their life is if you do this stuff. What my parents don't get is that it's teaching me things that are good for me. It's in a positive way, but they think it's in a negative way. And I don't think so.

Chase recalled telling his stepfather about *Glass*, who reacted with, "That's a pretty mature book for you." Chase assured him, "Well I'm pretty mature, but you just don't know it."

In a conversation about *Living Dead Girl*, one of the first disturbing books she read early in the school year, Elise brought up the problem with her peers: "It takes a brave author to write something like that, knowing like there are going to be kids whose parents are like, 'No way, you can't read that.'" Addie and Josefina said they didn't hide from their mothers that they were reading it, but they tiptoed around the details. Elise lamented, "You're safe, like, picking a safe topic." Josefina said she would probably be less forthcoming with family than with peers when talking about this book, but Addie insisted that it was too important *not* to open up about it.

Things did open up, according to students, when parents and other care-givers read the books for themselves. Yolanda provided a detailed instance of this. Upon reading the first few chapters of *Living Dead Girl*, her aunt was unsettled. According to Yolanda, she was worried and said, "This is a dreadful book. . . . You shouldn't read stuff like this." Yolanda reassured her, "It really changed my thinking." Convinced to keep reading, Yolanda's aunt became as engaged as Yolanda and even had some uncertainty at the end of the book and needed to talk it through.

PARENT PERSPECTIVES ON STUDENTS' READING

We got a better sense of parents' perspectives by going straight to the source. In early summer one year, when parents could reflect on what had transpired over a year of engaged reading, we interviewed some of them, asking directly how they felt about their child's book choices. Overwhelmingly, parents were clear first about how their children had changed as readers. Violet, a kindergarten teacher, told us her daughter had been placed in special reading classes for years and had failed several end-of-year state reading tests. After someone's suggestion that her daughter might have an attention disorder, she took her to a psychologist for testing, all the while second-guessing herself. She confessed, "I think I've been teaching long enough to know Riley does not have that." She was reassured when the psychologist posited, "She's fine; she just doesn't like to read." Summing up the 8th-grade change, she observed: "Well, never in 13 years had Riley wanted to tell me about a story. Never. I mean she got so uptight about one book—she wanted to tell me the ending." Riley passed the end-of-year benchmark test and was released from the reading intervention class. Violet was relieved, and hopeful, adding, "She's reading now more than ever before, and that just thrills me."

Tessa, Heidi's mother, had a similar story. A 1st-grade teacher's suggestion that Heidi might have ADHD prompted Tessa to consult a psychologist who, she said, "ended up diagnosing [Heidi] with an auditory processing problem, that she wasn't able to read and comprehend what she was reading." In response, Tessa and her husband bought several computer programs purported to solve reading problems, but they saw little improvement over the years, and at least once, they fought a decision for Heidi to repeat a grade. Like Riley, Heidi began to read in 8th grade, not with a focus on explicit instruction in reading skills and strategies, but instead because her teacher focused on engagement. She passed her 8th-grade state reading test, but what stands out most to Tessa are the changes she observed at home:

> She's reading a lot more. She's reading a lot more constant. Her book lengths are getting thicker. I've seen her reading magazines now, which is something she never did before. . . . She's asked me to take her over to [a local bookstore] to buy her books all the time. That's really new. . . . It's like her confidence has just gone up. She came home with a list [of books], and we went and bought 'em!

Heidi also began searching for song lyrics on the computer, studying recipes for baking, and reading the weekly church bulletin, all of which were new practices for her, according to Tessa, and the kinds of everyday reading she had previously resisted.

Jack told us that his son Martin had never resisted reading prior to 8th grade and usually completed his reading assignments. Their house, according to Jack, was "full of books," and he said he had read to Martin since he was a young child, from classic literature such as Kafka's *The Castle* and Dostoevsky's *Crime and Punishment* "just so he could get used [to] the flow of words written the way it should be." It was not until 8th grade, though, that Jack felt Martin was "reading for reading's sake" and "starting to appreciate the craft," adding:

> He now goes up and reads every night before he goes to bed. And it's continued since school's been out. It's become a part of his deal now. He goes up and reads. I've caught him reading in the daytime, too.

Jack was candid, though, about his discomfort with the kinds of books Martin was reading, but not because of their mature content. He confessed he was struggling with the idea that students might not be assigned what he considered "the great works," as he had been as a teen. He also observed, though, "When I grew up, the young adult literature scene was much smaller." Several days after we spoke with Jack, he sent us an email message to say he had thought more about how engaged reading had affected his son's literacy development. He explained, "Martin has improved noticeably in his storytelling" and "Over the course of the year, his stories have become more cogent and compact," jokingly adding, "This has greatly improved our dinner conversation." It appeared that no matter what students' reading experiences were prior to 8th grade or what parents' expectations for reading had been, parents were sure that when their children read the books that matter to them, they develop as readers in significant ways.

Corroborating what students reported to us, all of the parents with whom we spoke reported that their children told them about the books they were reading. As one parent put it, "It's not a closet thing." The adolescents approached their parents with questions when they got hung up in their reading. For instance, Tessa recalled Heidi asking her about the meaning of "conscience," and it was only after a conversation about it that Heidi explained, "That's what's going on in this book." She also remembered having complex discussions that she described as more of a "spiritual type." She remembers Heidi asking her "When you die, do you think you come back?" and later learned that Heidi's reading of several books had inspired this question.

Jennifer described deep involvement in her daughter Ellen's reading experiences. According to Jennifer, Ellen insisted that she read particular books, and when we asked which titles stood out most for her, she mentioned *Thirteen Reasons Why*, a story of suicide, and *Wintergirls*, a story involving eating disorders. She confessed to us that she and her husband were watching these choices closely, noting that most of Ellen's choices seemed on "the darker side." However, she described how knowledge of these books had proven to be a useful tool in her parenting, specifically that "it has sparked some conversations." For instance, relative to one book, "We had a long conversation one night about cutting, and a girl she knew that was cutting, and she was worried about that."

When we asked specifically how Ellen's reading and Jennifer's involvement in her reading had affected their relationship, Jennifer offered specific examples:

> The books give us an excuse, permission to discuss things with her that might be harder to talk about otherwise. And we, last night, had a pretty serious discussion with her about her feelings, how she's feeling. She's on medication for depression, and how is that going. She also has been dating Harry for a year. . . . And Ellen is young. She's thirteen . . . So, I've been sort of grasping at straws about how to handle this. We talked last night again, about, it's

been a year, and you know, it's hard to go back to just holding hands if you do other things. So, I think the books, because there are things happening in the books, we can use that as a jumping-off point. And even last night, my husband hadn't read the book, but I was able to say, "Now, it's just like when so-and-so character did . . ." It somehow gets it out of the personal, and she doesn't feel attacked. . . . And I like to know what she's reading.

Jennifer described conversations about books as "a safe way for us to kind of get into some of these things." In other words, the books allowed the teenagers to think through life's decisions about drugs, sex, and other complexities in advance, in slow motion, with assistance from others, reducing the likelihood of subsequent poorly thought-out decisions.

Jennifer also reflected:

I personally find the books very interesting, so I have a hard time saying, "Okay you shouldn't be reading this." They appeal to me . . . I can remember reading a book—I do not remember the title—I was probably about her age, and the main character was Francesca, and she had an eating disorder. And I remember being very drawn to that book, and I've never had an eating disorder. I eat anything I want and too much of it! So it wasn't that I really related to it, but there was something in it that, you know, I had to read this book, I had to find out what happened to her.

Jennifer shared that her experiences with Ellen over reading had prompted her to nudge other parents, so she had organized a book club for some of the other 8th-graders' parents and their children, which met regularly in different families' backyards. In the spirit of this new intergenerational practice, near the close of our conversation with Jennifer, Ellen, along with her boyfriend Harry, showed up with two additional books they were encouraging Jennifer to read.

NOTES

1. Erikson (1963).
2. Larson et al. (1996).
3. Bowlby (1969).
4. Armsden & Greenberg (1987).
5. Cooper et al. (1998); Howard & Medway (2004).
6. Cooper et al. (1998).
7. Burge et al. (1997).
8. Raja et al. (1992).
9. Brumariu & Kerns (2010).
10. Armsden & Greenberg (1987).
11. Boele et al. (2019).

Part II

THE BREADTH OF TEEN DEVELOPMENT

CHAPTER 5

Social-Emotional Development

Emotional skills trump standardized measures of intelligence in predicting academic and personal achievement.[1]

—Mary Helen Immordino-Yang

Eighth-grader Marion reflected:

> I thought *Destroying Avalon* was really good, really sad at the end. But it just makes you think about, to pay attention to how people react, to pay attention to how they're feeling about stuff. Like when you see people, you don't really think, you know, you think, well, they don't have problems or whatever. But then some of the ones I've read, you can just understand people better.

Engaged reading, Marion observes, has expanded her ability and propensity to imagine people's thoughts and feelings and the contexts that might produce them. She hints that reading gives her a sense of diversity, but also commonality, a sense that life's struggle is not just her own. She notes the importance of attending to people's reactions—the physical and facial manifestations of their thoughts and feelings. Her claim is similar to Hattie's claim that we shared at the end of the Chapter 3. She is reporting not only a more observant, reflective, and human approach to others but also a recognition of her own thoughts and feelings.

This effort to understand others' thoughts and feelings is not somehow incidental—it becomes a quest, almost a compulsion. Tory confesses: "It's made me really want to understand, I just want to know, like, what's going on in [character's] head? Does she want to be, like, the center of attention? Does she want to be like her sister more? I don't get it [yet]. . . . If I keep reading it. Yeah. Then I might get a better understanding of it." Similarly, Shelly, observed, "I started trying to find deeper reading, something that, like, put me emotionally into the book."

It's not merely intellectual, as Eric commented, "I have a bit more sympathy now. After reading *Not Simple*, it's hard not to." The more readers become absorbed in the stories, the stronger their ability to empathize, which does not happen when they read expository texts, or when they are not engaged.[2] Reading these books gives students the experience of entering another's mind with the time and aesthetic distance to reflect on the experience. The process is transformative, even for people who are habitually emotionally disengaged or who avoid attachment.[3] Listen to the puzzlement of Maisy wrestling with her own transformation:

> I think I've become more respectful to others this year for some reason. Like, I care more. Like, I don't know . . . it's kind of weird . . . like, books, they tell you about, like, how some people feel. Like, I don't know if that's really how they feel, but, like, once I read the book, it's like these people who are being bullied, then I can tell how they feel, and then, so, like, I'm more respectful to people.

These students are describing a cluster of dimensions of human development: the ability and propensity to imagine and experience others' and one's own, beliefs, perspectives, feelings, and thoughts; the inclination to attend to facial and bodily indicators of those thoughts and feelings and the factors leading to them; and thus the ability to accurately make sense of them. For the sake of brevity, we'll call this cluster of abilities "mind reading," sweeping under the rug theoretical wrangling over distinctions among empathy, theory of mind, and mentalizing.[4] Mind reading is the core of a larger cluster commonly referred to in education literature as social–emotional learning (SEL). SEL generally refers to the ability to recognize emotions in others and ourselves, to manage them appropriately in challenging situations, and to establish and maintain positive and productive relationships with others.[5]

THE SOCIAL HUB OF DEVELOPMENT

Mind reading is a hub of human development with substantial effects on social interactions. For example, children who show angry or aggressive responses in personal interactions commonly have limited or distorted mind reading such that they adopt a blaming attitude, assuming hostile intentions in others, coloring their whole social experience.[6] By contrast, people with more developed mind reading collaborate better and have better social skills. They are more agreeable—one of the top five measures of personality, consisting of altruism, warmth, friendliness, and attentiveness to others' needs. All this leads to more friends, better friendship relationships, and a stronger social support network. It also leads to a lower-maintenance classroom life because students are less likely to misbehave and disrupt class, be absent, or get expelled from school.[7] Parents should appreciate that children with better mind reading are similarly less likely to misbehave outside of school.

Having a good understanding of one's own and others' emotional life is important as adolescents establish the ability to regulate their emotions.[8]

It makes adolescents less prone to anxiety and depression and more likely to experience a sense of well-being.[9] It helps maintain optimism and resilient responses to life's challenges.[10] It also likely moderates the relationship between intelligence and achievement.[11] The more accurately we are able to imagine others' emotions, the better we handle social conflicts and access and manage social resources, which brings us back to the relationships in Chapters 3 and 4.[12] Understanding the thoughts and feelings of others makes positive relationships possible. In short, nurturing mind reading is a good way to support the academic, social, and emotional development of young adults.[13]

In Chapter 3, we pointed out the fundamentally social nature of human beings and that biological systems have evolved to support our social evolution. Mind reading is at the heart of those systems. We are born predisposed to try to figure out what's going on in other people's heads. If an infant (3 to 18 months) is playing with a toy and you cover it with your hand, the infant will assume the move is intentional and will immediately look at your face to figure out what you think you're doing.[14] Because this foundation is so natural, we tend to take mind reading for granted, but it is only a foundation. It needs to be developed through a history of social interactions. As it turns out, becoming fully engaged with the characters in literary narratives is a kind of interaction that provokes changes in readers' ability to empathize and to imagine themselves into the minds of others.[15]

Readers identify and build relationships with characters, entering into dialogic interaction with them, interactions that don't just end when the book is put down. For example, Kevin had been reading *Gym Candy* and was frustrated with the main character, whose father had taught him to stifle his emotions: "It kind of made me think that he thinks that football is his life. There's no crying in football, so there's no crying in life" and, as if speaking directly to the character, "It's kind of like some people need to cry. So, when something like that happens, just let it out," a recognition of appropriate emotional regulation. Similarly, Addie observed, "I feel so connected to the characters that I don't want to leave them . . . I have a special bond with the characters, 'cause I just feel like I was in the book, and I was there beside them the whole time."

Readers' full engagement with narratives produces an immersive contextualized simulation of real social life, augmenting their ability to understand and empathize with others who are different from themselves, including their peers.[16] Calista pointed out:

> Like with urban fiction I don't know what happens in the ghetto. I don't know what happens, but it teaches me new perspectives on life. Like *Bully* and stuff, I never knew how alone some people feel, or what it's like to be in a mental hospital. Someone who attempts suicide, I don't know how they feel, so it helps me understand how they feel and it gives me new ways to view life.

TALKING ABOUT THOUGHTS AND FEELINGS

Although this sort of engagement with characters, by itself, affects the development of mind reading, it is not the only relevant vehicle. Mind reading
develops through conversations that exercise it, conversations with characters in books, but also conversations with peers and others in real life—
particularly conversations that invoke the use of mental verbs and mental
state language.[17] These, of course, were routinely the focus of the students'
conversations about their books—their own feelings and the feelings and intentions of characters. Marion explained, "when you talk about books, . . .
people are all talking about the same thing, . . . focusing on feelings and
stuff like that. So, everybody just seems more compassionate about things."
Feelings compelled the conversations about feelings, which led to a more
compassionate learning community, as Nia described:

> Like it would just be so random. You'd sit next to your friend, and you'd be
> like, "Hey, what are you reading? I'm reading this, you know." . . . 'Cause I feel
> like when you read a book, and you read something so crazy, you just have to
> talk to somebody. You just have to get it out, you know? . . . We told how angry
> our character made us feel, 'cause they did this, that. And "I'm so happy they
> got what they wanted," you know?

Paul explained, "Like my friend Daphne. She got emotional, kind of.
Every time she finishes a book, she talks to me about it. She talks about it
like she's seen it, and like how much she cried."
   In other words, these book conversations offer the perfect space in
which to explore and expand the vocabulary of emotional–relational life.
Our understanding of others' and our own emotional lives depends on the
language we have available for making sense of it and the experiences we
can unpack using that vocabulary.[18] Literature is one of the best sources
of such vocabulary,[19] and conversations about characters' experiences,
motives, and actions offer teachers opportunities to further augment the
students' emotional–relational linguistic tools. The better we understand
others' emotions and the contexts that invoke them, the better we understand our own emotions, and the better our own self-regulation.[20] This understanding is enlarged by the conversations: "If I be mean to someone,
I have to think about it from their point of view. Like someone might have
gone through a lot. Maybe had a bad home life. . . . Like the *Crank* series . . . like, I kind of told my friend that she should read it so that we could
talk about it."
   There is another way the book conversations contribute. At the beginning of the chapter, Marion observed that reading these books "makes
you . . . pay attention to how people react, to pay attention to how they're
feeling." In real life, accurately imagining others' thoughts and feelings

requires the ability to correctly "read" the facial/physical indicators of those thoughts and feelings. This component is partly developed through engagement with literary narratives. But Marion's observation suggests that the intention to attend to these indicators can transfer from reading to real-life interactions. And the emotions in the book discussions are certainly real and complex. In a peer-led conversation, Ted shared, "In *Why I Fight* this boy burns his house down, and I was thinking how bad that would feel to burn your house down by accident and then to get blamed for it." Similarly, commenting on *Living Dead Girl*, Shelly observed:

> The whole time when I was reading the book, I really wanted to like jump into the story and help Alice, and kind of free her from Ray. And it made me mad at some parts, and then sad, and happy. And I could actually FEEL those emotions.

This experience of emotions makes the book conversations a fertile arena for paying attention to each other's facial and physical reactions, testing out theories about emotions, and refining the accuracy of mind reading. However, it also awakens alertness to those indicators in other situations, as Marion observed:

> Basically, it was the same thing I was saying before, like, how everybody's so relaxed. I think I have, too. You tend to be nicer to people. And, just think about, you know how we have all those books like *Living Dead Girl*, where you think about how that stuff really happens. You kind of watch people more, you know, outside of school, to see if there's anything going on.

Researchers in recent years have recognized how reading narrative fiction, even in adults, improves mind reading with all the relational SEL benefits that brings with it.[21] Students were commonly aware of this, sometimes using it to take others' development into their own hands. For example, 11th grader, Addie—one of the few students whose 8th-grade reading was not undone by high school, in part because she had ample book conversations at home—well into a lengthy interview with Peter explained:

Addie: Some boys are now reading the John Green books, which I think is cool. . . . A lot of people read it once they turned it into a movie . . . *The Hunger Games*, too . . . [and] *Divergent*.
Peter: I was just thinking that a boy who was reading something like *The Fault in Our Stars* would probably be a good catch.
Addie: Exactly!! Actually, I ask my boyfriend to read books that mean something to me, because I want him to understand, like, "Look at what you should do. Look at how you should act and what appeals to me and what touches my heart."

Peter: What's inside your head.

Addie: Exactly!! It's a great way of showing someone what you mean without having to say it. I've been encouraging all these boys. I'm like, "This is your keys to the kingdom. Like, I don't know why you would ever not! There it is!"

Without reading too much into her comments, it's clear that Addie understands the possibility of transformation through personally meaningful books and the associated conversations that cannot easily be approached directly. And Addie is onto something. Aside from the advantages of an empathic partner with better mind reading, greater exposure to narrative fiction (not nonfiction) is associated with greater egalitarianism in gender roles and reduced gender stereotyping, without affecting attitudes toward appropriate sexual partners, behaviors, or circumstances.[22]

ON REFLECTION

There are at least two ways in which readers insinuate themselves into narrative texts. One is the recognition of the similarity between part of the text and personal memories. The second is when the reader identifies with a character or narrator, essentially role-playing and blurring the boundaries between self and other, invoking and modifying feelings. This process can transform everyday life and also past memories.[23]

Immersion in the emotional–relational lives of characters requires constructing others' lives while offering some distance and time for contemplation. It allows readers to examine the feelings and motivations and to view the process as a thought experiment, particularly as they engage with peers to consider the uncertainties and moral ambiguities. The distance and time allow for reflection not normally available in life in real time. This reflection on the self had a profound effect on individuals and their relationships. Trinity observed:

> I think of [my family] a lot differently now, because the books have changed my perspective on them. . . . Because I used to think they were really mean, or whatever. But then after reading *The Perfect Chemistry* and stuff, I just realized that they're trying to protect me.

Similarly, Jocelyn found that reading *Episodes*, a book by a young man with Asperger's syndrome, was like "sharing an experience with a friend who has the same problem as you," a way "to read how other people deal with it." She effectively counted the author among her other friends with Asperger's. But the distance offered by the book had a significant effect. She had previously been bothered by the fact that her mother had been reading books about Asperger's syndrome. "It would make me mad because I would think she's trying to figure me out or something." On reflection, she realized that resenting her mother's efforts to understand her experience "sound[s] pretty irrational now."[24]

Recognizing themselves, their friends, and their families in the characters' emotions and relationships offered ways of seeing themselves and their relationships in a new light and a way to step back and look, a little dispassionately, at their behavior in the context of longer-term goals. Roberto noted, for example:

> Well, like my relationships with my friends do better, 'cause like, see, like, in that book, it showed me not to be cocky . . . *Shooting Star,* and *Gym Candy.* . . . Because like if you're cocky, you'll lose most of your friends. And if you try to do something like to just get popular, like fight or do drugs, you don't get nowhere in life.

Listening carefully to Roberto's and the others' comments, we also hear the development of self-regulation, also linked to the development of mind reading, which we will return to in the next chapter.

TO SUMMARIZE

Students who are fully engaged with their reading actually enter the social worlds of the narrative, taking up characters' perspectives, experiencing their emotions, and entering relationships with and among the characters. The process expands the reader's ability and propensity to imagine themselves into the minds of others. This, in turn, makes readers more inclined toward prosocial behavior, improves the readers' chances of being accepted by peers, and builds larger and stronger friendship networks, in part because peers recognize them as more prosocial.[25]

The ambiguities, uncertainties, and emotional experiences arising from narrative engagements provoke conversations that examine emotional–relational experiences, augmenting the effects of the engaged reading, including developing the ability to more accurately read the minds of others. In a previous chapter, we noted that Christopher Masi and his colleagues' meta-analysis of interventions to reduce loneliness offered four successful strategies, two of which were relational—increasing opportunities for social contact and enhancing social support.[26] The other two were enhancing social skills and developing more accurate social cognition, exactly what the students have been describing.

At the same time, the engaged reading experience provokes reflection on the reader's own experience with the "aesthetic distance" afforded by the reading—reflection that can be transformative, not least because it improves emotional self-regulation. The ability to manage one's emotions, in turn, is related to personal resilience, the ability to maintain a positive strategic attitude when faced with life's inevitable negative events.[27] In other words, it makes people less vulnerable and offers them better mental health and well-being.[28]

The importance of SEL is lost in school language arts curricula. Economist Steven Levitt, Distinguished Professor at the University of Chicago, laments this absence, pointing out that if we want kids to do well in life, in schools:

> The real travesty is that we don't teach kids how to manage their emotional life. Why not teach kids anger management, how to get along with people? . . . It's weird. . . . I think if sensible people sat down to think about [the fact that] we hold kids hostage for 6 to 8 hours a day for the first 18 years of their life, what would we want them to know at the end?[29]

Good question.

NOTES

1. Immordino-Yang & Gotlieb (2017).
2. Mar et al. (2006).
3. Djikic et al. (2009a).
4. An array of constructs occupies researchers in this general domain who work hard to tease out and test the details of constructs and their causal relationships. We apologize in advance for this shortcut. For some of the complexity see for example: Cerniglia (2019).
5. Social–emotional learning is sometimes used to refer to the social–emotional competencies and sometimes to the process of acquiring them. We will use it in the former sense.
6. Mohr et al. (2007).
7. Sharp (2008); Petrides et al. (2004).
8. Rieffe & Rooij (2012).
9. Mavroveli et al. (2007); Sarrionandia (2018).
10. Schneider et al. (2013).
11. Agnoli et al. (2019).
12. Niven et al. (2012).
13. Zhao et al. (2020).
14. Phillips et al. (1998). Intellectually similar children with autism do not do this; they are more inclined to just try to remove your hand.
15. Djikic et al. (2009b).
16. Mar & Oatley (2008).
17. Furrow et al. (1992); Adrián et al. (2007); Ornaghi & Grazzani (2013).
18. Barrett (2017); Lindquist et al. (2015).
19. Stanovich (1992).

20. Sodian et al. (2003).

21. Mar et al. (2006).

22. Fong et al. (2015).

23. Kuiken et al. (2004).

24. The book had also generated conversation with a friend's mother whose words stuck with her: "She was like, 'You know, once you meet a kid with Asperger's or high functioning autism, you meet a kid.'" Jocelyn added, "We're pretty much as different as normal people are from each other. What is the extent of that word *normal*? If everyone is different, then what is normal?"

25. Mavroveli et al. (2009).

26. Masi et al. (2011).

27. Joseph & Newman (2010); Schneider et al. (2013).

28. Armstrong et al. (2011); Liu et al. (2013).

29. Ward (2021, p. 16).

CHAPTER 6

"Who Will I Be?": Building a Life Narrative

I'm especially inspired by *If I Stay*. That's one of the books I won't ever forget. That's one of the stories that's going to stay with me forever. 'Cause it changed that family's life a lot. And I've pretty much changed as much as the girl in *If I Stay*. I'm not dead, but (laughing) . . . I'm alive. And I'm just going to change the way she changed her ways a lot. . . . I've made some really big decisions this year.

—8th grader Darla

Reading *If I Stay*—in which the main character contemplates life, death, and the future as the only family member surviving a car accident—was transformative for Darla. Her comments reveal a young adult asserting agency over the narrative trajectory of her life—who she intends to become. Robyn Fivush, director of the Family Narratives Lab at Emory University, argues that we talk ourselves into existence through stories:

> We talk about ourselves, our thoughts, and emotions; our intentions, hopes, and fears; as well as about others, how their lives intersect with ours, and how all of this interrelates with our present and our future. In essence, we construct coherence and meaning for our own lives through reminiscing with and about others.[1]

The narrative *If I Stay* provoked Darla to take herself as an object of study, just as she might a character, and exercise some authorial agency over her character's narrative trajectory. Jeff Sugarman and Jack Martin explain: "In the process of enacting psychological descriptions of ourselves as certain sorts of persons, we become the kinds of beings we are. . . . It is an active structuring of existence."[2] In other words, as humans, we have the capacity to examine our lives and exercise some agency over who we become and how our lives will play out. Darla's claim is that books like *If I Stay* are a tool for that agency.

We encountered these acts of self-construction over and over again in our interviews—not surprising really, since constructing a life narrative, a self, is a major task of adolescence.[3] In interviews, the self-construction process was invariably linked to reading emotionally engaging books and the resulting conversations with peers, teachers, parents, and selves. These acts of self-construction were transformative, and always in positive ways. Consider Jeremy's comments after reading a book in which the main character has to make decisions about whether to act in ways that perpetuate cycles of gun violence or to do something different:

> *Homeboyz* [caused me to change]. It, like, takes you through stages of him growing up, while you're, at the same time you're reading the book, you're thinking about him growing up, so that makes you want to grow up with him, and like be mature and not do, like, stupid stuff. Yeah, so that book helped me become a better teenager or something. It's what I feel like.

Like Darla with *If I Stay*, Jeremy used the process of reading *Homeboyz* as a tool for building a better self-narrative and, consequently, a better self. Before we consider the many facets of these transformations, the contrast between these two examples invites a temporary sidebar: It seems unlikely that Darla would have had the same transformative experience with *Homeboyz* that she had with *If I Stay* and equally unlikely that Jeremy would have had a similar experience with *If I Stay*. What is the likelihood of these experiences happening if these students and their peers were all required to read, say, *The Scarlet Letter*? More on this later.

Students found themselves making transformative self-revisions in several ways. Some simply lived into a character—always a positive character when taking it up as a mentor. Some, like Jeremy, used the character's decision-making and narrative trajectory as a cautionary tale, taking steps to exclude possibly problematic life paths. Some synthesized principles from the collection of books they read. Some were transformed through the conversations in the context of their daily life complexities.

LIVING INTO A CHARACTER

It's common enough for adolescents to look for aspirational role models—historical figures, media "influencers," peers, sports figures, hip hop artists, and so forth. It turns out that books are a good a place to find them, and in books, it's easier to explore the thoughts, feelings, and decision-making—the most informative parts—of these role models. For example, Addie assured us that *The Book of Bright Ideas* was good, encouraging us to read it, explaining:

> There's a character in the book named Freda, and I know that I base myself off of her a lot, because she's strong and she's witty, but she's still kind of sensitive.

But she helps to guide other women, and she helps them to feel good about themselves. And I think I love her character. I fell in love with her character. And that book, like, every day I'm thinking what would Freda do? . . . I think it's in the characters and their thought processes.

"What would (should) Freda (I) do?" Students often reported this merging of the chosen character and the self for purposes of decision-making and making sense of the world. This strategy, at least with young children, offers emotional distance that improves executive function.[4] However, students also reported using the character as an internal conversation partner when in need of advice. Many recognized this instrumental value of books. For example, reflecting on what she had learned as a reader after a year of engaged reading, Marta asserted:

> Books aren't really just books. You know? I used to look at books like, yeah, it's a story on pages, and it's really fun to read. But now I'm relating them to real-life situations, and I find myself, like, going to characters in books for advice.

Given the range of potential role models in books, some might worry that students would choose negative models or hang out with unsavory characters in their heads. Audrina, a student in an alternative school, reported taking up negative role models—but only within the narrative. Asked, "What draws you to those books?" she explained that she took up the identities of the characters as she read, becoming "technically, this bad kid in this book," but "still this good child that hasn't done that. . . . When I do come back to reality . . . I'm thankful that I'm not that kid because I don't want to be in that circumstance." In other words, some imaginary time spent in the heads of questionable characters allowed her to understand the consequences of bad decisions in a safe space without actually having to experience them, making it less likely she would engage in risky activity in the first place. Others either did the same, or simply adopted aspirational characters. Students, such as Marta, distinguished clearly where their interests lay:

> I'll find myself thinking about that, like, what would this person do, and I'll try to, like, follow them—if it turns out good. Obviously not like in *Crank*, but like in *A Child Called It*, that kind of inspired me to be, like, a spokesperson.

Role model inspiration came from narratives, whether from fiction or biography. Sadie was inspired by *Soul Surfer*:

> It's a very inspiring book. It changed my view in life . . . she has a struggle because she only has one arm, so she puts her faith in it, and I'm really strong in my faith of things. So seeing how she struggles, it shows me that I can do things that I don't usually do.

These changes were noticed by others. For example, Holly independently observed, "My friend Sadie, when she read the book *Soul Surfer*, she's changed a lot from the self that she was. She's a lot stronger in her faith from reading that book. She takes more time to figure out things."

A REFLECTIVE METAPHOR

Students routinely entered and experienced characters' social worlds, engaging with a protagonist's emotional, relational, and moral challenges. However, reading also allowed them to simultaneously experience and identify with the perspectives of multiple characters while taking the time to ponder behaviors, decisions, situations, and consequences, affording some distance between themselves as readers and themselves as characters. This distance allowed the recognition of metaphorical relationships between elements of a character's life narrative and their own—recognition of a self-narrative that made them uncomfortable. For example, having read *If I Stay*, Darla reflected:

> It really got to me, *If I Stay*, cause the way the girl treated her parents, I kind of treated my parents just like that. Like I kept on pushing them away from me. I didn't want them to know anything about my life. I was always sneaking around doing things that I shouldn't have, and I realized that my parents were going to be there every step of the way, whether I like it or not. They were going to be there to calm me down. They were going to be there if I was upset or crying. They were going to be there if I was mad.

This process of at once standing inside and outside a character, effectively zooming out to see the bigger picture, was another nudge to narrative reconstruction. Lola had a similar experience in a different book, commenting, "some of the things that happened kind of like reminded me of myself, like her not listening and stuff, to her mom trying to say stuff. Like, I would do that."

The self-recognition in a metaphorical relationship could be quite powerful. Darla reported that "when I read, I can be in the book with that person." In reading *Living Dead Girl*, Darla became angry not only at the protagonist's abuser but also at the abused protagonist for accepting the relationship. In the process, she recognized a similar relationship in her own life and decided not to be like the character in the book. Darla took control of her self-construction by rejecting the toxic relationship she had been accepting:

> From when Ray beat her and did those things to her—this girl, she kind of bruised me with what she did. So, I decided to get rid of her. I was tired of her treating me the way that she was treating me. I didn't want to deal with it

anymore. Like, every day I would wake up and I would feel that I would have to rely on her for everything that I did. Everywhere I'd go she'd have to come with me, and I was just tired of it. I wanted to be independent. I wanted to do things by myself. It was always me by her side looking for someone to be with 24/7.

Darla made major changes in her peer relationships, taking control of her self-narrative.

Students were aware of their transformations and their source in the books, offering them a tool for self-construction. For example, Lawrence asserted that his "attitude" had changed:

I've gotten way more mature than acting like a little 4-year-old. . . . Reading how people in books, how the characters are, how they act and stuff, makes me think how they shouldn't do that. How they should change what they're doing. Just quit doing that and go home. And it just made me think, because I did some of that stuff they were doing.

This recognition of the instrumental value of books in the construction of a self-narrative opened new relationships between the students and books, a reason to read not normally considered in discussions of adolescent reading, but, as you will see, evident in many students' comments.

NARRATIVE AS A CAUTIONARY TALE

Many of the books chosen by the students were edgy, including reference to drugs, gangs, sex, incest, and other elements that make adults nervous. Indeed, some students described their reading preferences as "intense and disturbing." But they saw the content as relevant to their lives, to issues they were either in the midst of or saw as impending. Gavin observed:

'. . . cause we've been reading things about people our age and the things they go through and the choices they make. . . . It kind of helped, because we go through those things, too, and it helps us learn about ourselves. And you can kind of relate to the characters in the book. If they make a bad choice, then you shouldn't make that choice. It's kind of like your life in a book. You get to know what happens ahead of time.

This idea that their reading allowed them to preview the consequences of particular decisions was ubiquitous. With regard to engaging in sex, Aisha commented:

Like, some books, girls they do drugs and then they have sex and stuff, and then, like, it shows, like, the outcome and all that, and it makes me think why should I do that? I might end up like that. It makes me reconsider things.

The same was the case with drugs. For example, Marta commented:

> . . . . I guess like every teenager, you hear about drugs all the time, and your friends are doing it, and they make it sound so wonderful. So, for a little while, I'm starting to second-guess myself. I'm like, am I really right not to be doing them? They seem to be having a good time. And then I read the *Crank* series, and I was like, okay this is where my friends are going to end up, and I don't want to be there as well.

Similarly, Michael was one of several football players whose paths were clarified through books: "In *Gym Candy*, he's a football player and he gets on steroids, so it ends up turning in a bad way. So, I guess that, 'cause I play football, so I guess that changes some things, like not to do."

Again, this conscious use of books as life-crafting tools was common, as Jana confessed:

> Sometimes I'll have the same idea as a character in the book, and I'll see a character do it first to see if they work it out, or if it works for them. So, I think before I do things now. . . . Um . . . just to see some of the characters, like, crash and burn in their lives, makes me want to do something with my life so I don't end up like them.

The advice students constructed from the narratives of others' lives was often exactly the kind of advice parents might have offered. However, such advice coming from parents is often unhearable by their adolescent children who are busily trying to separate themselves from their parents. This point was not lost on Shelly who, after reading *Living Dead Girl*, observed:

> Like my mom is, like, "Don't run off. Be where you are supposed to be." That's because if I'm somewhere I'm not supposed to be, and something happens to me, my parents will never know where I am. Like, if I say I'm going to go to my god-sister's house, and I go to my friend's house [hypothetically, of course], and something bad happens while I'm there, my parents will never know what happened, and that scares me the most. 'Cause if something happens to me, and I get kidnapped or something, I want my parents to know where I was when it happened. Like, if something ever happens like that, it would scare the crap out of me. My parents are like "stay where you're supposed to be." Now I'm like, "Yeah, okay, I will."

In the face of a disturbing book, parental advice or rules—previously seen as harassment, plain and simple—suddenly seemed entirely sensible and motivated by love rather than distrust.

These life-changing realizations had a viral quality. Having changed their own life narrative, students took it upon themselves to bend the narrative arcs of their peers. Unlike parents, who might directly offer advice, students were more canny. Realizing that unsolicited advice doesn't always go well, they commonly took a different route. Jeremy pointed out that:

> In the beginning of the year, some of my friends would, like, Danny, he was thinking gangs were all cool, right? And then I read *Homeboyz*, and then I told him to read *Homeboyz*, and now he don't like gangs. He ain't into them. He's like friendly now, into sports, just like me. So, alright. Cool.

More generally, Jeremy recognized that reading books was serving him well, so he also proselytized about that: "I'm trying to, persuading other people, to like, read books too, now." And it wasn't "pleasure reading" that Jeremy and others were pushing on their friends. It was "disturbing" books. The students appreciated that the books disturbed their thinking.

SYNTHESIZING PRINCIPLES

For some students, it was a specific book that had transformative properties. Others synthesized principles or plans across the books they had read. Perhaps it was the fact that a repeating pattern in different stories suggested an element of truth. Shelly recognized the bad decisions of characters across two different stories and her own history and abstracted a principle. While talking about *Crank*, she connected it to *In Ecstasy*:

> Because I don't make the best choices in the world, and that book, you can say, "Well, it's not THAT bad," like it will only be a one-time thing, whether it's drugs or stealing or whatever, like, but it becomes a habit eventually. It's like the same thing in *In Ecstasy*. That's how it was in that book, too. It was, like, just for fun, and then it got really bad. It made me think, well, if I'm going to do something just one time, well I better think again before I do something because it can really mess up my life.

These realizations were often momentous. In end-of-year interviews, we asked all the students whether they had changed as a person over the year. Most recognized that they had, and "maturity" was the most common term they used, and it seemed related to a reflective sense of agency with respect to their life-narrative. Marta, for example, observed:

> I think I've grown up maturely. I've been able to look at myself and say, "Okay, this is what's gotta be done. Okay, we need to relax and take time and smell the roses, but we also need to plan for the future."

Explaining changes she made after reading specific books, Darla noted that reading these texts:

. . . has really brought me out to be another person, to be someone that I used to not be. Because I used to be all mean, and just, hateful. I used to be rude and disrespectful, but I'm polite now, and I learned how to not be so rude, and have manners. . . . In the future, I believe if I keep reading, I can achieve more things than now. That I'm going to be better than anybody, and I'm gonna be able, if somebody's gonna try to take me down, or tear me down or upset me, I'm just going to be a better person. I'm not going to listen to what they're saying. I'm just gonna walk away. Usually now, if somebody says something, I'm not gonna walk away, especially if it's insulting.

Similarly, Elise explained:

I've read books about mean people, and I used to be, I was a person who was, like, very guarded, and if you didn't like me, then that's your problem. And I'm who I am, so if you have a problem with me, get over it. And then, like, reading about all those mean girls who think like that, the things that happen to them, it made me sit back and question it. So, it's been, like, I've been a nicer person. But I'm more energetic.

Students like these were abstracting a pattern from a collection of narratives and deciding how that pattern would inform their own life-narratives because, as one student sagely put it, the books give you "different views on, like, life, and you only got one chance at it."

SELF-REGULATION

In the diverse stories about students' transformations, there is a common thread of asserting agency over self and life narratives—an aspect of self-regulation or executive function. As we noted in Chapter 5, stronger mind reading begets better self-regulation. However, students also report other paths to self-regulation.

It's common enough to talk about opportunity costs, but we should also consider opportunity benefits. It turns out that the simple act of becoming engaged in reading meant that problematic behaviors diminished through lack of opportunity. Tory noticed this: "I used to get, like, mostly I'd get into a lot of trouble, but since I've read a lot, I don't get into as much trouble anymore, because I'm mostly into my book all the time." She explained further:

I don't know, but I think, just like me reading has helped me get through school. 'Cause like last year I don't know how many times I got ISS [internal school suspension], 'cause I didn't read last year or in 6th grade, so I got sent to the office so many times. But then when I started reading, like, I don't get involved in so much drama anymore, so I just keep to myself, so I don't get in trouble. [My mom] saw that I don't get in trouble as much. She said, "Is it because you're reading?" I'm like, "Yeah." And she's like, "Well I think you should keep going, then." 'Cause she wants me to get a scholarship to college, to be actually a woman going to college and not screw up my life by getting pregnant or doing drugs or going to jail or something like that.

Jeremy, who was in special education, told a similar story.

I used to be like super, super, super hyper when I'd come to school. That was like in the beginning of the school year, too, this year. Now I'm like chill, I'm chillaxin', you know. Relaxin', chill in class, doing my work now. And I think that part of that is because of books. They give me something, like, to do when I'm fidgetive. I'll just turn to the next page and read, instead of getting in trouble.

Notice Jeremy is fully conscious of using reading for self-management and altering his self-narrative. He noticed this once he was engaged in reading. Without the engagement, there would be no way to convince him that reading would be a good way to keep himself out of trouble.

Engaged reading, by itself, was an effective strategy for self-regulation for other reasons, too. Addie reported emotional self-regulation:

Like the cool thing about reading is that when I'm really upset or something, and I need to get something off my mind, I'll just go read a book, and I'll snap out of it during the reading time, and I'll just feel much better. And it calms you down, I guess.

However, the recognition of cause and effect, gained from reading narratives that reveal the consequences of decision-making, was particularly powerful. It made students take the narrative trajectory of their lives seriously, particularly at the immediate behavioral level. Consider Quinton, a young man in special education who, for the first time, passed the state reading test.

I read books about people's lives. *Homeboyz, Rucker Park Setup, War of the Blood in My Veins.* They're in gangs and they seek redemption. That word comes up a lot in the book I'm reading now. . . . My mom was shocked when I asked her for books. She said, "Quinton, I don't know if you've matured or what." I've told her it's a new lifestyle. It makes me think about things that I do before I do them. I used to do things before thinking. Now I think about the consequences.

The clear recognition of a new self, both by Quinton and his mother, is striking. Others, such as Lindsay, reported the same experience:

> I have changed because I think more about things before I do them, and reading is more a part of my life than it was ever. Like, I enjoy reading way more, and I read more meaningful stuff, not just like random stuff. It gave me a different perspective on things, like how people actually feel when things go on. It just tells me that I should be a better person, and that I need to put a stop to things before they get too far.

While Quinton's and Lindsay's stories of self-agency speak to relatively short-term narrative management, others also looked to the longer term. For example, reflecting on her reading of *The Rose That Grew From Concrete*, by Tupac Shakur, Maisha explained:

> His poems and words. Like when I read them it makes me think about how his environment was growing up. I mean, I lived it. My mom, she had me when she was 17. Didn't know exactly where she was going. So, it was kind of hard, but. . . . His words reminded me of my own self, in a way, but it made me feel like I should be more thankful. 'Cause I used to be a brat. It makes me feel I should be more thankful and take more responsibility and doing things that I think are right and trying to help other people out. When I grow up, I'm going to college to become a criminal justice detective, or a social worker or something like that. I feel like I have a way in life of helping a lot of people.

We can hear in Maisha's story both a recognition of herself and her life and the decision that she wanted a more meaningful, morally satisfying life. Having a purpose in life reduces the likelihood of self-absorption, the source of many anxieties.[5] Note that the provocation for her rethinking was in the moral discomfort experienced in her reading. This provocation from moral discomfort is also clear in Holly's account:

> Some of them that I've read, like *Before I Fall*, it's like how this one girl tried to change everything to make it like it should be, and I feel like in my life sometimes I need to make changes and make things right.

We will explore the matter of moral development more fully in the next chapter.

RECONSTRUCTING THE SOCIALIZED SELF

This learning about other, different people's lives sometimes expanded to an understanding that individual selves are socialized products of interactional histories, and thus, different interactional futures might shift the direction of their lives. Rashad, a second-generation gang member, experienced in

8th grade an ongoing dialogue about his life, both within books and with his classmates and teacher. A pivotal moment came when Rashad read a memoir of a man who, as a young child had been raped by a male cousin, later joined a gang for connection, became a sexual predator himself, and committed countless other unspeakable violent acts before making a major life change (*My Bloody Life: The Making of a Latin King*).

Rashad was startled by the information made available to him in this narrative, and he recruited many classmates, as well as his teacher, to read the book. Not able to reconcile the author's brutal actions with their own experiences, other readers called upon Rashad to explain and also to ask how he viewed his own future. These conversations prompted him to recognize similarities between his life and that of the author, but also some unsettling differences. For instance, he shared that he believed that for him, as with the author, joining a gang meant securing a family. But simultaneously, he explored news stories of his gang's activity in other locations and learned, for instance, that members were sex trafficking young girls, disturbingly similar in magnitude to the violent, depraved acts he read in *My Bloody Life*.

Recognizing similar historical patterns of behavior in himself and the potential for future patterns, and also that the author of the book had eventually made changes, he appeared to recognize that through his decisions he had some agency over what seemed previously destined. For instance, he began to take seriously his classmates' questions about whether it was possible for gang members to go to college, searching the Internet and other books for positive examples. He also began outlining a draft for his own memoir, using characters and incidents from books he read to help organize his story in an elaborate graphic organizer. When Gay asked what motivated him to write, he recalled the introduction to *My Bloody Life*, in which the author wrote, "I hope this book can save the life of at least one kid" (p. xvii).

Rashad recognized both self and other as products of interactional histories. He recognized the possibility of agency in changing his future. At the same time, he recognized that decisions about his own actions affected others' futures: With agency comes moral responsibility.

WHO AM I? WHO DO I WANT TO BE?

The sense of agency in constructing a self is an obvious thread that runs through these stories. But the sense of self is also determined by other factors. For example, passing the state test for the first time had an impact on Darla:

> . . . . . I'm so proud of myself. I didn't believe that I could do it, and I did it. And I'm just going to go spread joy because all my other scores, I've never passed a [state] test in my whole entire past life, and I finally passed one. . . . Yeah. I'm gonna bring myself out more. Now that I've done that, I believe I can do anything.

Though we can't establish unequivocal causation, our data suggest that the reason she passed the state test for the first time might be attributed to the sheer volume of reading she did and the conversations she had about those books with her peers and her teacher.

The conversations had their own consequences on students' self-stories. Many students found themselves to be more outgoing, like Jackson: "I was kind of in a shell last year. I was almost like, shy, sort of. Not so much this year, like, at all." Likewise, Michael observed, "I don't know, I just think I've been more outgoing this year than last year. I think I've gotten more friends." Though in Jackson's and Michael's interviews, they make no attribution for this shift in sense of self, our data suggest that it is simply a reflection of their experience. They read a book that they can't stop thinking about and *have* to talk to someone about, which overcomes their shyness. In the process, they find other people are engaging to talk with, not judgmental, and are interested in talking with them. This changes who they think they are. It makes them feel like bona fide members of a community of engaged readers—an academic community. Elise explains her self-transformation, "I feel like I used to be a very social person, and I'm not a very academic person, but I can actually, like, have conversations about books, now, which is kind of weird for me." You can almost hear the old identity and the new identity, developed over different time scales, colliding as she speaks.[6]

Asked to explain, she said, "Yeah. 'Cause I'm not the brightest cookie ever. . . . Like, I struggle with my grades, but I can push myself," which she says has allowed her to find a different side of herself. This sort of shift has been referred to as "restorying."[7] It reflects the unavoidable entanglement of the academic and the social and the fact that, within the academic talk of the classroom, students are not only learning subject matter, they are also becoming "identified as recognizable types of people."[8]

These changes in self-construction are maintained partly through self-talk. For example, Darla observed in her end-of-year interview, "This year I really didn't put myself down." Asked what caused the change, she asserted, "Books. Me reading, 'cause I've read a lot this year." Of course, self-talk is not enough. Besides, self-talk begins in social interactions that become internalized. The self-changes have to be socially maintained, which means others, particularly peers, have to interact with you in ways consistent with the new self. They have to change their view to match so that the new self is reflected in the interaction. Fortunately, peers readily noticed the changes, as we saw earlier with Sadie's changed self following her reading of *Soul Surfer*. But this was common because of the persistent conversations among the students, as Norma remarked earlier, "Yeah, everyone has gotten so much smarter. Like they're all . . . we always talk about books." Amber agreed, "A lot of my friends in class have changed the most. I guess their perspective on the world, certain parts of their lives."

The changing self-constructions were also sustained through a changing relationship with reading, specifically a recognition of its value and function. Addie nicely captures the significance of books for constructing a life narrative and the recognition of her peers as readers:

> You gain wisdom through reading. I stick to that. You gain so much wisdom through reading. If you've ever noticed, the people who don't read don't tend to make the best choices. I mean, it's better to experience something tragic through a book and then be able to come out from it and know better things about it than to experience it yourself and to deal with all the pain and grief.

NOTES

1. Fivush (2019, p. 835).
2. Sugarman & Martin (2011, p. 284).
3. Erikson (1963).
4. White & Carlson (2016); Myers et al. (2014).
5. Damon et al. (2018).
6. Wortham (2005).
7. Worthy et al. (2012).
8. Wortham (2004, p. 715).

CHAPTER 7

Moral Development

Don't be afraid to stick out. Be a snitch in bad case scenarios. In my book [*Leverage*], my character sees the football players picking on a cross country runner . . . the boy is like, "I will never forget this day." He is never the same after that . . . he stuck up for him, but then the boy committed suicide . . . this last chapter the boy . . . he doesn't know whether he should tell because [it's the two best players] who are responsible . . . I've learned in my reading, don't do what other people do just to fit in. Do what's best, in your opinion.

—8th grader Wilson

Schools worry about students' academic development. They generally don't take seriously the fact that young adults are also developing as moral beings. The reasons for this doubtless include that parents do not want schools messing with their children's moral development or, as some fear, "indoctrinating" them. Parents will disagree about the nature of morality and its development. Nonetheless, we should face the fact that moral development is an important dimension of adolescence. At least we should consider whether there are elements we can agree upon in some way and how moral development relates to school learning and activities. For example, schools can't operate well if students think cheating and bullying are perfectly fine.

Adolescents' moral development doesn't simply happen by adults asserting and enforcing black and white rules for values and behavior. Rather, it happens as young adults think through decisions within their experience of the complexity of human existence. As they enter adulthood, they will face decisions about who they wish to become; what they value; and how they wish to act in the context of drugs, sex, gangs, peer pressure, and the many other complications of modern human life. Some will have already made such decisions in middle school. For example, by 9th grade, about one in four students have already had sex.[1] In general we suspect adults might agree that forethought and planning before the heat of the moment is preferable.

In the previous chapter, we heard students taking control of their lives through moral decisions they would make, as Lawrence observed:

> See, like, when I was reading *Homeboyz*, it really made me think of how your life can be really messed up, like, if you do the wrong thing, and you have to pay the consequences. So, I've been thinking about that some. It kind of got to me.

The books helped many students commit to making what most parents might think of as more moral choices. But like Lawrence, their logic was self-centered, a recognition of the likely consequences for themselves, albeit with a longer-term perspective. They chose not to take drugs, get drunk, or join gangs because they saw what might happen to them if they did. Parents might be pleased about this because in 2017, over 28% of U.S. 8th through 12th graders reported using illicit drugs.[2] In the same vein, over 17% of 12th graders report binge drinking within the previous 2 weeks. That's five or more drinks in a single event, and the rates are higher for female than male students.[3] Let's not even think about the problem of joining gangs.

Reducing these poor decisions is a good start, but moral development is about more than self-interested decision-making with positive outcomes. We wouldn't give high moral marks to chief executive officers (CEOs) who made decisions to protect the environment simply because not doing so would diminish their compensation package. We might give higher marks if, for principled or caring reasons, they made the decisions for the greater good *in spite of a reduction* in their compensation package. In other words, we judge moral development, in part, based on intentions and the tension between self-interest and prosocial behavior or evolved moral principles.[4]

Reasonable people will disagree about the values underlying certain moral decisions. Nonetheless, there are decisions most will agree represent a positive moral stance. Contrasting two 8th-grade readers who read about a similar issue in two different books drives home this point. When one student read *Hate List*, which begins with a mass shooting and suicide in a high school cafeteria, his response was a commitment not to ridicule classmates because he worried about revenge. This is a sensible strategy in service of self-preservation, but not one meant to reduce the pain and suffering of others. Shelly, on the other hand, described a prosocial stance:

> I read *Some Girls Are*, and it made me really think about how bullying affects people in like a really big way, and um, in that book, a girl was iced or frozen out of her clique, or whatever, and it really affected her really bad. People harassed her like all throughout the school year. And that's just an example. I learned that bullying people is, not the best in the world because it can affect people in a really bad way.

DEVELOPING THE MORAL SELF

As we saw in previous chapters, mind reading underlies much moral development. It encourages the possibility of decentering oneself and caring for others. More empathic adolescents, in fact, develop more advanced moral reasoning and are more likely to engage in prosocial behaviors.[5] However, there is also another force at work—identity construction, a critical task of adolescence. As adolescents build their sense of who they are, they develop a collection of selves they integrate into an "ideal self." They can centralize in this construction a range of different selves (musician, athlete, geek, etc.), one of which is their moral self— "the extent to which people identify with, and are invested in, being a moral person and doing what is moral."[6] For example, when altruistic people describe themselves, moral characteristics are at the center of their description. Self-construction that centralizes moral identity in the life narrative predicts later community service,[7] less antisocial behavior,[8] more prosocial behavior,[9] and less behavior that jeopardizes health, such as drug and alcohol use or risky sex.[10] Think of this as young people constructing the central character for their life narrative. The moral features of that character constrain the possible behaviors in the narrative.

How does this development of moral identity relate to reading the young adult books the students preferred? First, the majority of the books they chose feature moral dilemmas, the very thing that made them engaging (and "disturbing"). For instance, Roberto read lots of stories built around football players, and as he explained, they "give you situations":

> Like in *Shooting Star*, the trainer thinks [the main character] is on steroids. She talks to the coaches, and they get with him, and ask if he is juicing, which is using steroids. He thought in his head, then he stuttered, and he was like "No . . . no sir." If it was me, I wouldn't use it. But if it was me, I'd tell my coach the truth. 'Cause, too, he probably could help you. Instead of getting up there fast, you could build muscle up by weight training.

But Roberto had been talking to friends about this and other books, because many of the situations he encountered in books offered no easy answers and necessitated talking with others. About *Gym Candy*, another book involving steroid use, Roberto said to a group of boys, "In that situation, you think how you would think about that, like how you would solve that problem." This led to a conversation in which the moral crisis they deliberated was what you might do if you learned a friend or teammate was taking steroids. Several of the boys said they would keep the information private but try to help wean the friend off the drugs. Wilson disagreed: "I think if you take it step-by-step, they'd probably think you're agreeing with them, that it's right to do the drugs . . . I'd tell his parents to sign him up for rehab." There were no easy or agreed upon solutions. Conversations like this became the norm. These deliberations—about how they, as themselves or as a book character, might handle particular moral dilemmas—became foregrounded in the construction of self-narratives.

Stories about the self, in particular those that involve doing or experiencing harm, raise questions about our concept of who we are. The struggle to make sense of those events complicates and elaborates our sense of self, producing growth.[11] Sharing these stories invites reflection on values and moral stance. It has the same effect on listeners. Robyn Fivush, director of the Family Narratives Lab at Emory University, points out that adolescents hearing such stories from their parents, for example, particularly when there is an explicitly articulated moral lesson to the story, have a better sense of well-being and meaningfulness in their lives, along with a better sense of autonomy, mastery, and purpose.[12]

The bridge between the moral self and moral behavior is a sense of moral agency, which Holly Recchia and her colleagues describe as "an understanding of themselves and others as agents whose morally laden actions are based in their motivations, cognitions, and emotions."[13] In other words, moral agency is the awareness of the implications of one's actions in terms of justice and care. Having a sense of moral agency means recognizing the self as the unifying element responsible for a history of actions with consequences for others. Building the moral self requires acting accordingly, building a history consistent with that sense of self.

Sometimes our actions are inconsistent with that sense of self, so we have to find a way to explain our behavior to ourselves that keeps the central character's morality intact, so we adjust the narrative. This can lead to self-serving cognitive distortions, such as victim-blaming or harm-minimizing, which can neutralize empathy, a process that, if unchecked, can become normal and general. Consider, for example, the book *Thirteen Reasons Why*, which was read and discussed endlessly by the 8th graders (years before the controversial Netflix series adaptation). Around that same time, Gay attended, at a different school, a teacher reading club that had selected the book. The teachers' reactions to Hannah, a main character who had taken her own life, were strikingly different from those of the 8th graders. For the most part, the teachers were frustrated with Hannah, suggesting she had overreacted to things her peers said and did to her, things that, we learn through tapes she had recorded prior to the suicide, she blamed for her downward spiral. Their consensus was that Hannah had needed to "get over it." A clear case of blaming the victim.

The 8th graders, in contrast, consistently responded similarly to Laura, who observed, "I guess it makes you less quick to judge because you don't really know how things affect people. What you say, it might not hurt one person, but it might hurt another person." Laura intimates that whether or not she or others she had talked to about the book would have been offended by what was done and said to Hannah was not the point. It was about trying to understand how Hannah felt. When students did initially shame victims in books or make statements that minimized harm to victims, their peers would often push back, helping them to see things more clearly from the characters' perspective.

MORAL JUDGMENTS

Some of us are quick to judge others' behavior. Having seen a particular behavior and judged it as good or bad, we then assume the behavior is typical and motivated by a fixed character trait rather than by a situation or mental state. We do this quite quickly. Carol Dweck refers to this as an entity mindset.[14] From an entity mindset, if a person steals something, they are more likely to be judged as a thief than as hungry. From this mindset, not only does judgment come quickly, but also, having judged, we subsequently focus on information that confirms the initial judgment, ignoring information that might disconfirm it. This mindset is very prone to stereotyping. And yet "character traits" like courageous, lazy, or immoral are a common element of English literature instruction. Traits appear to explain behavior without needing to attend to the detail of a character's thoughts, feelings, or context, or to the possibility of change.

By contrast, people who adopt what Dweck refers to as a growth mindset are more likely to consider explanations that feature context and mental processes. Many students, such as Desiree, noticed themselves shifting toward a growth mindset:

> I don't look at people the same anymore. And, like, gang people, in the same book, the guy in the gang, he didn't want to be in the gang. He wasn't really, like, a bad person. He just put up the front like he was. And then, he had to be in the gang to protect his family . . . I can't assume that everybody in gangs is bad. They might *have* to do that.

From a growth mindset, people's psychological processes are more interesting because they offer a more nuanced understanding of a person's needs, views, behaviors, and what they know or don't know.[15] People taking up this mindset are aware of stereotypes but just don't see them as accurate descriptions. They find disconfirming information more relevant and interesting than confirming information, and, as it turns out, the more advanced moral development, the more information individuals feel they need to judge the reasonableness of an action.[16]

These mindsets are also moral stances with moral consequences. Growth theorists, for example, think a transgression is probably temporary and are inclined to help make it so. They lean toward restorative justice, forgiveness, and education, because they expect change, or growth.[17] Entity theorists, on the other hand, because they view transgressive behaviors as representing fixed characteristics, judge more harshly and tend to seek punishment or retribution rather than education. For these reasons, we view a growth mindset as a more nuanced and advanced moral stance than an entity mindset. Since being judgmental or not also applies to the self, the growth mindset is more psychologically healthy. As students gain a deeper understanding of social–emotional life and change, they are less prone to depression.[18]

We suspect, as did the students, that the book-based conversations, which invariably involved learning about classmates' and book characters' thinking, might be the reason for this common shift. Not only did students recognize changes in their judgment of others and its roots, they also recognized a shift in their *propensity* to judge:

> [*Living Dead Girl*] gave me so much better insight onto how people actually feel. And I think this year, because I've read that type of book, that I've become more understanding. So, I think it's good to read books like that, just to learn something different. . . . It's made me really want to understand others and other things better, what others go through that may be hard to tell.

Moriah confessed being historically judgmental of others, but explained how reading the complicated lives of characters confounded her perceptions:

> I've always thought people have, like, normal lives, like more a normal life than a hard life. Then, like, reading *Smile for the Camera*, and the girl in *Love and Leftovers*, like, especially the girl in *Smile for the Camera*, 'cause it's a true story. She talks about all these people she meets. And I was starting to open up a little bit, realizing I could be wrong about people. Probably there are an amount of people who have a normal life and an amount of people who have an interesting life. I don't know. *Living Dead Girl*. I started to be more aware of what people are.

The writer of the memoir *Smile for the Camera* participated in abusive relationships. The protagonist of *Love and Leftovers*, for a while, wallows in self-pity. The main character of *Living Dead Girl*, who is being sexually abused while held in captivity, contemplates trading the safety and well-being of another young girl in order to save herself. Rather than assuming the flaws she perceived were fixed traits in these characters, Moriah began to believe they, and people in general, are not one thing and that they live in and through situations that are beyond her understanding and experience:

> 'Cause I'm the kind of person who always thinks, "I hate people." I'm starting to think maybe they have a good reason. I know this might sound kind of mean, but . . . like, I guess I was the kind of person who would sort of judge, you

know. And I'm sort of being more aware. I've never had a right to judge. I'm becoming more, like. . . . I have a better reason not to judge, if that makes sense.

You can hear in these students' observations the roots of moral development in their empathic response through their expanded mind reading. The focus on others' thoughts, feelings, and experiences is key to the growth mindset, and it undermines the possibility of taking up an entity mindset. But it's also key to moral development. Carol Gilligan has argued for an ethic of care to be a central element in moral development based on her analysis of women's moral problem-solving.[19] Though her arguments are based on gender, we see no reason why a morality of care should be exclusive to women. It is one necessary piece of moral development. The ethic of care is firmly based in relationships and mind reading rather than in the abstract general rules proposed by Lawrence Kohlberg.[20] Nonetheless, both male and female students showed links between an ethic of care and principled moral behavior while taking into account the costs and benefits of acting in particular ways in particular situations.

Their propensity to engage in uncaring behavior, and judge others in ways that might allow it, are blocked by the expanded imagination of the consequences for others and the recognition of the relationships between human beings—the foundation of the golden rule. Audrina puts it clearly:

Thirteen Reasons Why changed my . . . I don't judge people at all. If you judge people more often, it can mess with their minds, like make them choose bad things. And Twisted, it's about a bully and, well, so I think bullying is bad. In Twisted, this boy, he gets bullied by this girl-that-he-like's older brother and, like, it's really sad, 'cause. . . . You shouldn't judge somebody by the way they act or look. And you shouldn't bully nobody, 'cause it's really mean, and it can make them choose bad things.

Notice that this recognition is not only an assertion of caring. It has evolved to a rule backed by a solid, self-generated logic. This was both an individual and collective experience, because it wasn't a single book that produced it, but multiple books and the conversations across them producing a nuanced view. It was an added benefit of students reading different books. For example, in a conversation about abuse in A Child Called It, a small group of students observed that they might not know what hardships another person is enduring and how their own actions or words might exacerbate the stress. As Reese put it, "I pick on some people, and you know what? I don't know what happens in, like, their home." When Leigh agreed, "It's like, think twice before you actually pick on somebody," Riley reminded them of a troubled character in another book: "Like that book Thirteen Reasons Why, how even a little thing made her commit suicide." Wyatt echoed, "Thirteen Reasons Why, even the littlest thing."

RECOGNIZING LANGUAGE AS A POTENTIAL ACT OF VIOLENCE

To make moral decisions, first we have to recognize something as a moral matter, and it's easier to see moral failures in others than in oneself. When readers identify with a character who is being bullied and at the same time recognize the bullying behavior as something they themselves have engaged in, it provides an opportunity for them to see themselves as the other and ask whether that is who they wish to be. Victoria commented, "*The Beckoners* is about bullying, and I was, like, 'Oh my god, I'm a bully! Oh no!' So, like, but not, like, really bad . . . but, like, so I'm not going to do that anymore."

This reckoning was a common outcome of reading, and it spread, changing behavioral norms. This was evident one day when Marty was reading *A Man Named Dave*, the sequel to *A Child Called It*, a memoir recounting the childhood abuse Dave Pelzer suffered at the hands of his mother. Marty interrupted the other readers in his cluster, thinking aloud, "Moron. Moron. Where's the dictionary? I know what that word means but now I need to read the meaning." Putting down his copy of the book, he reported the dictionary definition:

> The first definition is a person with a mental deficiency. There's a second definition. This one says a stupid person. His mom calls him a moron. I know what that means, but now I'm thinking about what it really means.

Now he had the attention of others in the cluster who had either read or heard conversations about the memoir *A Child Called It* and its sequel, which Marty was reading. Scott observed, "Like you call somebody a moron or a retard." Patterson and Jason then reminded everyone of some specific ways Pelzer reported that his mother had physically and psychologically harmed him. Following a few seconds of thoughtful silence, Scott, chagrinned, observed, "We call people that all the time," and Marty responded, "When I read this definition, I'm thinking that's not a good name to call anybody."

Marty's new understanding of "moron" arose through his identification with the character in the memoir's first-person narrative. Experiencing Dave Pelzer's confusion and pain, he protested the words and actions of Dave's mother.[21] His recognition of the potential violence of his own language was likely augmented by the space reading offers for pause, reflection, and conversation, the latter also distributing his new understanding.

A quite different word brought Desiree's reading to a screeching halt:

> Oh my gosh. We had a moment. Like me and Shannon. Okay, Shannon was sitting there, and she was reading *Something Like Hope*, and I read that book right after her, 'cause she told me about it. She was like, "Oh, this is a good book." And I was reading *Perfect Chemistry*. We were both at sad parts. We

were both reading. She almost started crying. I almost started crying. We got like really emotional in the book. Ms. Tucker was like, what's wrong? In my book, or whatever, the boy called having sexual relations with a girl—uh, can I say a bad word?—He called it a "fuck," and she was like really upset. She was like okay calling it sex is one thing, but calling it a "fuck"—I was like, oh my gosh. Ms. Tucker was like, "What's wrong Desiree?" and I was, like, he called it a "fuck" and I was all crying. We both got into it. It was really good. [Why did that cause such emotion in you?] 'Cause I felt like, you know, you're IN the book. It's like you're in there, and you're, like, oh my gosh, I can't believe he did that. . . . I felt like so bad, 'cause she really did love him, you know.

When we ban books for problematic language like "fuck," as is often the case,[22] we lose opportunities for expanding young people's moral grasp of the potential violence of language.

MULTIPLE PERSPECTIVES AND MORAL REACH

The conversations these students had about their reading invited multiple perspectives in a safe, trusting, space of uncertainty which, in a democratic society we cannot help but value. While there are common dimensions of moral development across cultures, the relative value placed on different dimensions varies substantially among societal groups.[23] In a pluralistic democracy, we have to figure out ways to relate productively to those whose moral constructions are different from our own. We can think of schools and classrooms as scaled-down societies that simulate for adolescents the democracies they will inhabit and shape as they enter adulthood. When Wilson, a self-described "prep," reported that in 8th grade he started routinely talking to "goth people, emo people, people who have hard times at home [like he does]" and that he considers this a positive life change, that's a big deal. Sharing stories produces a shared history, invites a shared world view, and increases interpersonal respect, which enables conversations across moral differences. The sharing of emotions leads to greater empathy. It allows people on opposite sides of controversial issues, like immigration or gun control, to develop greater respect for the other.[24] This is particularly so when those stories involve physical or psychological harm, either experienced or inflicted, and the emotional fallout from the experience (vulnerability, shame, etc.). This is one reason why students' preference for reading and discussing "disturbing" books is important.

Taking up multiple perspectives prompts another aspect of moral development, an increase in moral reach, the social distance over which our moral commitments extend. Do our moral commitments extend only to ourselves and our immediate family, or do they extend to a broader swath of humanity over a broader time period? Do circumstances and intentions matter in our moral judgments when it comes to friends and family, as it does even in tribal cultures, but not when it comes to people of different religions, nationalities, or races, as it must in a multicultural democracy or a more global society?

Most of the instances we observed in which adolescents appeared to expand their moral sphere were leveraged by differences between themselves and peers sitting next to them in class, differences brought to the surface by what they were reading and talking about.

We observed one such conversation that included a mix of some students who identified as gay and others who identified as straight.

> *Marta:* When I read *Keeping You a Secret.* I thought, "Yeah, like, this could happen to me." Like I'm really glad my mom understands, but my dad was like a complete homophobic. I know if he was still living in my house with my mom, I'd be in a situation where I'd have to go live in a let's-be-gay shelter.
> *Phoebe:* Are there any around here?
> *Maisy:* Yeah . . .
> *Marta:* There's one in Appleburg. I want to work there. The sad part is that parents actually kick their kids out.
> *Jamie:* I think my stepdad would understand, but . . .
> *Marta:* My dad's half of the family, like when they found out, they started sending me hate mail, and they would leave threatening messages on my mom's phone. Like, "If you don't get that son-of-bitch out of the house . . ."
> *Jamie:* My mom, my two aunts, my grandma and grandpa know.
> *Maisy:* My nana knows, and my sister knows. I think my uncle might.

At this point in the conversation, Alan is grimacing, and Laura glances uneasily over at Phoebe. Marta notices the discomfort.

> *Marta:* This is really awkward. Now all the straight kids are being really, really quiet.
> *Alan:* I don't know how to get in this conversation.
> *Phoebe:* I know everyone here supports it . . .
> *Jamie:* They just don't know how to talk about it.

It is unclear that "everyone" supported their gay peers at this point, but a door was now open to the possibility for conversation, with the straight students nudged to say something.

> *Alan:* I just can't see how you could kick your kid out of the house just because they choose to live their life in one way.
> *Marta:* Yeah.

Phoebe: My church, I go to a Unitarian church, and it accepts, they accept homo—oh my God, they accept gay people. They're totally okay with it. It's like a really, really open church.

The "straight kids" were clearly a bit shaky on what to say and how to say it, but were nudged further by their gay classmates' interest:

Jamie: Where is it?
Maisy: Is it more spiritual?
Marta: What church is this?
Phoebe: It's Unitarian Fellowship. It's on the corner of 13th and Oak. Hudson Jones, from our school, goes there. We're the only ones from this school who go. Me, my sister, and Hudson. I like my church. I think it's good to be open to everyone. The pastor's son is gay.

As a side note, it's important to note that Hudson has two moms, and importantly, he has multiple debilitating conditions, is bound to a wheelchair, and has few social connections in school, except with teachers. In fact, when Phoebe mentioned him, it was the first time we had heard another student say his name. We reemphasize here that it is the books and conversations that pave the way for his inclusion and for potential relationships. Phoebe told us weeks later:

I know some books, like *Keeping You a Secret* is a book that a lot of people, that some people didn't really want to read because they don't agree with the whole background of it, the whole gay thing. But some people were really taken to it and then talked to some of the people in our school that are like that. I guess got closer to them, too. I thought it was really good. It was so sad, though, how the girl's mother didn't want her anymore just because of the choice. We were talking about it in class a little bit. I remember Marta was the first one to read it in our class, I think. She was saying how she loved it and how she, like, cried during some parts and how she laughed. So that helped more of us to read it. It's really good.

Doubtless, some people will worry over Phoebe's suggestion that sexual orientation is a "choice" or Alan's earlier comment that gay people "choose to live their life one way." Others will worry that homosexuality or religion is a topic of adolescent conversation at all. Our point is that these young adults are beginning to know more about the lives of people who are unlike them in certain ways and are open to hearing and inviting their perspectives.

For Akeem, it was a relationship with an author, rather than a peer, that made the difference. He was a big fan of Paul Volponi, whose books mainly feature male characters and often involve sports. When *Crossing the Lines* was published, Gay found a preview on her phone and first handed it to

Roberto, because he was reading a string of sports-related books that highlighted the implications of bullying, and this new book fit the bill. He read the description, thought for a few seconds, then handed the phone back, saying it was not his type of book. This book was indeed about bullying, but featured a transgender character, which may be the reason Roberto passed on it. When Gay handed the phone to Akeem, he paused for a second when he read in the preview a reference to what seemed like a boy wearing lipstick and a dress: "Is [the character] a guy?" Without further hesitation, though, he told Gay he would be interested in reading it and asked her to order it for him. Regardless of his comfort with the topic, he trusted Paul Volponi, the author. Saul took the phone next and commented that this book, because of its bullying theme, would connect to *Leverage*, a book he, Akeem, Roberto, and three or four other boys had talked about. It would only be a matter of time before a transgender character entered their conversation, via Akeem and Paul Volponi.

Stereotyping is the arbitrary restriction of perceptions of difference and the denial of a relationship of care. Breaking down stereotypes is not an easy thing for any of us. Human beings are predisposed to stereotyping as an efficient way of managing perception. But citizenship and moral development require that we outgrow stereotyping because it undermines, from without and from within, both moral development and the possibility of democracy. Democracy requires an undoing of the narrower moral reach of small-group identity instincts.

Stereotyping, typical of in-group/out-group behavior, allows us to hide the stereotyped other's humanity and deny them the care and moral principle we offer those with whom we have closer relationships. The more we become aware of the range of differences and similarities, the more stereotypes break down. Perspective-taking, both through engaged reading of narratives and through conversations about those narratives, reduces prejudice and stereotype. For these adolescents, breaking down stereotypes appeared to be accelerated and expanded through relationships in and around books with people and characters whose lives and values were very different, relationships and perspectives that might not have been possible otherwise. In school, students know the right answer when the teacher asks, "Is genocide wrong?" or that the takeaway they ought to report from *To Kill a Mockingbird* is that people should see beyond skin color. But these are not deeply felt and oversimplify the process of truly expanding moral reach.

SO...

Moral development is not about teaching a set of values; it is about students developing their own moral compass and a sense of moral agency—a sense that they can recognize moral problems, think them through, and, as Lindsay did ("If I see anything, I stop it"), act accordingly. Although teachers did routinely ask the students how reading was changing their thinking, they did not tell them *what* to think. Marcus's teacher did not assign him to read *Leverage*, much less tell him what to get out of it, but weeks after reading it, Marcus shared that he could not shake the memory of the events leading to the tragic death of a character. Importantly, he recognized himself as a potential part of the problem. Invoking his moral self, he observed, "I'm not a bully, or anything, it's just that I haven't made wise decisions." He added somberly, "I could've been nicer to somebody," signaling a commitment to more positive moral action in the future.

There is no way for language arts to be divorced from adolescents' moral development. Language itself is morally laden, and students come to recognize that, along with the power and responsibilities it confers. Engaged reading and discussion of narrative texts expand students' mind reading, which, along with negotiation of the moral dilemmas books present, expands their moral development. This is not about public schools telling students their moral obligations outside of school. Rather, it is about students becoming mentally healthy moral agents, with a sense of their own moral commitments—what they will stand up for and how matters of morality fit in their identity and life narrative. Holly's recognition that as a result of her reading, "I feel like in my life sometimes I need to make changes and make things right" seems like a clear and positive assertion of expanding moral integrity, an editorial correction of her life narrative to bring it in line with her moral self. The students' recognition that others will often have different commitments and that those differences will need to be equitably negotiated is not only a healthy indicator of moral development, it is the foundation of a democratic society.

NOTES

1. Ethier et al. (2018).
2. Johnston et al. (2018).
3. Chung et al. (2018).
4. Eisenberg et al. (2014). Although once research on moral reasoning was dominated by Kohlberg's stage theory, which focused on moral conflicts emphasizing rules, obligations, and principles of justice, more recent work has emphasized conflicts between prosocial and self-interested behavior as being more relevant for prosocial action than judgments about right and wrong or cultural injunctions.
5. Eisenberg et al. (1987).
6. Hardy et al. (2014, p. 45).
7. Pratt et al. (2009).
8. Barriga et al. (2001).
9. Pratt et al. (2003); Hardy (2006).
10. Hardy et al. (2013).
11. Pasupathi & Wainryb (2019).

12. Flvush (2021).

13. Recchia et al. (2014).

14. Dweck (2006).

15. Molden & Dweck (2006).

16. Saltzstein & Takagi (2019).

17. Chiu et al. (1997).

18. Levy & Dweck (1998).

19. Gilligan (1982).

20. Kohlberg (1981).

21. This is what Louise Rosenblatt referred to when she described reading as transactional. Reading is not simply a transfer of information. Rather, in the process of reading, both reader and text are transformed and, through the conversation with his peers, they too are changed. Rosenblatt (1978).

22. American Library Association (n.d.).

23. Haidt (2013).

24. Kubin et al. (2021).

CHAPTER 8

Happiness, Well-Being, and Other Trivial Matters

A little bit ago, I had this realization, that, oh my gosh, I'm a happy person. It might have been some of the books I've read, like, [The] *Rules of Survival and November Blues*. . . . I'm, like, I have such an awesome life compared with other people.

—8th grader Lisa

Who doesn't want their children to be happy? Though it doesn't show up on state standards or most school district goals, should we ignore the fact that these 8th-grade students reported being happier? They reported happiness in the sense of the pleasurable life, using words like "fun," "enjoy," and "joy". In part, the pleasure lay in the engagement itself, which they pointed out in so many ways: Shannon observed, "I actually enjoy reading now," or Audrina, "Now, I just can't stop reading the book." But this pleasure spilled over beyond the contact with books. Josie reported, "Like, because when I'm reading, like, after I read something, I seem like more happier than I was when I started. Like, I'm the happiest that I'll get." Engaged reading was, in fact, pleasurable, but the broader experience of happiness might also be attributed to the social relationships engendered by the engaged reading.

But the pleasurable, hedonic life is a shallow version of happiness. The eudaimonic view of well-being argues for a deeper, more meaningful happiness, grounded in a sense of competence, autonomy, and relatedness—all human needs.[1] We have already offered evidence that students, individually and collectively, had established that foundation. However, they also seemed to have a sense that their lives were more meaningful and engaged.[2] Part of that meaningfulness might be attributable to their realization of their social agency, that they could positively influence others' lives, and the realization that their relationships with others added meaning to their own lives. Some of the meaningfulness might also be attributed to recognition of the possibility of a more meaningful, purposeful future, as we heard when, propelled by her reading of *The Rose That Grew From Concrete*, Maisha observed, "When I grow up, I'm going to college to become a criminal justice detective, or a social worker or something like that. I feel like I have a way in life of helping a lot of people."

GRATEFULNESS

The happiness was in spite of the fact that the books many chose were "intense and disturbing" rather than uplifting Hallmark narratives. Experimental studies have shown that reflection on death and other disturbing experiences tends to induce gratefulness and happiness.[3] For example, Addie noted after reading *Living Dead Girl*, "It was a different feeling, one of gratitude and thankfulness that that wasn't my life." Some students confessed they began the year with a festering anger because of family, economic, or personal situations, but experiencing the lives of relatable book characters with much harder lives recalibrated their own troubles. As Amber noted, "I've learned a lot from books, I guess, because you do get an appreciation for what you do have and, like, for being thankful for the happiness and joy in your life. Some of those books, it's crazy what's in there."

This blossoming gratefulness affected even students who, on the face of it, had little to be grateful for, as Maisha noted:

> *Tyrell*, it made me think, first, 'cause I was kind of raised in that kind of lifestyle. But as I looked at it, I looked at it like it was kind of hard, you know that? But seeing how it was for somebody else, and seeing how it was for them to live it every day. But to read about someone's life like that, it made me think, there's so many kids that brag about what they do and don't have. And then people like me, that didn't really have anything growing up at all. . . . Like I used to think that I was terrible. Now that I look at it, I felt that I was kind of important, because I was like, this person got that, this person got this. I should look at it as, even though I didn't have too many things when I was little, I should still be appreciative that I had my parents in my life.

This sense of gratitude was a common outcome, and the more grateful young people are for what they have in their lives, the happier they are, the more socially connected and socially supported they feel, the stronger their psychological well-being, the more positive their social behaviors, the stronger their coping abilities, and the greater their life satisfaction.[4] Gratitude reduces risk factors in African American adolescents and increases protective factors.[5]

Gratefulness promotes prosocial emotions of empathy, trust, compassion, and forgiveness. These spill over to the classroom community, producing a more positive emotional climate, sustaining feelings of well-being, and inviting creative thinking.[6] In other words, the students' happiness and sense of well-being, while experienced as individuals, was, in part, a by-product of their co-construction of the classroom life in which they participated. Individual students' happiness and well-being happen in the mutually transforming context they are busy creating.

Students recognized these positive feelings and relationships. For example, reflecting on 8th grade from the distance of 10th grade, Nia observed:

> I just remember it was fun. It was always a good environment. It was never, I don't know, it was never tense, you know? It was always happy and good moods and fun, you know? If one person wasn't in a good mood, they'd end up laughing by the end of class. That was just fun. It was like we were a family, you know? We always had each other's back. What was said in that room, stayed in that room. It was very fun. And trusting.

Students, unprompted, explicitly articulated this memory of a "caring," "trusting," positive classroom life. Is there a parent, student, or teacher who thinks any of these outcomes is not worth pursuing—whether or not they are valued in state standards or tests?

LOSS AND GRIEF

Young people deal with a surprising amount of trauma: deaths of family and friends, abuse, divorce, and many forms of heartbreak. Here again, students reported that the books helped them get through it. For example, Elise noted changes in her state of mind after reading *Chasing Brooklyn*, in which characters experience loss and grief: "When I was younger, I lost my best friend. It was really hard for me, but books like that really take me back and help me remember her but without getting really upset." Hattie had a similar experience:

> *The Sky Is Everywhere*. It was really good. I could really relate to it. I'm rereading it now. I lost two people really close to me when I was younger in elementary school. One was my grandmother, and one was my dad. So, her losing someone that close to her, a sister, I could really relate to that. What she's going through, like feeling you're lesser than your sibling. They outshine you. Like, my brother is smarter than me and usually does a lot better, so I can understand how she felt about that. I can really relate to that book, so I think that would be one of my favorites. . . .

It might sound like Hattie relates to the character and thus simply comprehends better than if she didn't relate to the character's experiences. However, better comprehension is probably not why she's rereading it. It is more likely motivated by the understanding and management of self, emotions, and relationships that it affords. Consider Clark's observation:

> I don't know. My friend died a couple of months before that, and then, like, I just wanted to read books about suicide and all that stuff. . . . She was my best friend, and once I read that I got my anger out and stuff.

This sense of book-enabled catharsis was not unique, and it was not only the students who recognized the books as tools for personal healing and development. Parents also recognized the significance. For example, Naomi offered an explanation as it related to her daughter, Elise:

> She's been on this journey, and I think several of the things that she read brought a lot of closure this year. She had lost her best friend in 6th grade, so the second half of 6th grade was a lost year for her. She was developing an eating disorder. We put her on Prozac for depression. . . . In 7th grade, she was angry, and that came out very, very clear. She would be angry with me. She was putting up walls between her and her friends, walls between her and me. . . . In 8th grade, she is healing, and I have my daughter back. . . . She read some things that were edgy. She read some things about death. . . . I think it helped her get things in perspective. . . . I think through the reading that she did, it really helped her to get to a better place. . . . I think she kind of experienced some things through her reading and just grew as an individual with the type of stuff that she was reading.

Naomi explained that Elise's transformation was more than just coming to terms with her grief. She had become more open and communicative about her life and everyday problems: "Up until this year, it was kind of a need-to-know basis, and now it's more like, 'What do you think about this?' or 'This is what's going on in my life.'"

In an interview, Elise talked about the books she had been reading:

> My favorite book this year was probably . . . *Chasing Brooklyn* [a book about death, grieving, and recovery], I don't know, probably because it's personal to me, because, I don't know, like, I don't know how to explain it. It really, like, touched me, and really like made me feel bad for people and to understand, like, that is just a part of life, and you have to grow on what you're given. Like, what happens to you happens for a reason, and you may never know what the reason is, but you just have to push forward and grow as a person and as an individual.

Naomi's, Elise's, Clark's, and Hattie's observations suggest that choice of books, the conversations around them, and the subsequent relationships that form hold promise for helping youngsters deal with forms of traumatic life experience. Like the rest of us, adolescents encounter a range of traumas, and supportive peer relationships (see Chapter 3) often provide a lifeline.

Bereaved children who have supportive relationships with peers have better socioemotional and behavioral adjustment. Those who report talking with friends about the death have more self-esteem, a better sense of self-efficacy, and even feel more connected to the deceased.[7] As with adults, social relatedness is a key component in bereaved children's ability to develop positive self-systems.[8] Listening, feeling heard, sharing narratives, and emotionally connecting with others can result in a restored sense of relatedness, trust, community acceptance and engagement, and expanded strategies for managing trauma.[9]

MORE HEALING OPPORTUNITIES

Elise's initial responses to grief are common, but there are other responses, too. The National Alliance for Children's Grief asserts that in response to grief, 39% of teens have trouble sleeping, 45% have more trouble concentrating on schoolwork, and 41% say that in the face of grief, they acted in ways they knew would be physically, mentally, or emotionally not good for them.[10] The majority feel that others don't understand what it is like. But surprisingly little attention is paid to the fact that many children experience some form of trauma during their school years. Nationally, an estimated 7% of children, 5.3 million of them, experience the death of a parent or sibling. In some states the rate is 10% or 11%.[11] Less is known about the percentage experiencing the death of a friend, which we only seem to attend to when there is a school mass-shooting.

There are many other traumatic events that students experience. When asked whether he had changed as a person because of his reading, Clark pointed to *Walking on Glass*, a book in which a son walks in on his mother's suicide. Clark observed, "Like my mom had an overdose, but she didn't die." And then there is divorce. During their school years, about 40% of American children born to married parents will experience divorce. Relatedly, some children are taken from parents into foster care. Trinity reported:

> The books I read kind of hit home a little bit. 'Cause in *Something Like Hope*, she was dealing with her daughter being put in a foster home, and I was in a foster home, and she's facing these troubles. And I'm always in trouble . . . I feel like I'm putting myself in the character's shoes when I'm reading the book.

And there is also abuse. Marta responded to the "have you changed" question with:

> *A Child Called It* and *The Lost Boy*. I was abused for eight and a half years, and it was like I was able to relate to it, and I'm like kind of a spokesperson for child abuse, so it's like I'm able to book talk it a lot, and it's easier to get across

to people when they can actually put themselves in their shoes. It's why most people can't much imagine it.

As with grief, the ability to talk about the experience, be heard, and receive support is healing, but difficult. The books make possible otherwise inaccessible conversations and self-disclosures.

It is not only traumatic events that the books seemed to help with. Ongoing tensions and frustrations were also mollified. For example, Trinity connected with Brittany, a character in *Perfect Chemistry* whose brother has autism. Trinity plays a major caretaker role with her own brother who has autism. Confessing that she was often resentful, through her experience with *Perfect Chemistry*, she contemplated the alternative:

> It just showed me like not to take life for granted, 'cause something could happen in the blink of an eye, and someone you love a lot can be gone. That's why, like, my brother, if anything ever happened to him, I would probably die. That's my best friend. . . . He gets frustrated, and I don't know what to do. 'Cause I'm only 13, and I shouldn't have to deal with it. But then again, my brother is 16, and he can't express how he feels. He doesn't know how to deal with it.

The roles and struggles of siblings of children with handicaps are frequently neglected. Efforts to address them, such as with the Sibling Support Project, find that emotional exploration and making friends are critical parts of the siblings' needed support.[12] The emotional–relational talk encouraged by the personally relevant books helps create exactly those conditions.

It might seem impossible to address directly young adults' many obstacles to happiness and well-being, not only because of the range and uniqueness of those obstacles but also because doing so requires a context that elicits and supports them. However, the books and the contexts they provoke appear to make the impossible possible.

POSITIVE EMOTIONS AND WELL-BEING

Positive emotions such as happiness can be viewed as ends in themselves. The pursuit of happiness is claimed in the U.S. Constitution as a human right, and who doesn't want it for their children (or themselves)? However, positive emotions have benefits that stretch beyond the obvious, producing a cascading web of links to well-being. Positive emotions and meaning are mutually related and similarly linked to engagement.[13]

Cognitively, more smiles produce greater attentional breadth and flexibility and have a positive effect on decision-making and likely on cognition more generally.[14] Positive emotions produce more creative and open thinking, which, in turn, directly enhances resilience and mental health by creating a wider array of strategies for coping with life's stresses and adversities.[15] Consequently, positive emotions decrease the likelihood of a range of health problems such as obesity, diabetes, cardiovascular disease, immune disorders, and depression, each of which affects quality of life and life expectancy.[16] The costs to society in terms of healthcare and workplace performance are enormous.[17]

Relationally, positive emotions expand the attention paid to others and their needs, reduce psychological distancing, promote prosocial interactions, and generally improve interpersonal relations.[18] Simply witnessing prosocial acts also leads others to act prosocially, particularly when participants expect that others will also tend to act prosocially.[19] Positive emotions also reduce stereotyping[20] and expand acceptance of others, including those with disabilities, which surely affects the latter's well-being.[21] Good social functioning in general leads to greater subjective well-being.[22]

Emotions, and that includes happiness, are also contagious.[23] We are, after all, social animals, and people gain pleasure from interacting with others. Even people who think they don't want human contact find that connecting with others brings pleasure, a pleasure that is also contagious.[24] This both enables and is a consequence of students' individual engagement with books, with each other, with their teacher, and with others in their lives.

FEELING HEARD, UNDERSTOOD, AND CARED FOR

A common enough lament of teenagers is that adults just don't understand. However, Justine observed of her teacher, "Mr. Simmons helps me out because he understands me." Daphne was even more specific about her teacher and the process through which this comes about:

> Like, Ms. Tucker knows more about you from what you read and what you like to read and through the discussions that we have with her, like as a class and separately. . . . You can tell she has recognized what we like, what we don't like, and she keeps that in her mind. So that will come up throughout the year. And I just realized that that's one of the gifts she has. . . . [Previous teachers] they're good teachers, but they're not that personal person who will find what you like and discuss with you through the book. Ms. Tucker is just one of those people who just *gets* you, basically. So, you can just talk about anything with her. And then, through reading, she can get to *you*.

These adolescents felt they had been heard and understood. Feeling heard invokes the sense that one's presence in and contributions to the community are valued, along with a sense of belonging, all of which are important contributors to a sense of well-being. They also had the sense that their teachers cared about them, which is linked not only to higher achievement and engagement[25] but also to their self-esteem and overall well-being.[26] The more teachers know about students, the more they are likely to care, and, as Daphne suggests, the book choices and conversations make this possible.

Feeling heard matters as much as the content of what is said.[27] As Nia observed, "You talked about it . . . it was good to have somebody listen and understand. . . ." Similarly, to requote Priscilla, "I was like, 'YES! Someone understands!'" The sense of being heard and understood came not only from conversations with their teacher but also with peers and family members.

Of course, the other side of feeling heard is that someone is actually listening, making talking about life's complexities easier, as Amber suggests:

> I think how when you're talking like that, out in the open, you see that, like, that you have the same relation . . . and they think like I do and see the world in the same way that I do, but they just change my mind a little bit, and they see what I think about.

Being willing to listen and possibly have one's mind changed is big. In fact, listening without the possibility of having one's mind changed might not be considered listening. As Sherry Turkle in *Reclaiming Conversation*, observes: "When [conversations] work best, people don't just speak but listen, both to others and to themselves. They allow themselves to be vulnerable. They are fully present and open to where things might go."[28] For these students, the ability and propensity to listen spread beyond the classroom, as Ella noted:

> I'm really more open to my sister's thinking now, and my mom's thinking, 'cause, like, before, I only thought about how I thought and I didn't think about anything else, but now I see like all the different types [of] thinking.

Many students, such as Jason, reported this open, listening stance toward others: "I think I've gotten more open minded because of the stuff I read. . . . So, I think more open-minded and more willing to listen." Similarly, Jana reported, "I'm more open to people, talking to them instead of being quiet and awkward. . . . [Others] talk more, too. They're open to discussion."

Being interested in others and in conversations with them helps not only to build relationship, but also to understand why people do things—which brings us back to mind reading. For example, this student encountered a primary character who was abusive to his girlfriend:

> *Breathing Underwater.* Well, I'm not done with it yet, but now I sort of think, maybe they're mad or mean or something because of their home life. And you can't really control what's going on in their home life, so it's like giving them an extra break. And I think it opened my perspective, and I think, maybe they're not actually mad. Maybe they're just upset because of what their parents did to them.

This greater understanding of people's lives seems to reduce the likelihood of attributing problematic intentions to others, which in turn increases the likelihood of more tolerant, positive relationships—and thus of well-being.

SOURCES OF HAPPINESS AND WELL-BEING

In earlier chapters, we have argued that building a positive life narrative, establishing positive relationships, and centering the moral self, for example, have powerful health benefits, particularly in terms of the life decisions young people make. We also contended that moral development goes hand in hand with a sense of meaningfulness and purpose, which make for greater well-being. In Chapter 7, we introduced what Carol Dweck refers to as a growth mindset, because of its moral implications. That mindset includes the idea that people are affected by context and learning and that they can change. But aside from its moral significance, a growth mindset is important for students' well-being because it positively affects relationships. When disagreements arise, those with a growth mindset try to work together to resolve them, working toward change.[29] They end up feeling more positive about their partner in the process. Entity theorists don't have the option of change, so their disagreements easily turn into confrontations, stereotyping, blaming, and putting their partner down.

In this chapter, we've added a few more contributors to happiness and well-being. Students reported being transformed, feeling happier and more open, with an improved sense of well-being, even managing trauma better, because the books they chose invited conversations about, and new perspectives on, the complexities of their lives, books that, because they were "intense and disturbing," invited a sense of gratitude for the small mercies in their lives. The conversations with peers, parents, and teachers invoked a sense of competence and relatedness, which, along with the sense of autonomy afforded by choosing books and how to respond to them, satisfied students' basic human psychological needs. The classroom construction of literate competence valued individuals' contributions to the collective conversations. The value of contributions depended on a combination of unique and shared perspective and personal history of experiences and books. In other words, it valued individuals' strengths, and opportunities to use one's strengths lead both directly and indirectly to general happiness and meaningfulness.[30] Students also had a sense of meaningfulness both in their school work—their English class—and in their lives because of their sense of aspirational possibility and because of their recognition that their lives mattered to others.

Positive emotions provide an important foundation for lifelong intellectual, social, and even physical advantages.[31] U.S. citizens are guaranteed the freedom of "the pursuit of happiness." The paradox is that when individuals actively pursue their own happiness, their (largely hedonic) efforts often undermine the possibility of achieving it by damaging their relationships with others, producing loneliness.[32] In these classrooms, however, happiness and well-being were *by-products* of engagement with personally meaningful books and, consequently, with others equally meaningfully engaged and equally in need of and appreciative of each other.

NOTES

1. Ryan & Deci (2000).
2. Seligman et al. (2005).
3. Frias et al. (2011).
4. Algoe et al. (2008); Emmons & McCullough (2003); Hill & Allemand (2011); Lili (2016); Wood et al. (2008).
5. Ma et al. (2013).
6. Bono & Froh (2009); Diebel et al. (2016); Lin (2015); Tian et al. (2015).
7. Dopp & Cain (2012); Worden & Silverman (1996).
8. Dopp & Cain (2012); Sandler et al. (2008); Wolchik et al. (2008).
9. Balmer et al. (2021).
10. National Alliance for Children's Grief (n.d.).
11. Judi's House (n.d.).
12. McCullough & Simon (2011).
13. Kwok & Fang (2021).
14. Johnson et al. (2010); Shukla et al. (2019).
15. Burns et al. (2008); Cohn et al. (2009); Gloria et al. (2013); Gloria & Steinhardt (2016); Li et al. (2019).
16. Jood et al. (2009); Kemeny & Schedlowski (2007); de Luca & Olefsky (2006); Steinhardt et al. (2011).
17. Stewart et al. (2003a); Stewart et al. (2003b).
18. Isen (1999); Isen (2000).
19. Sparks et al. (2019).
20. Ric (2004).
21. Urada & Miller (2000); Taubman—Ben-Ari et al. (2011).
22. Joshanloo et al. (2018).
23. Sparks et al. (2019).
24. Epley & Schroeder (2014).
25. Roorda et al. (2011).
26. Lavy & Naama-Ghanayim (2020).
27. Murdoch et al. (2020).
28. Turkle (2016, p. 9).
29. Darnon et al. (2006).
30. Vuorinen et al. (2021).
31. Stifter et al. (2020).
32. Mauss et al. (2012).

CHAPTER 9

Reading Competence

This year I'm a little more dedicated towards my homework. I guess 'cause homework's more funner this year. It's more entertaining. We get to read books. I love books. I think books are a whole lot better than TV.

—8th grader Anthony

"Fine," you might say, "but what about these adolescents' academic development? Can they read better? Do they learn to do the things they'll need to do in college?" Fair questions. For what it's worth, the students' scores on the state reading test actually rose. In comparing students' test results in 7th grade, where they had experienced a traditional curriculum, to their end-of-year 8th grade scores, where engaged reading was prioritized, the percentage of students passing increased by seven points, while the passing rates for students statewide remained constant.[1] Plus, a significant number of students rose out of the lowest passing score band, and the number of boys, African-American students, Hispanic students, and students from economically disadvantaged groups who passed also increased.

This might seem surprising, since the students primarily chose to read narrative fiction (with some narrative nonfiction, such as memoir), whereas reading material in the test was strictly informational. It is less surprising when you consider the sheer volume of reading the students did, their deep engagement, and the kinds of conversations the books provoked. In fact, a large-scale study examining data on over 250,000 15-year-olds from across 35 countries indicated that those who read fiction had stronger reading skills than peers who did not, which was not the case for students who reported reading nonfiction, newspapers, magazines, or comics.[2] Suzanne Hidi points to another reason we should not be surprised. Summarizing research on interest, she observes:

Children as well as adults who have individual interests in activities or topics focus their attention, persist for longer periods of time, and enjoy their engagements more, are more likely to use strategic processing and tend to learn and write better than those without such interests.[3]

Nonetheless, these findings do fly in the face of much institutional wisdom, which, in recent years through the Common Core State Standards, has pushed for the majority of reading in upper grades to be nonfiction. The logic is based not on research evidence—we could find none—but on anticipation of the kind of reading that will be encountered by the two-thirds of students who will attend college.[4]

As present and former university professors, we can certainly attest to the predominance of informational texts in college—outside of English literature coursework. However, preparing for that reading is not as simple as providing lots of preparatory practice with nonfiction. It is complicated by the range of different kinds of texts postsecondary students might be asked to read, the variety of disciplines they might choose, and the constantly changing technologies around text. These make it difficult to pin down a set of strategies that, if learned or practiced, would enable general competence in, much less motivation for, reading informational texts.

READING STRATEGICALLY

A common instructional approach is to explicitly and sequentially teach students a set of reading strategies. That was not what happened in these classrooms, though strategies were made explicit by both teachers and students in the context of meaningful book discussions, both those orchestrated by the teacher and those occurring spontaneously among students inside and outside of school. Perhaps more importantly, the students became fluent, strategic readers—readers who initiated and innovated strategic action and talked about it. Because they were engaged, they *automatically* acted strategically. Take Josie, for example:

> *Where She Went* was a little confusing at first, but I went back and started over and it helped. I think I might have went more in depth to it. The first time, I don't know if I went too fast. So, I tried to take my time more, to make sure that I understood.

When students really want to understand, they automatically monitor and act strategically. Over time, they also build an expectation of understanding and acting strategically and a confidence that carries them through difficult spots and transfers in surprising ways. For example, for the very first time, Darla passed the state reading test:

> I realized I had been doing reading all year and that [I'd] had difficult passages to read. So, I mean, I just read like I would any other time. And I think that's what got me through it, is that I've read more difficult passages . . . I would take time. I'd read a sentence. I'd tell myself, explain it to myself, and then I'd keep

reading more and explain more to myself, talk to myself a little bit through it . . . I've read a lot this year. So, when it came to [test] passages, it was like, oh, it's just like another book, except for that it has a different heading on it.

Darla's more confident stance toward reading was quite widespread and generalized to other classes. For example, Corinne observed:

I'm able to tolerate [reading in other classes] now, cause I'm like, okay, it's not as much fun as reading my own book, but like my reading has gotten better. I have a bigger vocabulary this year, so I'll just be able to finish it faster, and I'll be able to know what's going on. I won't have to read it two or three times.

Similarly, Riley observed:

Like last year I was on like a 5th-grade level, and I feel like I am on this [higher] kind of grade level. Last year I didn't like reading at all. . . . [This year] I'll go home, and I'll get engaged in a book instead of just get on the computer and watch TV and stuff like that. . . . My vocabulary has gotten a lot better from reading.

The expanded vocabulary was mentioned frequently by students, particularly those for whom English was not their first language. Though students didn't mention greater flexibility with syntax and orthographic patterns, those capacities also likely developed.[5]

Our point here is that given the many benefits of engaged reading of narrative texts and the fact that the skills and attitudes acquired appear to transfer to nonfiction texts, there appears to be no reason to retreat from narrative fiction in English language arts classes—the kind of class we are documenting here. Besides, the rest of the school day was wide open for other kinds of reading in science, social studies, math, and civics, including informational texts.[6] In other words, engaged reading of narrative fiction in the English class has many benefits and apparently few, if any, opportunity costs with respect to developing the ability to read nonfiction.

READING STRATEGICALLY, ON STEROIDS

Without doubt, the students engaged in reading were vigorously strategic. It was normal, for instance, for students to notice when their comprehension went awry, but rather than just reread a few sentences to regain their footing, which we are certain they did throughout their reading, they reread whole chapters. Michael said about reading *The Rivalry*, "Once I got to about page 50 on it, I decided I was going to read it again, 'cause it was kind of confusing." The second attempt cleared things up. Students also reported routinely rereading entire books when they recognized something was amiss. This was particularly true for books ending with a twist.

Students also used strategies we could not have predicted, including those they created specific to the books they were reading at the time. For Meleisha, surveying the landscape of the book first, then making a plan, had become the norm:

> I just looked through *The Catastrophic History of You and Me* before I started reading it. I always look through books like that, and if there's something interesting, I write it down. I'll keep track of what each part is about. I wrote for the first part, "how she died" and "flashbacks." And then, also, each chapter title is the lyric from a song. See, the first one is "Don't you forget about me." . . . [I started doing that] just this year, because a lot of the books I've read did that. So that way, I can know what's going to come up, and I can know what part ties in with the other ones, how to move through the book and put it all together.

Marcus cautioned his classmates that shifts in *Friday Night Lights* might hold up their reading: "Sometimes it would talk about different people, then it would go and talk about the history of the town, then it would talk about football. Then after games, it would talk about how the players felt in their minds, and stuff." He advised them that "If you organize [the parts] in your head beforehand, you can understand where all the stuff is coming from." If any of this seems trivial or commonplace, think back to instances in school when you might have skipped around in a text just to locate answers to questions the teacher asked or when you finished an assigned reading without remembering a thing from it, but closed the book anyway, just thrilled to be done with it.

One of the reasons we could observe vigorous, purposeful reading so frequently was that students were choosing books based on interest, and interest in talking to others, rather than ease of reading. Routinely, this meant reading was hard, but a number of students referred to it as "good confusion" because they desperately wanted to figure things out and enjoyed problem-solving while reading. Rashida, for instance, who sometimes found the unreliable narrator in *Glimpse* baffling, stated matter-of-factly, "Like you have a lot of questions," but went on to explain, "I write them down on sticky notes, then I go back and see if I can answer them later . . . after I've read more." Is there better preparation for critically reading nonfiction texts? Rashida and many of her classmates brought to life research suggesting that interest in a text can offset the potential negative effects of text complexity.[7] This realization should also mollify concerns that when given freedom to choose books, adolescents just pick the shortest or easiest text they can find. Instead, they appeared to relish complexity in the texts they selected.

We learned about the cognitive dimensions of students' reading incidentally, for the most part, as they talked through and about the moral dilemmas and self-reflection they experienced. When Peter mentioned he had packed *Identical* in his bag for an upcoming flight, a student cautioned him: "It was good throughout the whole book, and then when you got to the end it confused you, and then you had to go back and read it all over again." The rereading had revealed it was the narrator's struggle with dissociated identity disorder that had contributed to both his confusion and his engagement. He resisted spoiling Peter's experience with the book, though, hinting only that "Some people, I think, [the story] kind of opens their eyes, and seeing, like, they don't have it that bad, and then the way they're treating people isn't the best."

The students' interest in complexity and their energetic strategic response were despite the fact that teachers did not offer preplanned, sequenced lessons in how and when to use cognitive strategies. We will take up more of what the teachers systematically did do in the next three chapters. In the meantime, we simply point out that it is one thing to have learned a set of strategies that lie rusting in the corner for lack of use and quite another to be driven to invent or solicit strategies to advance pressing personal interests. It is not the ability to execute technical strategies or to simply identify the literary tools an author used to write a book that fuel students' reading experiences, even though students did exactly that. Rather, participation in conversations transcending the book—with others sitting next to them, with characters, friends, family members, and with themselves—drives their strategic reading experiences.

COMPREHENDING SOCIALLY

While reading *Stolen*, which features an abducted character with Stockholm syndrome, Shea confessed, "I'm like really, really confused . . . but it's, like, good." She said while reading, she thought, "Oh my gosh, what's going on?" At the same time, she recognized this was precisely what the author had in mind: "The way Lucy Christopher wrote it, it's like she wants you to think about what's happening." Now, we could view these comments through a traditional English curriculum lens, and if so, we would probably note Shea's persistence at understanding what the text means and also her appreciation of the author's craft. But that limited interpretation would miss the point of why Shea is reading *Stolen*—or why any of us would read literature—at all. Puzzling over the uncertainty in a character's psychological and relational life is a way of puzzling over the same in ourselves and the people around us.

Unsurprisingly, the propensity to imagine the minds of others and to infer their motives is related to higher levels of reading comprehension.[8] Even so, these students do not read merely to comprehend a book, per se, but to make sense of their lives and the world and to do *better*, to be competent agentive participants in both. Consequently, the social strategies they invoke to select, attract, and engage others in conversations around the books are reading strategies just as much as the strategies they use to analyze or reanalyze words, sentences, paragraphs, or books. In fact, their cognitive engagement is inextricably linked to engagement in a composite of the social contexts of the stories they read, the social life of the classrooms where they are puzzling over complex texts, the social worlds of their everyday lives, and the social futures they imagine.[9]

This is but one way that engaged reading is inseparably cognitive and social. Stepping back to examine the classroom context in which Shea is reading *Stolen* brings yet another layer of social strategy into focus. Addie told us, "I know there's a giant line for *Stolen* right now." The phenomenon of "hot" titles, according to Addie, was about social participation: "Just because everybody, I mean, it helps us communicate, in a way. It kind of helps you make new friends, almost." For these adolescents, the motivation to read, and thus to have opportunities to develop cognitive muscle with respect to reading, was triggered by the desire both to make meaning of the world and their lives and to be an active participant in a vibrant community.

Students routinely turned to each other to help sort out confusion while reading. For instance, when the shape-shifting characters in *Shiver* and *Linger* stumped Monica, she consulted a friend: "Me and Shea were reading the books at the same time, so we would talk to each other about it, and then I would have to go back and reread or whatever and figure out what they were trying to say." Meleisha explained to her classmates one day what they would have to think about if they chose to read *You Against Me*, which she was the first in the class to read:

> It's like in third person point of view, when a narrator not in the story is telling you about it, right? So, it was in third person point of view, but in two views. At one point it was Ellie, and then it was Jack. On a Post-it Note, I put, like, Chapter One was Ellie, and Chapter Two was Jack. Then Ellie, Jack, Ellie, Jack. . . .

When her teacher asked whether this strategy made her a better reader, she clarified, "It helped Gwen (a classmate), 'cause I understood it after the first chapter, but she just got confused."

READING CLOSELY

In recent years, "close reading" has become a popular preoccupation for curriculum developers, recommended in the Common Core State Standards and related frameworks. Although it has roots in literary scholarship, its application in K–12 schools focuses on texts of all sorts and emphasizes textual analysis limited to what is explicitly written, with the idea that the reader's past experiences get in the way. The goal is to ascertain what the author intended, providing supporting evidence found only between the four corners of the page. From this perspective, expertise is demonstrated by the ability to answer text-dependent questions.

If you've followed our argument that the point of engaged reading of narrative texts for students like those we interviewed is to help them to make sense of and expand the meaningfulness of their own lives, close reading, as described, probably already sounds like a bad idea. Bringing one's own experiences to bear on the narrative is both necessary and useful. Besides, who is anyone to say what a narrative text means in the first place—or that it means just one thing? Sara Holbrook, a poet, provided an ironic perspective on this.[10] She learned that two of her pieces had appeared on the Texas State Reading Assessment (STAAR Test), one on the 2014 7th-grade test and the other on the 2013 8th-grade test. When she read the tests and tried to answer the accompanying comprehension questions written by the test maker, she, the author of the poems, came up short. We suspect Shakespeare and Hawthorne might be equally perplexed to see what is being done with their work in the name of "the author's purpose."

We did observe, though, that 8th graders were doing some of the closest reading we have ever observed in classrooms. The difference was in the nature and location of the meanings they made. Dennis said that *Snitch* made him rethink joining a gang, as he put it, "You're going to be controlled by somebody, basically, and I didn't want to go down that road." To the point, however, consider how much he thought about and remembered what the author had written:

And [the gang] turned on [the main character] because he lost one of their sweaters. And I just thought to myself, how could you do that. It's just a sweater. It had their colors on it, but then after realizing it, he said that losing gang colors is a big deal, but losing gang colors when you're not a gang member is an even bigger deal. And it brings consequences. And those consequences are going to be severe. He said, "All I can think to myself is I'm going to die." And the guy said, well, we're going to go kill [somebody]. And he said, "He handed me a Glock, and I put it in my pants, shoved it in there." And he said, "It felt uncomfortable, but I knew it was something I had to do." He said, "I was going to kill somebody tonight." And he ended up not killing anybody, he just pointed the gun at this dude that had the sweater that he had to get back. And he was going to shoot but he just held it there, and he said, "I started sweating bullets, I got really cold." . . . He said Mouse came over and took the gun and shot him a few times in the leg, and then he shot the girl in the face. He said it went in through her jaw, in through her cheek and out through the other side. He said, "All I could feel was blood all over my face from how close I was to her." And I was like, dang. That's deep. And it made me think how being in a gang would really change my life. How you can go from being a straight "A" student to being somebody who is going to be able to kill somebody.

It is possible that Alison Van Diepan's intention in writing *Snitch* was somewhere in the neighborhood of what Dennis got out of it. Regardless, his focus on the details and dialogue was driven by his own questions, about his future, not by what someone might ask as a way to gauge how analytical he had been in his reading.

READING: NO SOLO ACT

What do we recognize as reading competence? Consider an observation we made one morning. A group of six girls were involved in a lively conversation, huddled in a corner of their English classroom before the start of the school day. When the bell rang for the first period, they pleaded with their teacher to let them keep talking. She consented, but only if they caught the rest of the class up to what they were discussing. One of the girls had finished reading *Living Dead Girl* the previous evening, and her impulse to discuss it met with conflicting understandings of the ending which, indeed, is ambiguous. Opening up the issue for the class to consider, Norah offered to reread aloud the last few pages to settle the issue. As she finished the last few words, there was a moment of silence, then:

Amber: I didn't think she died.
Marissa: I guess I was just in such a rush to finish.
Calista: And she was stabbed.
Norah: I guess given what she went through, with the abuse, she couldn't have like, lived.
Marissa: I didn't realize that she died the first time, but now hearing it again . . .
Calista: She was in front of the . . .
Rosemary: It's still a happy ending.
Norah: Well, it's a sad ending!
Calista: Well, it's happy and sad.
Norah: It's sad because she got shot, but she's finally free from like . . .
Amber: . . . from years and years of being, like, tortured.
Rosemary: If I was in her situation, I would have wanted to die.
Marissa: You would be free from all that emotion. Like if you lived, you'd have to deal with the thought of those like four or five years when all of that, like, happened. You'd have to remember that.
Calista: I think it's better off this way.
Marissa: I just didn't think she died.
Sasha: I guess we're all, like, in denial.

The rereading seemed to bring the girls to agreement on the ultimate fate of the main character, a girl not far from their age who had suffered physically and psychologically at the hands of an adult male abductor. The whole of that character's experiences, though, remained discomforting, as the girls turned to how it shook their own sense of reality:

> *Calista:* You wonder, like, if you look close enough, you might not think it's here, but it's everywhere. I've read a lot of books like that, with sexual abuse, physical abuse, and just neglect, and so overall, it has gradually changed me. I'm more aware of the things that are happening. I just finished *Shut Up*, and it was kind of a sexual thing, too.
> *Amber: Living Dead Girl* changed my whole . . .
> *Rosemary:* I know. I stick with my parents in stores and stuff.
> *Sasha:* Yeah. I used to walk home from the park, and my dad was like, "Don't walk by yourself. You don't understand. I've seen it on the news, like girls getting attacked." I was like, "Whatever," you know. And after I read that, I'm like, "Yeah, you may be right." I'm certainly more aware.
> *Calista:* Like every conversation I have with my parents, I always like, refer back to the book. Like, I'm lucky to have that. I'm lucky to have conversations with my parents.

Looking around then, Calista noticed that so far, only girls were talking, so she announced, "I'd like a guy's point of view." Shifting in her seat to face a cluster of boys in the back of the room, she said, "We're going to make [reading this book] a requirement for you." It's worth noting that when students expect these discussions after reading, they tend to read more carefully.[11]

If previous chapters struck a chord with you, you probably recognize some important markers in the conversation. The students have been deeply engaged in reading a book they selected. They're eager to talk to each other. They have imagined themselves into the mind of a character facing a difficult situation, and they have considered the implications for their personal lives. Through self-initiated conversation, they compared conflicting understandings of the story. They noticed (and cared about) potential problems in their reading, which they strategically resolved. They considered meanings that transcended the literal interpretation of the story. They began to open their minds to others' perspectives, including parents'. Plus, realizing the possibility of even more different ways of thinking, they deliberately sought new sources of information, in this case, from their male peers. Remember, too, this whole scenario emerged from an interaction that started before the school day began, stemming from reading that was accomplished voluntarily, both inside and outside of class. In short, the students took control of expanding their learning. They were intellectually and collaboratively engaged in their reading.

That the students are individually asserting agency over their reading lives is certainly important. But the self-generated dialogic interactions with peers, disagreeing, seeking evidence, and building meanings together, have many further benefits.[12] Thinking together dialogically improves comprehension,[13] expressive language and willingness to speak in public,[14] creative thinking and reasoning ability,[15] use of analogical reasoning,[16] persuasiveness (including frequency of providing evidence, logic, and use of rhetorical strategies, which transfer to writing),[17] expansion of academic vocabulary (particularly among children from underserved communities),[18] conceptual reasoning and understanding in math and science,[19] quality of moral reasoning,[20] ability to lead successful problem-solving groups,[21] and self-esteem and confidence.[22] They also improve perspective-taking and disposition to consider others' ideas,[23] which, in turn, produces more positive attitudes toward peers and reduced stereotyping and bias against out-groups,[24] including improved relationships across ethnic and handicapped and non-handicapped students.[25] On top of all these benefits, we should not ignore the fact that students enjoy these interactions, which also generate more interest and engagement.[26] Though we have seen evidence of these benefits, little of this would be detected by the state reading test.

READING COMPETENTLY

There are those who worry that without teachers choosing the reading material, providing direct instruction, and holding students accountable with assignments, students' reading ability would fail. As it turns out, however, when reading engagement is the focus of instruction, students, particularly those who are normally seen as at-risk, do better in reading even on standardized tests. Second, students developed close reading and other textual analysis skills without presequenced direct instruction, though not without explicit instruction from peers and, as we shall see, from teachers. The students in the study became more strategic, with a stronger sense of agency in their reading, and were prepared to actively select and engage challenging texts.

Third, some students attended to the esthetic qualities of narratives and authors' craft, stepping back to comment on text construction, essentially as a work of art, as this student does:

> The Book Thief. I actually read that, and I've been in love with it. It's so good. It's written in the perspective of death, and it's like not . . . death isn't the main character, but he's a significant character. It's really cool, and it's really beautifully written, and I can't get over how death himself describes life in colors, and

the richness, and the coldness of certain colors, and him observing the book thief.

This sort of esthetic admiration was sometimes taken up in students' own writing—"Yeah, like the things I read inspire what I write"—and distributed through the conversations.

Fourth, students pointed to narrative literature's potential to provide "mirrors and windows."[27] Narratives serving as mirrors of personal experience provided a sense of affirmation of students' cultural and social identities. Tyriss, for example, was drawn to *Love and Leftovers* because "Like I am, and my dad is gay, too." Priscilla, by contrast, described *Wintergirls* as a window into a perspective to which she might not otherwise have access:

> I learned what trouble bulimics and anorexic people go through. 'Cause you never really think about it, but when you read it, it's like, Whoa! I understand it now. And, like, what happens in their life because of the struggles they face.

Dennis hints at additional consequences when he observed after reading *Tyrell* that "some of that stuff that he actually went through, a lot of homeless people actually go through. That kind of had me feel a little different about homeless people."

In sum, students engaged in reading narratives of their choice reported commonly cited forms of meaning-making competence, including personal response, enjoyment, esthetic appreciation, personal connection, and awareness of other. In other words, attending to students' human development need not come at the cost of their conventional literacy development. However, given what we have seen and heard, these standard indicators appear to underestimate the complexity of reading competence and might need some revision. What do we make, for example, of Dylan's expression of comfort with uncertainty?

> I'm reading *Rules of Attraction*, and everything changed in my head since when I was reading *Crank*. I had to go from all that stuff that was in my head. . . . My thoughts are kind of messed up now. . . . In a good way. . . . There was lots of things going through my mind.

In terms of comprehension, this sounds like an appreciative assertion of incomprehension.

Most of the students' descriptions of their experience with reading this way suggested fundamental shifts in the function of reading narratives, and thus, in how they experienced the texts. In many ways, reading became more about making sense of themselves and others than of the books. As we take stock of the reading competence students gain in school, what do we make of these shifts? How do we count the cathartic reading experiences described in Chapter 8? How do we value the conversational skills the students have developed, particularly their ability to engage face to face, to inquire, disagree, and build knowledge and relationships together? How do we value their understanding of books as tools for self-construction, or their comfort with uncertainty, or their desire to seek multiple perspectives, or their commitments to make a difference to their own and others' lives?

NOTES

1. Ivey & Johnston (2013).
2. Jerrim & Moss (2019).
3. Hidi (2001, pp. 203–204).
4. Vlasova (2023).
5. Share (1999).
6. Understanding reading practices in those classes would be another study, a different book.
7. Fulmer & Frijters (2011); Fulmer et al. (2015).
8. Dore et al. (2018); Guajardo & Cartwright (2016); Lecce et al. (2021).
9. We might remember this in both challenging assessments that focus narrowly on whether students use cognitive strategies or get the main ideas of stories they read and reimagining curriculum and instructional standards that, presently, lead with such limited objectives.
10. Holbrook (2017).
11. Miller et al. (2014).
12. We're drawing here on research in a range of fields, including dialogic engagement, collaborative problem-solving, collaborative reasoning, and philosophy for children—research in which multiple perspectives, including disagreements, are used to advance understanding.
13. Rojas-Drummond et al. (2014).
14. Trickey & Topping (2004).
15. Mercer et al. (1999); Wegerif (2005).
16. Lin et al. (2012).
17. Dong et al. (2009); Latawiec et al. (2016).
18. Ma et al. (2017a).
19. Mercer et al. (2004); Mercer & Sams (2008); Osborne & Chin (2010).
20. Xin et al. (2013).
21. Sun et al. (2017).
22. Trickey & Topping (2006).
23. Johnson & Johnson (2009).
24. Galinsky & Moskowitz (2000); Todd & Galinsky (2014).
25. Johnson & Johnson (1981a); Johnson & Johnson (1981b).
26. Xiaoying et al. (2013).
27. Sims Bishop (1990).

Part III

NEGOTIATING LITERATURE, TEACHING, AND TEEN DEVELOPMENT

CHAPTER 10

What Do We Think We're Doing?

Paulita never liked reading. But when I paired her with a book—*Esperanza Rising*—in literature circle, I thought that would be such a great book for those [Latina/Latino] kids. She hated that book! . . . I still wasn't engaging them. But with [the new approach], they get their choice of the book, so they're gonna read it. They're gonna be on fire about it.

—Ms. Tucker

This project began with teachers reflecting uncomfortably on their teaching. In their hearts, they wanted their students to find reading as engaging as they did, and by that standard, their teaching practices had been failing them. They read research that led them to believe access to and choice among personally meaningful texts would make a difference.[1] So they abandoned assigned reading, made a range of excellent young adult literature available for students to choose, abstained from asking comprehension questions or assigning projects to control the reading, and provided ample time for students to read and talk about books. The practices they stopped are what Nobel Prize–winning economist Richard Thaler and coauthor Cass Sunstein call "sludge"—the things that make it difficult to accomplish one's goals.[2] The result? As we have seen, among other things, lots of engaged readers.

Would this engaged readership last beyond 8th grade, though? We were curious, so we revisited some of the same students at the end of 10th or 11th grade. Alas, avid readership had plummeted. Most students' reflections, particularly the boys', echoed the sentiments of their pre–8th-grade nonreading lives, lamenting, "We don't read that much anymore" and "I used to love to read." Sadly, but usefully, they offered us an opportunity to return to and dig further into what causes adolescents *not* to read. Their perspectives underscored for us the differences in their reading before, during, and after 8th grade. Importantly, as we will discuss in this and the next two chapters, their reflections highlighted what an essential role the 8th-grade teachers played, not only in arranging for them to be engaged but also in expanding the meaningfulness of their reading and social lives. First up, though, is what we learned from the students as they looked back from high school.

FIZZLING OUT OF ENGAGEMENT

As high schoolers, the students offered four primary reasons why they no longer read as much: lack of time, lack of personally meaningful experiences with books, lack of choice, and lack of access to books they had not already read. Students spoke of the lack of choice among "diverse" relevant ("real," "relatable") books—a matter of both autonomy and relevance. Amelia observed, "[Now you are] being handed a book and say read this, answer the questions on this, . . . books you don't really have interest in." The autonomy argument was presented positively, for example, "If you have the choice to pick, you're most likely to do it." It was also presented negatively, in terms of being "made" or "forced" to read particular books. Concerns about lack of choice also extended to the pace of reading, as Amelia added, "It's not always enjoyable to follow the same pace, you know, read this many chapters a night." Of those who still read beyond required material, most reported rereading books they read in 8th grade.

There were exceptions. We found one student who liked all of the assigned books. Another, Roberto, liked some of them. He noted that one of his teachers "assigned us a book, and it would just be, 'Read this section, read this section.' I never read it . . . I can't read anything that just doesn't catch my attention, or I'll just fall asleep. . . ." Assigned *Romeo and Juliet*, he confessed, "I cannot pay attention to that story at all." A different teacher, however, assigned some readings that he liked, ". . . mythology, and since they caught my attention, I—he'd assign us a section, I would do that section that night, and I'd even do the next section because they were good. They attracted me." In other words, for those who did not protest out of a sense of autonomy, the assigned books were potentially engaging, but on a hit-or-(mostly)-miss basis.

The resulting lack of passion had its own consequences. For example, when asked whether she had recently persuaded someone to read a book, 10th-grader Nia exclaimed with surprise, "No, I haven't." Asked about the surprise in her voice, she observed:

> I am [surprised], 'cause in 8th grade I would be like, "Oh my God you have to read this book." You know? And now, I'm just like . . . not really. . . . You know, I guess I never really realized that before now. Well. But I used to do a lot more reading in 8th grade, and I wish I still did a lot of reading. I don't have the time to get into it as much.

This attribution to lack of time was common. Students pointed out that teachers no longer set aside sufficient, or any, time to read in class. Josefina interpreted this as a statement of values, observing, "I feel like no one makes time. We don't read. It's really not important to them."

what we make time/space
for highlights our
values

Michelle noted, "I used to love to read. Right now, I don't have a lot of time for reading. I wish I did, but I just don't have it." She said that because she no longer had time scheduled:

> . . . to sit down and get into [a book], when I have free time, I'm just like, I think I'll just go play video games or something . . . [because] I got a lot of technology after 8th grade. I got an iPhone, I got an Xbox . . . I was just so focused on all the technology that I kind of just shoved my books away. I kind of regret that. . . . And it's like well, I can always do it tomorrow, and you never do, 'cause you put it off.

Of course, in 8th grade students had reported pushing technology away in order to read, even though a few admitted to using their phones late at night to talk about their books. Not having time in class to become caught up in the narrative removed the press to return to the narrative outside of school.

Access to good books was also a problem. Meaningful books were not stored in the classroom, and students pointed out that they had no time to visit the school library, and even when they did it contained either "not ones you'd want to read" or "the same books we read in 8th grade." There was doubtless some truth to their claim, but even if it were not the case, students pointed out that they did not know which books to read. Nia explained that her 8th-grade teachers "took the time to get to know me personally—know what I like to read, know what I don't like to read, know what to recommend to me." Teachers, the students claimed, varied in their capacities as reliable, knowledgeable, enthusiastic sources of book information.

[handwritten margin notes: Guide; Relationship; resource]

UNRAVELING OF THE SOCIAL THREAD

Losing teachers as a source of reliable book information was compounded by the loss of a peer community passionately endorsing books. According to Scarlett, "Not a lot of people at the school enjoy reading," so there's a "shortage of readers to talk with." With the passionate reading community gone, their book endorsements and conversations followed. Students no longer had the reliable information sources about what to read and about each other's interests. But the conversational relationships themselves had been central reasons for reading. Paloma put it this way:

> I kind of just don't read any more. . . . [In 8th grade] I used to read every single day even when I got home, I could not put the book down . . . it's just that I have nobody to get up with and to ask questions for myself and if I do ask questions, they get answered but they're not in-depth questions like I used to.

Although students identified time, relevance, choice, and access as significant factors contributing to their engaged reading, they also made it clear

peer influence

these factors were linked by a persistent social thread. Back in 8th grade, Xavier had explained part of the thread, pointing out that he was reading more than he ever had before:

> Like, me and Otis we're best friends and we hang out and sometimes we talk about our books. He read *Good Behavior*, and he liked it a lot, and I just got finished with it, and I liked it a lot. He just got finished reading *Blood on My Hands* (has the book with him) and he gave it to me . . . I didn't think I would like [*Snitch*] because it had a girl on the cover. I didn't think I would like it until Otis recommended it to me. Otis and Calvin, actually. . . . I think it's kind of easier now for me to find a book. . . . My friends, I watch them while they read and I see how much they enjoy their book, and I wonder what it's about. I like reading after them.

Xavier's observation highlights why, in high school, students no longer knew what to read. The trusted social relationships and conversations were gone. From her perspective in 10th grade, Paloma offered the negative version from her high school experience:

> It's just not the same rush as when I did 2 years ago . . . I don't read as much . . . I don't really have [conversations] with anybody any more I just. . . . If I read . . . the next day I won't remember as many details as I would have because I haven't talked it, and nobody's really interested in talking about it with the English teacher. . . . Like teacher and student relationships went away . . . [peer relationships too]. We never really talked because everybody read the same book and it was just like *Tom Sawyer* . . . we started reading the beginning of *Precious*, and we talked about that, then we just stopped talking about it . . . I don't know what it was, we kind of just dropped the conversations and we just stopped reading. And everybody in class just stopped talking about it. The only reason we're talking about books now is because we're reading—all of us are reading, um, *Lord of the Flies*, and none of us like it, so . . . we don't like really talking about it. . . . Like we didn't even read this chapter, so let's wing this. . . .

Although a few of the students who continued to read had parent conversation partners or had made chance connections to adults at school—a secretary or biology teacher who shared their reading interests—these conversations didn't satisfy the deeper needs students had experienced in 8th grade. Recall from Chapter 1 Paloma's wistful insight, reflecting again on 8th grade:

> [It] gives you different points of view, and so [in] that class you were just basically talking about yourself, but at the same time you weren't, and you just

don't have to give it away like that. . . . And I just felt, like, instead of being students and teachers, we just became friends and like Ms. Tucker said, a family. 'Cause we just shared so much.

Paloma's analysis of her 8th- through 10th-grade experience invites us to think more about the complex associations among reading, talking, relationships, self-construction, even memory, and the havoc caused by apparently simple instructional decisions. Her observations suggest the collapse of an entire social support system. It's not just the reading that disappeared. All the dominoes fell. Note how she emphasizes in 8th grade the trust that evolved from, and made possible, otherwise difficult conversations. Students could talk about sensitive issues through the characters, without admitting that it was their own selves and relationships they were working on. At the same time, there was a tacit recognition of this fact and a trust stemming from the understanding that they were all sharing vulnerabilities and that they were not alone.

To sum up, the formerly engaged readers, looking back, reinforced the crucial role their 8th-grade teachers' research-informed instructional decisions had played in their reading: Time to read, access to meaningful books, and choice, were essential. But they made clear that the relational dimensions of their experiences—with teachers and each other—were inextricably linked to these memories. They grieved most the loss of transformative opportunities to learn with and from others inside and outside of texts and to deepen relationships.

MORE TEACHING CHANGES

At the outset, the teachers wanted their students to be engaged, so they successfully removed the sludge obstructing that goal, and we have emphasized the consequences for their students. We have said little about how it affected the teachers. Having seen in the first year the effects of engaged reading on the students, Ms. Tucker observed in the second year:

[The goals] change, don't they? Books are not the destination like we thought they were. We thought books were the cure (laughing). Not true! I want to see them more compassionate, more empathetic. I want them to see each other without stereotypes. I want them to read without realizing it. I want them to be empowered to choose their own books, to be readers for life. . . . That's a whole shift. I think just getting the books in the classroom, that was the original plan, but that's not the plan any longer. I think we've realized there's a lot more to it than that.

Independently, Ms. Pearson said much the same, that the end-of-year goal was no longer just to turn out better, more engaged readers, but more evolved human beings:

What's the purpose?

> I hope they're more compassionate. I hope they're more aware. I hope they're more tolerant of other people. I hope they have more world awareness. I hope they lose that self-centeredness, somewhat, and I know part of that is a product of age, but I hope they begin to see they are just a tiny piece in this world. . . . I would also hope it's caused them, if not to form friendships, at least [to] respect cooperative relationships with other people because they've had an opportunity to share and to have shared reading experiences, and they appreciate that they have more commonalities than they thought they did and that they're developing a culture, if you will, of respect for each other in terms of their thinking, that nobody's ideas are stupid, that everybody has valid ways of thinking about things.

In the beginning, the teachers could see what they wanted: engaged students. They could not yet see what else was possible. As the students showed them what engagement brought with it—what was possible—their goals for their students were elevated accordingly, and their teaching practices fell into line with the renewed goals.

It was not that the teachers no longer worried about the conventional aims of reading instruction. We'll get to that. It was that, like the students, they were mindful of something bigger. This was echoed in their reflections on student progress, like this from Ms. Pearson:

> Timothy wanted to share his journal with everybody today. What he wrote in his journal is "Second block is my best class because we're like a family. Nobody's allowed to hurt anybody else." It was all I could do not to cry, but how awesome is that? This was a boy that was in [alternative education] last year and has a history of being a bully, that has lived in the office most of his school career, and he's reading book number 13 of the year right now and talking to other people about books and excited about books and worried about his grades, wants to do well. And now he's friends with people he used to have a bullying relationship with. He and Jason were not friends. And today, Jason looked around and said, "You know what Big T, I love you." And somebody was gonna make fun, and he was like, "Come on, you know what I mean, not like that. I do. And Darion, I love you and Hudson, too. Y'all are my guys." And they were like, "We love you, too. We got your back, man." . . . I don't think I had anything to do with that other than being in the room. Well, maybe I did a little bit. Hopefully with the atmosphere that I go for and the openness of our conversations. But I think they're seeing something in each other, and they're willing to listen to each other a little more.

Appreciating Ms. Pearson's modesty, we know that the influence of all four teachers—Ms. Pearson, Ms. Tucker, Ms. Kirby, and Mr. Simmons—involved much more than just providing access to, and choice among, meaningful books, along with time to read and talk about them with no strings attached, though these were clearly important. So far, we have said little about what teachers offered beyond this opening of the gates. Let us start with Nia's observation that her 8th-grade teachers "took the time to get to know me personally—know what I like to read, know what I don't like to read, know what to recommend to me."

creating environment

KNOWING BOOKS AND INDIVIDUALS

Teaching, in the context of the standard English canon, positions teachers as experts on books like *The Scarlet Letter*, *To Kill a Mockingbird*, and *Lord of the Flies* in order to teach those books. The 8th-grade teachers needed a related, but different expertise. All four of the 8th graders' teachers read as much as students did, which the students noticed, recognizing that teacher recommendations might be well-informed. Teachers began the year by giving a series of book talks to large groups of students from across the classrooms gathered in the school auditorium, and thereafter, regularly talked about what they were currently reading and the personal impact of the books on their own thinking. Mr. Simmons routinely printed digital images of the covers of books he read and hung them on his classroom wall, so that anyone could ask about them. Students consistently named teachers as great sources for books:

students need to see teachers reading

> I like the way Ms. Pearson kind of explains what it's about. She doesn't, like, just put it on the shelf. Most teachers would be like, "Okay, here's the bookshelf. . . ." She's, like, "I love this book," and she personally reads almost all of them. That makes it easier to figure out which ones I would like.

Knowledge of good books was a source of capital for the teachers, and whereas some teachers might worry about giving up control over what students read, they relished the high degree of positive influence they had in helping students decide what to read. In some cases, teachers nudged the students toward certain books, but students were clear they made the final decision, as Kristoff explained, "They talk about the book and then they'll come to me and like, you should read this, and I'll think about it, and I'll read it."

There were instances where, on the surface, teachers might have appeared to exert a bit more force, such as when Trinity shared the following:

> Well, Ms. Tucker kept pulling [*Something Like Hope*] for me, and pulling it for me, and pulling it for me, so I thought I'd just give it another try. 'Cause she

said it was a really good book. I told her I read it once and I really didn't like it, and she's like, "Well give it another try," and I read it and it was really, really, really good. So, Ms. Tucker's the one that made me read it.

This account of how a teacher "made" her read a book might seem contrary to our argument about the importance of autonomy. But while the teacher chose the book and badgered Trinity to read it, the difference was that not only was the book not required but also Ms. Tucker knew Trinity. Outside of their healthy teacher–student relationship, this heavy nudging would backfire. But over time and through lots of conversations, as Trinity explained:

I think we've [become] a lot closer because we have the same taste in books, and we know we're on the same page. And our thoughts, when one person finishes off, the other person starts and picks up where the other person left off.

When Trinity made this comment, Peter had to double-check, "You're talking about the teachers and you?" because we had heard the students make similar comments, but about peers.
Yolanda had a similar experience:

Okay, I've read so many books this year, I can't even keep track . . . well, I do keep track actually. . . . The books I read are completely different than the books I read in 7th grade. I tried to finish the whole entire *Drama High* series, and then this year I went looking for a book like that. And then Ms. Tucker was like, "That book really doesn't seem like you. Here's a book you'll like." And when she did that, I didn't really want to read *Living Dead Girl*, so I was flipping through the pages and I wasn't reading, but then I saw a part where I started to read it, and I was like I'm going back to the beginning, and I started reading from the beginning. Usually, I wouldn't have done that. But that was when I completely got hooked on all the books that I've read. I'm just really glad she helped me find a book because I can guarantee I wouldn't have read all the great books I have.

Trinity and Yolanda were not just special cases for this teacher, though. She knew all of her students this way as people and readers. In an interview, we asked Ms. Tucker whether she had noticed changes in any particular students recently, and without hesitation, she said:

James, he's reading *Leverage* . . . he said it's the best book he's ever read. And it's great, the way he said it. It was like, "I like his character." He's not talking about the character in the book or the character in the movie . . . he said, "I like the way he's willing to be an athlete and a good student." I thought that was pretty powerful. . . . Tobey—he's reading *Clean*—and you can't pull him out of it. . . .

I said, "Do you realize you gained over a hundred pages last night?" He actually said to me, "Do we have to talk now, or can I just keep reading?" He could care less about talking today. He wanted to read. We paired him up with some John Green. He's gone deep. Ava, who takes two or three books at a time and can come back and tell you what's good about each book or what she doesn't like about each book—she's become very articulate. In second block, have you noticed Wendy? That's a different kid. It used to take her 12 weeks to read a book. *Glimpse* has been her breakthrough book. Or those three girls—if you put Jada, Deandra, and Wendy together, they are actually talking about books. They are not just chattering. They're talking about books and making someday lists. And they're taking recommendations from totally different people. And the way Wilson will ask girls for recommendations on books—he just read *Leverage* and *Break*, but now he's willing to go back and try *In Ecstasy*. Today you could have had the earthquake again, and he wouldn't have realized it. He's totally involved. Greg, he's in the second book [in the *Solitaire* series) and he realized there's a third. He found the first book on his own and he got it for Christmas. Tess has moved on from the *Twilight* series, moved on to *Evermore* and *Shiver* and *Linger*. She's talking about books in a different way. Thad, who goes out and buys books just so he can have all three *Perfect Chemistry* [books], and then [pitches] them to everybody. I like to watch Dennis . . . he just keeps comparing everything to *Tyrell*. He wants a book like *Tyrell*. But he doesn't give up. . . . He is trying to find that book. He is taking recommendations from other people and is trying. He just has a standard.

Did you count the number of students she named—not to mention the details of their reading—in the span of just a minute or two? Eleven. How many books or series are mentioned? Twelve. She could have gone on. We heard reports like this routinely, outside of our formal interviews.

That their teachers made it a point to know their students and what they were working on did not escape the students, nor did its impact, as Daphne pointed out in Chapter 7:

> Like, she knows more about you from what you read and what you like to read and through the discussions that we have with her. . . . Ms. Tucker is just one of those people who just *gets* you, basically. . . . And then through reading, she can get to *you*.

Students felt that their teachers cared about them, which is reflected in higher academic achievement and engagement,[3] self-esteem, and overall well-being.[4] How does this happen? Ms. Tucker explains:

> I can sit down next to a kid and say, "I have no clue what this book's about." But simple questions, like "Catch me up," the kid is just spilling it. They are so excited about what they're reading and they love what they're reading. They sit

[handwritten margin note: children need to know that someone cares about them]

and tell you everything. They don't care whether you know the book or not. They don't love the affirmation. They just want the avenue to talk. . . . They certainly didn't do that with an anthology.

NEGOTIATING RELATIONSHIPS AND RELATIONAL CAPITAL

Teachers could not have known their students so well without so much time in conversation with them about books. Certain kinds of talk make conversations and listening possible, together producing relationships that make possible deeper conversations. This is particularly true with the least experienced readers. Mr. Simmons was masterful at jump-starting these students. He commented that at the beginning of the year, Bristol seemed "almost hostile," but chalked it up to, "She really didn't know me." That changed as Mr. Simmons made it a point to have regular conversations with her as she tried out new books. For instance, when she read *Glimpse*, Mr. Simmons said they had been "talking almost daily" about the "dirty little secret" that was at the center of the book and the idea that for the reader, "something's not lining up right." He remembered when things came together in *Glimpse* for Bristol:

> I was back here talking to a student at my desk. She walked back here, almost angry, when she finally read the part in the diary where she found out the mom was prostituting her daughter. She came back to me . . . it is hard to describe. She was angry, and I don't know, I get emotional just thinking about it. Just to see how emotional she got, that she was that much into that story. We had an awesome conversation about it. She was completely immersed in those characters and what was going on. . . .

Mr. Simmons was not only able to name countless other books she had read but also how her demeanor and their relationship had shifted: "She used to come in with all this drama. Now, every morning she comes in and she just smiles at me, and we exchange little comments. She smiles at me first thing . . . we've got this connection going with the reading." Their relationship developed because Mr. Simmons's initial interpretation of Bristol's behavior was that she just didn't yet know him. It could have gone differently if, for example, he interpreted it as her being surly and threatening his control. Students learn to trust that they are not being judged. Ms. Pearson explained to us the significance of ensuring students could feel confident they were not being judged or evaluated:

> I found if I come with a clipboard, they're not as much open with me. . . . It's a lot easier for me to walk by and go "What are you thinking?" or "What are you reading?" or get them to engage in a conversation. Or I sit up here and go, "You

know, I'd love for somebody to tell me about their book." And you know, every time I say that, they're, like, lining up, "Can I read to you from my book?" So, I let them just kind of generate coming to me. And I'm not writing anything down. I'm like, "What are you liking about this one?" or "What are you now liking? I've noticed you abandoned that one?" And they'll tell me, because they don't feel like I'm grading them or judging them in any way. We're just sitting, having a conversation. They pull up a stool and we have a chat about what they want to talk about. I know it's not great for data collection purposes, but it's been really awesome for building relationships for them, by getting them to talk about the books.

The importance of building relationships through talk that Ms. Pearson refers to here is magnified when you consider the kinds of things that came up when students talked about books with their teachers. Trust was key.

Consider this example where Ms. Tucker was chatting with Rashad about his decision to read *My Bloody Life*, a memoir by former gang member, Reymundo Sanchez. Ms. Tucker was hesitant about this decision because of the combination of mature content in the book and Rashad's own experiences as a gang member. As she read aloud to Rashad portions of the book's preface, in which the author explains why he used a pseudonym and why he wrote the book, she shared her own questions:

> I think for me, it would be pretty intimidating to write this. He does survive, so why would you write about this? Why would you put your life at risk? I'm so curious as to why he would put himself out there, put himself in danger.

She also asked Rashad to explain some gang symbols on the cover of the book. Rashad offered initial thoughts on the book based on his own experiences, as well as what he had learned from other books, such as *Blue Rage, Black Redemption*. He hypothesized, "It might be like the Tookie Williams book. Either trying to reach out to people to warn them about what could happen or to speak out to fellow gang members who want to get out." When he made comments that reflected firsthand knowledge, Ms. Tucker offered no judgment.

Ms. Tucker was concerned, though, for Rashad to take the book seriously, particularly since he had developed a reputation of going through a book a day since becoming an engaged reader. She asked Rasheed pointedly, "Why do you think I'd be hesitant to give you this book?" He guessed it was because the book had lots of sexual details. But Ms. Tucker clarified:

> That's not the issue. You don't want to read that fast if you're really going to take it to heart. Remember, he's taking a risk writing this, and he says his purpose is to save one kid's life. This is pretty serious. Your reading needs to reflect that. Take time to think about how serious this is, what he has to say. Can we make a deal?

Ms. Tucker's rules for the deal were "You cannot read it all in one night" and "Before you give it away to somebody else to read—'cause I know you will as soon as you finish—you have to give it to me and let me read it." Rashad happily agreed to the terms. We can imagine many scenarios in which Rashad or other students like him would have never approached their teacher with a book like this in the first place. As Rashad read the book—over a period of several weeks—he talked regularly with Ms. Tucker about what was concerning or confusing to him, as he was, indeed, rattled by some of the details. When peers wanted to read the book after him, he talked to them about it first much the way Ms. Tucker had talked to him.

As we pointed out in Chapter 3, these relationships have important consequences for students' academic growth and for their well-being. Arranging for these relationships and for students to feel known and understood was important. These were not goals in themselves, but rather collateral benefits of the collective inquiry into books and selves. However, there were other instructional subtleties that we will explore in the next chapter.

Relationships among the teachers also shifted. There was a sense of we're-all-in-this-together created by the joint focus on engagement and on something other than conventional achievement and test scores. The agenda of group planning meetings often centered on new books, success stories, and consultations on students facing difficulty becoming engaged in reading. Because so many books were in circulation, there was no way for any one teacher to know all of the relevant books, and so teachers became resources for each other when they or their students were troubleshooting. Ms. Pearson explained it this way:

> We each have our leaning of the genre we really like, very clearly, but we're all willing to read other stuff, and so we come at it from a different perspective. So that's really cool as adults to talk about things, or to be able to refer a kid to an adult who I know likes those things. Like I can say, "Ms. Tucker is the one to go talk to, 'cause she reads all those books. She can point you in the right direction." And she's done the same thing, she's like, "Go talk to Ms. P." So, it's really cool, even if we read the same books. You know we ask kids to rate books zero to ten, I would say, "Uh, it's a five," and Ms. Tucker would say, "Oh, it's a ten."

It was normal to see teachers and students crossing the hallways to visit other classrooms in search of books or help. For instance, when Akeem encountered a problem in *Response*, he first asked if anybody in his class—Ms. Tucker's class—had read the book, and when he came up short, he simply announced he was going next door to consult Mr. Simmons, who he knew had read it. On another day, we noticed Mr. Simmons in his classroom sharing *Estrella's Quinceañera* with two Latina students from Ms. Pearson's class, one with a 15th birthday approaching, and as they were chatting, both Ms. Pearson and Ms. Tucker appeared to look for different books in Mr. Simmons's collection. This sort of collaboration among teachers offered students a healthy and productive social practice to emulate. At the same time, it strengthened the teachers' own support network.

NOTES

1. Guthrie & Humenick (2004); Ivey & Broaddus (2001).
2. Thaler & Sunstein (2008).
3. Roorda et al. (2011).
4. Lavy & Naama-Ghanayim (2020).

CHAPTER 11

Seamless Teaching

Humans grow along a number of developmental pathways—the cognitive, the physical, the language, the psychological, the social, and the ethical. Because these areas of learning are so closely connected, underdevelopment in any one area inhibits growth in others.

—James Comer[1]

We suppose most people take for granted that the job of an English language arts teacher is to help students learn how to analyze characters, plot, theme, literary tools, and devices and so forth. By now it's likely clear these were not what drove instruction in the 8th-grade classrooms. The teachers were not unaware of these expectations, nor did they reject them. Rather, as we saw in the last chapter, they came to believe that those were subordinate to their other goals. Consequently, instruction on plot, theme, character, and such did not happen in major stand-alone lessons any more than there were lessons on emotions, relationships, self-regulation, and the like. Rather, they were all a seamless part of the ongoing book conversations. As you will see, these conversations and the weaving of instruction throughout occurred both as students were reading and raising issues in their own selected books and during daily teacher read-alouds as students convened around a common text.

SEAMLESSNESS

To understand this seamlessness, consider a sliver of instruction in Ms. Tucker's classroom. She was reading to the students *What Happened to Cass McBride?* which details the mysterious kidnapping of the title character from four different narrative perspectives, and in nonchronological order. At a pivotal point in the read-aloud, a student, Zion, confessed, "I get confused about when things are happening, in the past or the present." In a different classroom, this confession would amount to a public admission of stupidity, to be avoided at all costs. But Ms. Tucker responds, "That's not surprising, the confusion, because there are so many flashbacks that

Need for supportive environment *Natural flow of weaving*

help us get to what the character is thinking." Her response renders Zion's confusion not an indication of stupidity, but a normal, interesting part of reading, increasing the probability of subsequent such instructionally informative admissions.

In the same breath, Ms. Tucker has introduced, in a memorable context, the literary term "flashback" with its functional logic—to "help us get to what the character is thinking." To reinforce the lesson further, she rereads a flashback where the narrator is remembering when he taught his younger brother how to climb trees, a brother who has now hung himself from a tree. Ms. Tucker stops suddenly and says: "This is settling heavy on my heart." Sharing her feelings, she implicitly invites the students to attend to their own and to contemplate what the character is thinking. Students quickly offer hypotheses about the character's state of mind, each maintaining uncertainty with "maybe" and "wait a minute," except for one who asserts, "He can't feel guilty for that." Immediately Ms. Tucker responds, "Doesn't grief cause you to think in irrational ways?" Her question simultaneously reestablishes uncertainty and reinforces attention to the complexity of thoughts and feelings. After a couple more student hypotheses, she observes, "We don't know yet, do we? The author is leaving these huge gaps, and it's up to us to infer."

Wilson interjects, "I like that. It makes you think, and it makes you want to get into the book more. You don't want all the answers on one page. You want to think." Supporting his comment, Ms. Tucker elaborates on it: "Do you remember in *The Secret Story of Sonia Rodriguez*, how the inferences we made initially were wrong? We learned that when we kept reading. We were surprised at the end, and that was fun. We don't know yet." The teacher's response reinforces Wilson's assertion that the uncertainty and its ultimate resolution add to the enjoyment. In fact, just like Zion's initial confession of confusion, Wilson's observation was made possible by their expectation of Ms. Tucker's pattern of responses, normalizing confusion, sharing her feelings, and maintaining comfort with, even enjoyment of, uncertainty.

In this brief moment of classroom life, Ms. Tucker teaches about flashbacks, which would fall under the Common Core anchor standard for 9th and 10th grade as: "Analyze how an author's choices concerning how to structure a text, order events within it."[2] She also nudges the students to think about what is explicit and implicit in the text—another 9th- and 10th-grade anchor standard. But notice how the academic instruction is woven seamlessly and responsively into the read-aloud and how she effortlessly fosters their mind reading and, simultaneously, the meaningfulness of the book. Later, she will share how frustrated she is with a character. To a student who asserts what a character ought to do next, Ms. Tucker asks, "Is that what you're recommending to [the character]?" Notice too how she doesn't judge the students' responses. She persistently positions them as competent, thoughtful engaged readers. She normalizes confusions and problems as part of reading and learning and names uncertainty as not only *not* a problem but a source of delight. Her self-disclosure and persistent reference to "we" foster a collective sense of belonging.

Aside from teaching literary technique, her interactions fulfill the students' needs for a sense of competence, relatedness, and meaningfulness and promote a growth mindset. The central element of mindsets is whether people consist of fixed character traits or whether they grow and change with experience and context,[3] which intersects with English language arts (ELA) instructional standards.

Ms. Tucker's interactions touch yet another dimension of development. They nudge students to be more comfortable with uncertainty and ambiguity, lowering their need for closure. This is important because when people have a high need for closure, they find uncertainty upsetting, preferring simple facts and uniformity of ideas. They tend to judge ideas quickly and on the most obvious feature or quality and, having judged, stick to the idea regardless of further information, a process often referred to as "seizing and freezing."[4] They cling to their initial opinion in a conversation and refuse to consider other perspectives. In other words, they close their minds, undermine dialogue, and diminish creativity. They have a strong desire for certainty, stability, and conformity—knowledge that everyone agrees on.[5] Consequently, in a collaborative group setting they reject and even become annoyed with or hostile toward those who disagree and threaten stable consensus. When need for closure is high in a group, the dynamics become less symmetrical. Some members dominate the talking and thinking, pressuring others to conform.[6] Group members develop more autocratic opinions and view autocratic leaders more favorably.[7] In fact, a high need for closure has been linked to the rise of authoritarian regimes.[8] It makes people more biased toward their in-group and against those who are different or who think differently, who they then tend to exclude.[9]

None of this is good preparation for an egalitarian democracy (or a marriage, friendship, or business enterprise, for that matter). Thankfully, Ms. Tucker's dialogic interactions, her positive attention to uncertainty, and the reduced classroom stress diminish the students' need for closure. Even the use of narrative texts has a similar effect, nudging toward more open minds.[10]

CHARACTERS AND CHANGE

Although ELA instruction has long had students seeking character traits (e.g., courage, laziness),[11] the relevant 9th- and 10th-grade anchor standard requires that students "Analyze how complex characters (e.g., those with multiple or conflicting motivations) develop over the course of a text, interact with other characters, and advance the plot or develop the theme."[12] Many of us recall in school learning to identify a character's traits—the defining features of their personalities and dispositions—and to say whether a character was round/dynamic or flat/static, that is, whether they changed, usually for the better, precipitated by an important realization, or whether they pretty much stayed the same. Ms. Tucker and the other teachers used the traditional language of character change in their talk about books, such as when she paused while reading to students to comment, "See this is where I know [the protagonist] is a dynamic character . . . this is the point where I know she is changing. This is a big moment for her . . . she does something a different way." This certainly checks all the instructional boxes: The teacher explicitly defines it, provides a contextualized example, and does so at a moment when students are engaged and invested. We observed students taking this up in subsequent conversations, such as when Meleisha said in a different book conversation, "Do you think she'll ever change, be a dynamic character by speaking out or something like that? I can see her doing that."

The instructional rhetoric of character change also blends nicely with the notion of the growth mindset, the idea that people may not be composed of fixed traits, that there's more to a person that meets the eye, that transgressions may be temporary lapses, and that permanent judgments are likely inaccurate. Recall that students recognized that through reading and being privy to characters' minds, they became less likely to judge and stereotype. So, when Ms. Tucker draws attention to the idea of dynamic or round characters, the idea that characters and real people are complex, she seamlessly nudges this way of thinking about others (and selves).

But what about the static or flat character, who, in academic terms, reveals no evidence to change the reader's perception of them? Are there people in real life who are similarly static? What if, as a reader, I identify with a character who remains unchanged? All relevant questions. This wasn't a problem for Ms. Tucker, even while making the literary concept clear. She simply extended her mind reading for these less developed characters, in essence turning them into *potentially* dynamic characters. For instance, finishing her read-aloud of *The Secret Story of Sonia Rodriguez*, the students were troubled that Sonia never resolved tensions with her mother, who most judged harshly. Ms. Tucker agreed that it was possible Sonia's mom had not evolved, "given what we know about her character typically." Nudging the students to imagine a future, though, she added, "But suppose she's changed. Could she be more than a static character . . .?" She reiterated this same idea later in a different book, with a different mother–daughter dilemma, saying that the mother "has such an amazing opportunity to change." When she asked, "Do you know who that reminds me of?" a student responded, without hesitation, "Sonia's mother!"

These caveats were not lost on students, as we observed them taking up this kind of thinking about characters even when the teacher was not present. For example, several boys were discussing the real-life subject of *Yummy: The Last Days of a Southside Shorty*, who was murdered in connection to gang involvement. They pointed to hardships that explained some of his decisions: "He didn't have a mom or a dad or anything. He lived with his grandma, and his grandma had all [those] kids. Nobody didn't pay any attention to him." When Rico lamented, "[Yummy] was just a kid" when he died, Rashad's words echoed the thinking he was apprenticed into by Ms. Tucker: "If Yummy had lived, I think he would have changed his life."

INFERRING, ESPECIALLY THOUGHTS AND FEELINGS

Inferring what is going on in characters' minds is a crucial dimension of human development, as we pointed out in Chapter 5, so we will not dwell on it long here except to point out that it is also a required academic skill—understanding the "conflicting motivations" of "complex characters," inferring plot and action—necessary also for students to become critical readers, understanding the motivations of authors.[13] So, when Ms. Tucker said about a character, "I'm surprised he's crying so hard," then asked, "What can you infer?" she was not just reinforcing a reading skill—reading between the lines and inferring motives; she was getting students to slow down and settle into characters' minds in order to understand more about the relationship between thoughts, feelings, words, and actions.

First-person narratives, by their design, invite readers into characters' thoughts, but the teachers also directed the adolescents to other characters whose thoughts are not made explicit. For example, referring to a hospitalized character in *Retaliation*, Ms. Tucker said to Rashad, "See, that's the part that upset me, because when the mom got the call about her daughter, my heart went out to her." Similarly, we only get the author's perspective in the memoir, *The Burn Journals*, but Ms. Tucker invited Norma and Kendall into the head of the younger brother who was in the house when the author attempted suicide:

My heart goes out to the brother because it's my impression he stays behind. And that smell, imagine that's your brother. . . . He's thinking he's the last person he saw before he did it, and the first person he saw afterwards. He can't get over it. I still can't shake that book even after years of reading it.

The author's parents had not yet made an appearance in the book, but Ms. Tucker pointed the girls there, too: "Can you imagine his parents, though, now that you mention walking into the house and stuff. I can't imagine what they must have encountered when they walked into the house, and the smell. . . ."

LITERATURE, THEMES, AND LIFE'S DILEMMAS

Ms. Tucker told her class one day, "I never think a book has just one theme . . . it depends on your experiences," to which student Meleisha added, "Books are multicolored." This was the theory that drove the concept of "theme(s)" in these classrooms, and it was a good translation of how literary theorist Louise Rosenblatt described *aesthetic* reading experiences—the idea that the real narrative is created when the reader and the text come together, each affecting the other.[14] Elena's experience with *Perfect Chemistry*—the realization that she, like a character, was struggling with the fact that she did not speak or understand Spanish despite it being the first language of close family members—was likely unique among the students who read that book, which revolves around a good girl/bad boy romance. Sharing her experience enlarged her classmates' understanding of the book and of Elena, along with their mind reading and likely moral reach.

So, the teachers did not ask or expect students to get a particular big idea or to be changed in the same way by their reading, and not just because they were all reading different books, but because doing so would likely have curtailed the personal and social growth that came from reading on their own terms. What they did, though, was to use the multitude of texts in circulation to nudge attention to patterns across characters that reveal some of the complexities of what it means to be human, in and out of books, compelling a level of abstraction. Noticing the conversations that were springing up among students over seemingly unrelated books, the teachers decided to have the students collectively talk through and categorize big ideas on a bulletin board and then add to them as existing patterns grew and new patterns were identified. So, big life complexities encountered in the books, like "left by a loved one" and "in over your head," were pinned to the board, surrounded by situations from books pertaining to each written on Post-it notes. New and revised dilemmas were added by individual students as they encountered them in reading or during small-group and whole-class conversations.

For instance, early in Ms. Tucker's read-aloud of *The Beckoners*, when two characters with stark differences are introduced, Saul interrupted, "I think they're going to end up being friends, because haven't you noticed that in books? Two people can be total enemies, nothing in common even, and then somewhere in the book they get over it or whatever and they become friends." Not worried that the flow of the narrative was disrupted for the moment, Ms. Tucker encouraged him, "Keep going with that idea." One after another, students supplied examples from different books that fit the pattern, but also to conflicting situations, such as a real teenager from a newspaper story who was dealing with the legal and social ramifications of being falsely accused of rape by a girlfriend. Roberto at first predicted, "There's no way he's going to trust his ex-girlfriend again. What

[Handwritten margin note: Opportunity for collaboration / Not all working toward one answer]

she did when she lied about him raping her. They ain't gonna be friends."
He paused for a second, though, and said, "Well, I mean, they might," and
Lawrence added, "They might, but I bet it won't happen as long as he can't
get off that [sex offenders list]."

The example illustrates blurring lines between experiences with fiction and nonfiction reading for the students and for teaching. Most English
classes would not have a newspaper article arise in a discussion of theme.
But Ms. Tucker and the other teachers frequently circulated informational
texts touching on topics arising in the books. When Ms. Tucker shared an
article about a 15-year-old Afghan girl imprisoned by her in-laws for refus-
ing to work as a prostitute, Kendall quickly noted similarities with *Sold*, a
novel-in-verse about a young girl forced into the sexual slave trade in Nepal.
In another class period, discussion of this same article centered on Afghan
girls' difficulties accessing education, leading Nia to ask, "So if Sonia doesn't
finish her education, could she end up that way, too?" referring to a fictional
character at risk of not graduating high school because of overwhelming
responsibilities at home.

Digging in further, on a subsequent day, Ms. Tucker announced, "I have
another article about the mistreatment of females, but this one happens much
closer to home . . . about gangs in [our state] found to be sex trafficking."
Before she could finish distributing copies, students were already reading on
their own. Immediately students recognized the name of the gang because of
its presence in their community. The article linked the gang to El Salvador,
prompting a discussion of relevant local and international geography. As
Ms. Tucker began to read aloud, students had many questions, such as what
"off-kilter" meant, when it was used in the article to describe how gang
members coerced girls to comply. To that, she simply responded, "Great
question. Ask your friends," igniting a flurry of hypotheses. Chatter continued through the ending bell, but before dismissing students, Ms. Tucker
brought them back to the big picture:

> Tomorrow, I want us to reflect on how the information in this article impacts
> us. We read about horrific things happening in Afghanistan and other faraway
> places. Then [our own state]. It's getting close. I also want to talk about how it
> connects to the things we're reading. I've been thinking about the consequences
> of the loss of innocence.

In subsequent days and weeks, "loss of innocence" became a big idea
pinned to the board, and as students read and talked about their own books,
they posted notes around it referencing characters' experiences. In the context of some students' gang involvement, fiction and memoirs about gang
members were popular choices across a broad swath of students.

The point in the teachers facilitating conversations like this was not to
have the adolescents come away with major themes to live by, but rather

to help them use multiple narratives—in a range of forms—to navigate the ever-changing gray areas in life and relationships. We struggle to see how identifying the so-called theme of *Animal Farm* or even a modern young adult classic such as *Speak* would enable students to become more engaged in the narrative, much less equip them with a similar range of tools for making a better life.

TEACHING ABOUT HOW WORDS CAPTURE AND SHAPE THOUGHTS AND FEELINGS

The teachers didn't distribute weekly vocabulary lists, but their widespread conversations about books and characters with the students made the introduction of new words nearly inevitable, particularly when just the right word helped to capture a character's vibe, dilemma, or mental state. For instance, Norma and Kendall struggled with whether being placed in a psychiatric unit was the right thing for the author of *The Burn Journals*, who had attempted suicide more than once. Ms. Tucker asked if they knew what *fixated* means. She explained, "Some people have it within them that they get fixed on one thing, and they can't shake it out." Kendall piped up, "Like a book! Like reading *Hate List*, and you can't get off of it even after your 23rd book!," referring to a running class joke over her obsession with one book, but clearly grasping the meaning of the word. Turning back to *The Burn Journals*, Ms. Tucker reiterated, "So you can't get it off your mind, even if you try, and you go in these vicious circles. So, I wonder if that wasn't part of his problem—he can't get suicide out of his head." The concept associated with *fixated* then appeared to help knock an edge off Kendall's thinking: "I think the way you just explained that, I'm thinking now maybe he deserves to be in the psych unit."

Words also mattered to students, particularly when those words gave insight into characters' emotional states and how those words must feel to someone when they say them. They routinely asked for meanings or looked them up. Knowing that words and imagery expanded students' experiences, though, teachers drew attention to them, particularly when they read to students. So, when Ms. Tucker came to the phrase "how innocent evil could look when sleeping,"[15] she paused and alerted students to "Watch word choice . . . watch word placement in this sentence." The students' choral reaction of "Ohhhhhhh!" indicated they followed her signal in the moment, but she often referred back to instances like this to keep students thinking about the power of language.

Frequent episodes illustrated students' adoption of this attitude toward language:

> *Lola:* In the book *Beautiful* the dad is mad or something and the girl is trying to get more pretty. The dad calls her poor white trash slut.

Wilson: Isn't another white racist slur "a honky"?

Meleisha: In the book I'm reading this girl was dressing for this guy she had a date with. The father was reading the paper. He said to her, "If you dress like a slut, people are going to think you're one."

Roberto: That's cold. Words you use can hurt. It was like that, what you [Ms. Tucker] read from that Sharon Draper book the other day. That lead sentence, or whatever, "Sit your useless butt back down."

Besides the fact that they mention three different books and the phrase "lead sentence" in this exchange, they are collectively recognizing a pattern, both in narrative and in real life, that language can shape thought, for good or bad. Sure, you can teach separate lessons on vocabulary, tone, word choice, or imagery, but outside of engagement with characters and peers who matter to them, will students think about these ideas beyond class time, much less accept personal responsibility for them? Recall back in Chapter 7 Marty's realization of the violent impact of a word like "moron" and his and his classmates' reflection on it.

TEACHING FOR INTELLECTUAL FLEXIBILITY

Previously, we described how students came to believe, through their reading and conversations, that to really engage with an idea, you have to keep an open mind to, even seek out, perspectives that differ from the author's or your own. After the class read an article in which a young woman recounted her drug addiction experiences, Wilson remarked, "You know what would be cool, if the author was her parents, like in *Crank*.[16] 'Cause it would give a different point of view." Like the other students, he realized one side is just the starting point.

For the 8th graders, books told from unfamiliar perspectives were a catalyst, as were books with shifting narrators telling different sides of a story. But when the students remained rigid in their thinking, teachers deliberately shook things up. For instance, countless students who read *Living Dead Girl* got stuck on their belief that Alice, the main character who had been abducted and held captive, could have tried harder to escape, claiming things would have gone differently if they were in her place. So, the teachers introduced books that opened new perspectives on captivity, such as *Stolen*, the memoir *A Stolen Life*, and *Pointe*, which is told from the viewpoint of the victim's friend. In the process of intently reading these books, the students became aware of several theories regarding why it might be difficult to leave, including Stockholm syndrome, fear, and shame. The problem Alice faced, like many other problems, they would learn, defied a simple explanation. The new perspectives prompted new questions, thus perpetuating further conversation and the possibility of additional explanations not yet identified.

Similarly, when Ms. Tucker read aloud the part in a different book where a school advises homeschooling for a pregnant student, Norma complained, "That's rude." When a flurry of peers sounded off in agreement, Ms. Tucker disrupted their sense of certainty: "Play the devil's advocate on the other side. Play the school's side." Without hesitation, students responded: "They're doing it to protect her. . . ." "They think she's a role model. . . ." "It's bad for the school's morals. . . ." "My friend got pregnant. She kept on going, and she [eventually] started doing homeschooling . . ." "On *Teen Mom*, she stayed home. . . ." "There was this school in Kentucky where the mom could go, drop off their baby, and get their education. . . ." The goal was not to get students to agree with each other or with the teacher—who did not share her opinion in this scenario—but instead to have them see beyond their initial or singular impressions.

NOTES

1. Comer (2001, p. ix).
2. http://standardstoolkit.k12.hi.us/wp-content/uploads/2012/12/LA_9-10.pdf
3. Dweck (2006).
4. Kruglanski & Webster (1991).
5. Kruglanski et al. (1993).
6. De Grada & Kruglanski (1999); Pierro et al. (2003).
7. Jost et al. (1999); Kruglanski et al. (2006).
8. Turner & Killian (1957).
9. Shah et al. (1998); Kruglanski & Webster (1991).
10. Djikic et al. (2013a).
11. Example of a website with a list of character traits: TeacherVision (n.d.).
12. http://standardstoolkit.k12.hi.us/wp-content/uploads/2012/12/LA_9-10.pdf
13. http://standardstoolkit.k12.hi.us/wp-content/uploads/2012/12/LA_9-10.pdf
14. Rosenblatt (1978).
15. Giles (2006, p. 11).
16. Ellen Hopkins, the author of *Crank*, has written that this and related books in a series are based on what she observed and experienced with her daughter's struggle with drugs.

CHAPTER 12

Inquiry, Learning, and Authority

Negotiation of meanings and purposes—itself the mark of a democratic society—is . . . the means of developing the individual initiative, independence of judgment, and social commitment on which democracy in turn depends.[1]

—John Nicholls

When reading aloud to the students *Jumping Off Swings*, Ms. Tucker reached a part of the book where someone had scratched "slut" on the locker of a pregnant character. She paused to ask, "Does the school have a moral responsibility to cover what someone wrote about Ellie on the locker? The school not doing anything is a silence." Students chimed in:

Meg: They're saying I don't care.
Jed: Maybe that happens a lot and they're just tired of dealing with it.
Carl: That's sort of like, for instance, if her mom came to the school, and her mom said which one is yours, and she says, "It's the one with *slut* on it."
Rosie: Don't teachers walk by and see that?
Ms. Tucker: Corrine says she'll stand in front of it all day if she has to.
Farrah: She's a good friend.

The students do not actually answer Ms. Tucker's question. Rather, they inquire into the implications for a range of parties, including the school, Ellie, her mother, and the teachers. Ms. Tucker does not judge; instead observing simply that the character's friend vowed to take some responsibility to protect her. The initial question served simply as a tool to provoke students' collaborative inquiry into the book, positioning the students as capable inquirers with authority to question, hypothesize, and bring their own experience to the meaning-making.

This collaborative inquiry stance brings with it a range of implications worth contemplating. Who has authority in the classroom? In these dialogic interactions, students speak more than Ms. Tucker does, something that Martin Nystrand and his colleagues in their classic study of 8th- and

9th-grade English classrooms, found to be highly unusual.[2] They found the average amount of dialogic interaction in 8th-grade English classes was 50 seconds. In 9th-grade, it fell to 15 seconds. In most classrooms there was none. Instead, there was the familiar pattern of the teacher asking a question, a student hazarding a response, and the teacher evaluating it, positioning the teacher as the sole authority and the activity as not an inquiry into books and life, but as guessing the teacher's answer. Students in the rare classes with extensive dialogic interaction benefited academically. These benefits are on top of the many benefits we listed at the end of Chapter 9. They are more effective than direct instruction in many ways, particularly for students for whom English is not their first language.[3]

FOUNDATIONS OF COLLABORATIVE DIALOGIC INQUIRY

The spirit of collaboration in the classrooms was certainly fueled in part by the students' engagement with books. They just *had* to talk and would do what was necessary to secure a conversation partner. The teachers often provoked collaboration further by suggesting who a student might talk to. As we have seen in previous chapters, they also foregrounded uncertainty and multiple perspectives as foundations for dialogue. But more than that, they were quite strategic in helping the students hear each other and in leading them to see why learning together beats going it alone. For instance, in a conversation about the section of *Paranoid Park* in which a character who trespassed is struggling over his part in the death of a security guard, Ms. Tucker simply instructed students to "talk it out," which they promptly did: "He tried to get him in self-defense. . . ." "He didn't do anything at all. . . . " "It's more likely the man's fault. . . ." "He probably thinks he's responsible. . . ." Rather than insisting on a conclusion, ending their wrestling with the issue, she responded, "It's amazing that you have already named so many different possibilities," acknowledging the importance of multiple views, setting them up to think together more in the future, and positioning them as people who can manage their own conversational turn-taking.

When Juan announced to the class that he believed *The Absolutely True Diary of a Part-Time Indian* was just for boys, Ms. Tucker asked a girl who had read it, "Keysha, do you agree with that?" After some back and forth and without yet reaching a conclusion, Ms. Tucker pointed out how the multiple perspectives had enhanced the conversation: "We wouldn't have got to this point if Keysha hadn't pushed back on our thinking." It is, in fact, these spaces of disagreement that force students to explain, and thus distribute, the logic of their thinking. It is Mrs. Tucker's regular references to "our thinking" that keeps everyone feeling they belong and owning the process.

For students to speak up, they have to believe their perspective is important. Some strategies for accomplishing this were subtle. When one student shared her opinion on a character during a class discussion, Ms. Tucker added, about another student, "That's what Jada is feeling . . . I heard her say that earlier today," signaling to Jada and her peers that she had said something worth remembering. Nudging comments like, "Can you go on with that thought?," and "Keep going with that idea," and "Let me see if I can summarize what you just said," suggested to both speakers and listeners that these were meaningful and useful contributions.

Teachers capitalized on minimal cues from students, such as when Ms. Tucker said to a quiet student, "I can see you've got a lot going on in your head. Tell us what you're thinking." In the midst of reading aloud from *Jumping Off Swings*, Ms. Tucker reached a part where the friend of a troubled character agrees to meet with and listen to that character's problem in the middle of the night. Chandler, another quiet student, responded with, "Awww." Ms. Tucker responded, "I agree with Chandler. That is so reassuring, even if it is 1:30 in the morning." A few minutes later, Chandler said something else in a really quiet voice, and Ms. Tucker nudged, "What did you say, Chandler . . . I need to hear you." Later in the class period while discussing another text, Chandler spoke up loudly and clearly enough for his classmates to hear.

The return on this teacher talk, pointing to how multiple minds make for better thinking, was that students were more tuned in to each other, listening rather than waiting impatiently for their own turn to talk. They came to expect that peers had important things to say. We observed this in class discussions such as when Nia hypothesized about a character's line of thinking, and Kendall, pointing at Nia, said, "You're really onto something." Similarly, Roberto's interest was piqued by a quiet peer's comment at a pivotal point in a read-aloud and asked the class, "Did you hear what Marcus said?" then asked him to repeat it. To bring that instance full circle, during the read-aloud the next day, Ms. Tucker revived the comment: "Marcus did this yesterday; He got us thinking. . . ." Further return on teachers' strategic talk was that students made it a point to recruit others' perspectives, some even making appointments with each other to talk.

DISTRIBUTING AUTHORITY, DISTRIBUTING TEACHING

It was not that the talking-in-class culture was easy for everyone, students or teachers, to live into. Ms. Pearson initially had to assure her students it was okay to talk without permission, especially during reading times, but also confessed her own evolution: "Letting the kids have more control is frightening, but ultimately empowering, because they're capable of more even than I thought they could be. I think I have pretty high expectations." In fact, the teachers found that authority is not a zero-sum game. The more the students were engaged and taking control of their reading and learning, the less the teachers needed to exert their positional authority.

Students also had some say in how class would go. The teachers originally introduced the books in the context of "silent reading," but very quickly the students protested that they needed to talk about the books, so the talk began, then became encouraged. Students were confident that their suggestions would be taken seriously. For example, Wilson was confident in his suggestion to Ms. Tucker one day: "You know how we have conferences with you? We should have conferences with each other. You'll go out of your category." This recommendation was about not only giving students more control but also getting everyone to branch out and hear about books they would not normally choose to read. Amber described one of her contributions:

> We have a lot of group discussion about books. Like I got this book, *Go Ask Alice*, and I told Ms. Tucker about it. . . . So, I read it, and she read it, and because of me reading it, we got the whole class to read it. They wanted to borrow my copy and hers. And we've had, like, discussions of that, and we compared that book to, like, *Crank*. . . . I haven't read *Crank* yet, but we compared it to different books like that, and it just got us into this discussion. And *Go Ask Alice*, we always seem to go back to that one, trying to compare.

Likewise, on the day Justine found on her phone's Internet a description of *Pearl*, written by her favorite author Jo Knowles, Ms. Kirby went to the public library and secured a copy and handed it to Justine the next morning, saying she would value Justine's advice on whether this was a book that should be in the classroom collections. Several chapters into the book, Justine started sharing sneak previews with others, including Ms. Tucker (who was not her teacher), by marking parts of the book that were intriguing, asking them to read, and waiting for their reactions.

As we have shown elsewhere, the more students were collaboratively engaged, the more teaching happened student-to-student at the point of need, freeing the teacher to address problems that were not so easily solved. In Chapter 9, we gave the example of Meleisha explaining to her classmates what they would have to attend to if they were to read *You Against Me*, including her response when her teacher asked whether the strategy she devised made her a better reader: "It helped Gwen (a classmate), 'cause I understood it after the first chapter, but she just got confused."

Consider Meleisha's impromptu explanation to her peers of how she made sense of a difficult book she had just finished:

> I go through the book and see what's in it, to see if it has parts or weird titles of chapters. And I looked through this book, and it has, like, six parts, and the titles of the chapters are lyrics from songs. I do that with most of my books. I write the parts down on a piece of paper and use it as I read.

This offering prompted several other students to tell the strategies they had used in their books:

I make [books to be] about my friends and my family. I put them as the characters.

In *Identical*, I wrote the names of the two characters, Raeanne and Kayleigh, on Post-it notes and moved them around in the book so I could keep them straight.

Or, like, book talking with people who have already read it. Making connections with people who know the book, like me and Zoe do.

Similarly, Wendy, Deandra, and Jada routinely sat together on the floor and could be observed reading different books silently, but also interrupting each other occasionally for help. Deandra described her response to Jada's questions this way: "I'll see the stuff that she didn't understand, so I might tell her what she doesn't understand in the book."

The teachers made it clear that everyone in the room was a teacher and that sometimes they too need help. In interacting with Rashad over his decision to read *My Bloody Life* (in Chapter 9), Ms. Tucker did not hesitate to have Rashad teach her, by explaining the meanings of gang symbols, as she was also advising him. It was common for all of the teachers to recruit assistance from individuals or the class, as when Mr. Simmons said, "You guys need to help me out, 'cause I'm confused," as he read a tricky section of *Snitch*. In the midst of reading aloud from *What Happened to Cass McBride?* Ms. Tucker said to her class about a confusing point from earlier, "You all helped me to understand this the other day." We also observed Ms. Kirby dropping into Ms. Tucker's class one day when she was stuck in a particular book. She had heard through the grapevine that one of Ms. Tucker's students had read that same book and was talking it up. Ms. Kirby promptly sat down in a desk across from her and fired off some questions that were nagging at her. After all, the books students were reading were drawn from youth culture, and the teachers' knowledge of those social worlds sometimes failed them.

The teachers were clear to the students that being a reader, no matter who you are, means you will encounter difficulty and will need to be strategic to solve problems. As two students were giving a book talk one day on *In Ecstasy*, a book from the perspectives of two friends struggling with drugs and relationships, Ms. Tucker commented, "I found it hard to keep [characters] Mia and Sophie apart. Did you have trouble with that? How did you manage that?" By admitting her own confusion, Ms. Tucker reminds the students that having difficulty while reading is normal and not a sign of poor reading skills. By asking how they negotiated the book, she shows them that she views them as the kind of people who would be strategic. At the same time, as they talk, they explicitly distribute their strategic thinking.

The relationships among the participants are symmetrical. No heroic teachers here. This flattening of the power dynamics between teachers and students, and of the potential intellectual hierarchy among students, was possible because there was no one book that everyone had to read, nor one big meaning everybody had to get from a book. Ms. Tucker reminded students of this frequently, such as when she told them, "Here's the hard part. When we talked about theme . . . sometimes books have more than one theme, and you all have proven that point. When you all have talked about theme . . . sometimes we've gotten different meanings from a book."

When the teachers asked questions, they asked open questions for which there was not one answer, and often where there was much gray area, particularly in the case of moral dilemmas. Students didn't feel motivated to compete for the teacher's attention. When Ms. Tucker asked the class, "What would you be feeling right now if you were [the character]?" she was not looking for a single answer or for a response directed to her. She was simply provoking their attention to their mind reading. She expects the students will engage with each other and take up the question from multiple perspectives. She shows that by not judging students' observations and by adding disclaimers to her own. For example, she shared, "I never did trust that girl in *Hate List*," an opinion that differed from that of many of the students, she was quick to add, "I struggled with that, but that's just me." The disclaimer made clear that she was not the authority on the character's motives, that it was up for debate. In fact, it was more than likely an invitation to the students to try to change her mind.

TEACHING FOR IDENTITY SHIFTS

In their role as architects of classroom talk, the teachers enabled students to build productive identities. To quote Elise again: "I feel like I used to be a very social person, and I'm not a very academic person, but I can actually, like, have conversations about books, now, which is kind of weird for me." Similarly, Kendall confessed that in 7th grade, she and Dennis "used to sit in English class and talk [not about class] the whole time," but that now, "[Dennis] has his book, I mean his nose in a book," and that they still talk, but about books. More broadly, and colorfully, she admitted, "Last year we were like a bunch of little wild monkeys." The difference, Kendall claimed, was more than just the books themselves or talking to each other: "We have all these teachers to help us. . . . They tell us, like, 'Well I'll help you with this book.'"

The shifts in identity from "we were like a bunch of little wild monkeys" to "everyone's gotten so much smarter," which another student noted, can be linked in part to how the teachers talked to, and about, the students. For example, Deandra's comment to us that "It makes me think more educated in my mind when I read because of how Ms. Tucker talks to me" can be linked to one of many instances when Ms. Tucker intentionally demonstrated this positive identity talk. In a read-aloud of a book in which a teenager in a dilemma needed to confide in a trustworthy adult, Deandra asked, "Would that be like the person that the counselor was to Sonia [a character from a different book]?" Ms. Tucker expanded Deandra's question by inviting other students to share similar relationships from other books. After several examples, she said, "I love how Deandra made us think about the word for that—confidante," thus not only introducing and elaborating new vocabulary but also rendering Deandra an expert, fostering in her a sense of competence and increasing the likelihood that her peers might see her that way.

The teachers nudged other sorts of positive identities. For instance, when Norma remarked on how far suicide survivor Brent Runyan had come over the course of his memoir, *The Burn Journals*, Ms. Tucker said to her, "What a compliment. I would love for him to hear that compliment from you," Norma is positioned as the kind of person who could have a conversation with an author and whose opinion would be valued. When Ms. Tucker makes the statement, "Marcus, when you were reading *Friday Night Lights*, that was a complicated book," she identifies him as a person who tries difficult things. When she follows it up with, "Did you have to organize that in your mind?" she is asserting that he is also the kind of person who acts strategically to solve problems, at the same time opening an explicit conversation about strategies. When she says to the class, "Let's see if we can learn things as a writer" and "I want you to think about how this process changes you as a reader," she asserts they are already readers and writers, who are also still growing, regardless of past achievement or literate identities.

The shift to seeing themselves anew took some students by surprise. An amateur photographer, Ms. Tucker took pictures of individual students one day as they were reading, and because they were fully engaged, they didn't notice. So, after she printed the photos to attach to their writing folders, some were shocked not only that she had snapped the shots but also at how they didn't recognize themselves, so scholarly-looking and immersed in thought. Jonah, shown deeply engaged in his book, swore it wasn't him. His mind's view of his former self—a nonacademic, nonreader—was so schooled that he had no idea how his present self looked.

TEACHING: MORE THAN THE SUM OF ITS PARTS

In these chapters on teaching, we have illustrated how, while expanding students' literacy and teaching the academic standards expected of them, teachers were also addressing students' social–emotional lives and supporting their positive identity construction. In Chapter 7, we introduced Carol

Dweck's research on mindsets in relation to students' moral reasoning, and we have alluded to them in subsequent chapters. Recall that the foundation of the entity mindset is the idea that permanent traits, like intelligence, courage, and so forth, explain behavior. Viewing someone as smart, or courageous, however, does not require attending to the mental processes behind a character's actions. The growth mindset, by contrast, accepts that people, and their decision-making, thoughts, and feelings, can change with their situation, which is why thoughts, feelings, and context are important for making sense of people and events.

The tendrils of these mindsets stretch into many aspects of intellectual and social functioning.[4] In a growth mindset, people think learning is most important. They feel most competent when taking on challenge, contributing to community thinking, or teaching others. They see problems, challenges, and errors as normal, especially if a person is taking on challenge. If they find themselves disagreeing in the process of learning, they engage the disagreement and try to synthesize the conflicting views and, in the process, enhance their view of their partner's competence. By contrast, when people take up an entity mindset, they think being seen as smart is most important. They feel most competent when doing something faster or better than others. Consequently, they avoid challenge because it might cause problems, errors, or the need to seek help, which might make them look less smart. When disagreements arise, because only one can be correct (and thus, smart), they turn disagreements into relational conflicts in which they end up putting their partner down.

As far as classroom learning goes and, indeed, life in general, fostering a growth mindset makes a lot of sense, so the question is how does one do that? But if that is still a question, you've not been paying attention to the teaching practices we've been describing. Each indicator of a growth mindset is fostered by the teaching practices we have described, and our data are rife with examples of growth-mindset thought and action. English language arts (ELA) teaching is not merely about skills, strategies, and content; though it is that, its reach is much deeper, for better—or for worse.

NOTES

1. Nicholls (1989, p. 167).
2. Nystrand et al. (1997).
3. Ma et al. (2017a); Ma et al. (2017b).
4. Dweck (2000). A less academic, more popular press version: Dweck (2006).

CHAPTER 13

Heckling

Because parents, educators, librarians, and public figures are so invested in the academic and character development of students, the literature adolescents read often falls under scrutiny and into contention.

—Grace Enriquez[1]

We believe there is something to be learned from the experiences of the teachers and students we've described in this book. We're not claiming for a second that what these teachers did is the only and universally applicable way to teach English language arts. Our research includes only four teachers and only 8th-grade students. Nonetheless, our perspective is likely to be controversial. So, in advance, we'll respond to some of the heckling we anticipate.

CONCERNS OF INTELLECTUALS, PHILOSOPHERS, AND THE LIKE

Everyone Should Read the Same Books

Proposals that everyone should read the same books have come with numerous justifications. One argument is that, without that, the culture lacks a foundation for common cultural reference and communication. We hope we have shown that vibrant conversations do take place among students who have chosen what to read, in part because they choose to read many of the same books. For example, Colton described a common scene:

> We're sitting at lunch, and we're talking about things that happen, and we relate it to things that happen in one of the books. And we usually recommend books to each other. So, we all end up reading the same books by the end.

Besides, the narratives they read evince overlapping themes from different perspectives. As to whether it will diminish their adult lives, we encourage you to reflect on how many times, as adults, you've depended on your specific required middle or high school readings at your workplace, in your relationships, or at significant life events.

The second part of the argument is that, as Doug Lemov and his colleagues claim, only by ensuring that students all read the same "high-quality literature" will they develop the skills of balanced civil discourse, because unless you've all read the same thing, you can't really listen to someone else's perspective.[2] We found, instead, that when students are engaged in their books, they are hungry for others' perspectives, even those of peers or parents who haven't read the book. Besides, currently, at least in the United States, the real civic problem is how we develop balanced civil discourse when people have not encountered the same information and narratives—how we learn to listen.

Lemov and colleagues' third line of argument is that everyone reading the same book also "allows teachers to have conversations about books [with each other]. If everyone is reading *Lord of the Flies*, there are people with whom to discuss interpreting the book for and with students."[3] They argue that teachers can then share lesson plans, simplifying their lives and improving their teaching. But when you've taught the same book for 5 or 10 years—likely the same one you were supposed to read when you were in school—and you've shared scripted lesson plans with colleagues or purchased them on Teachers-Pay-Teachers, is it really likely that your enthusiasm will bubble over contagiously into instruction or that you will approach the books as a matter of inquiry? It's more likely you will approach the books not as meaning-making, but as meaning-made, excluding students from the engagement. The teachers in this study routinely collaborated, sharing strategies, experiences, and books, including new favorites.

The teachers knew a lot of books—not all the books kids read—but a ton of them. They used this knowledge to help students know the options, to have meaningful conversations with them, and to capitalize on opportunities for explicit instruction. They found the time to read themselves because of student engagement, distributed teaching, and the intensity of their experiences with students in the moment (being totally present). That meant much less planning for class, leaving more time to read—which in the end proved more fruitful for them. The advantage was that they consistently set the students up to gain a sense of agency in *initiating* analysis and interpretation, which teachers then helped elevate.

Some Books Are Simply Superior to Others

The argument for everyone reading the same book is usually attached to a claim, that the books our students read were not "high-quality literature" or were insufficiently "rigorous"—that students should be exposed to excellent writing rather than that trashy modern stuff—what David Denby refers to as "Pop literature, skillfully composed by formula, [which] wouldn't offer as rich a field of reference and action" (whatever that means) and Doug Lemov and colleagues refer to as "benignly appealing youth fiction written after 1980."[4] Sound a little condescending? A few years earlier, in the *Washington Post*, Mark Bauerlein and Sandra Stotsky opined that school literature had gone to the dogs, particularly literature for boys.[5] They lamented the loss of the "military valor," the "high adventure," and "strong and active male role models" that reflect the "dispositions of male students," whereas, they claimed, "stories about adventurous and brave women abound." At the time they leveled this complaint, 2005, the vast majority of 8th-grade classrooms assigned books on average over 50 years old, most written by men, and only 3% were student choice.[6] Untroubled by facts, Bauerlein and Stotsky further asserted that:

> At the middle school level, the kind of quality literature that might appeal to boys has been replaced by Young Adult Literature, that is, easy-to-read, short novels about teenagers and problems such as drug addiction, teenage pregnancy, alcoholism, domestic violence, divorced parents and bullying. Older literary fare has also been replaced by something called "culturally relevant" literature—texts that appeal to students' ethnic group identification on the assumption that sharing the leading character's ethnicity will motivate them to read. There is no evidence whatsoever that either of these types of reading fare has turned boys into lifelong readers or learners.

If that sounds a little condescending and classist, maybe a little racist and sexist, well . . . it's worth pointing out that the majority of school children are now people of color.[7] Their comments also smack of a lack of familiarity with the books. In fact, many of the titles are even more complex than the classic texts routinely assigned in secondary classrooms.[8]

We concede that, as far as we can tell, our 8th-graders' experience didn't turn all of them into lifelong readers—a high bar. But it sure as heck made them into engaged readers in 8th grade, with all the benefits we've documented (and supported with research), and we often wonder what would have happened had the students experienced engaged reading throughout their high school careers. By contrast, the proposal to have all students read the same classic, culturally and personally irrelevant texts offers evidence for neither engagement nor social–emotional–moral development. Aside from their assumptions about interests, Bauerlein and Stotsky were right to worry about boys. Whereas girls' reading performance is consistent whether or not the texts are engaging, boys' performance drops on low-interest texts.[9]

While we agree that not all books are created equal, when the goals of instruction shift, criteria for what counts as "good literature" also need to shift. The teachers considered a text to be of high quality if it got students to think, talk, and keep reading. Some critics concede that allowing students to choose books is actually a good strategy, but only to build their "stamina" and to "hook" them so that they will become excited about the "challenging," "high-quality" literature they really need to read. But do they? At what cost?

No Deep Understanding of Books

Some propose that allowing student choice precludes their developing a deep understanding of what they read.[10] Several problematic assumptions underlie this argument. The first is that a deep understanding of what they read is the most important goal, rather than a deeper understanding of themselves, others, and humanity. Second, it assumes that students choosing what they will read precludes them also reading common texts. Merely observing adults' reading behaviors shows this to be false. Like the students, when adults find a book engaging, they talk others into reading it. Besides, in these classrooms, teachers read aloud and discussed a shared book. The insistence that not having everyone read the same book prohibits a deep understanding of what they read also assumes that understanding one complex human narrative doesn't help in understanding another. If that proposition were true, that there is no generalizing learning from one book to another, what would be the point of any instruction in any one book? Our students brought conversations from one book to conversations about other books containing related issues, wonderfully complicating the conversations about each book. They also frequently reread books with the express intention of understanding them better. Do students assigned to read required books voluntarily choose to reread them?

Kids Have No Idea What to Read

David Denby, after asserting that we shouldn't underestimate teens, declares that "teens rarely have any idea what books they're looking for."[11] Doug Lemov and colleagues concur, arguing that giving students choice is a bad idea because young people don't know enough about books to know what might be good to read. We hope that our evidence shows that it is possible to create conditions in which they do know what to read. Nonetheless, there is an element of truth to the argument, in that often students can't articulate exactly what their interests are.

For example, Jabar reported that "My favorite type of books to read are sports or violence, like I can't really read . . . like the books about the love, stuff like that." However, when asked about a book he could not stop thinking about or had to talk to someone about, he described narratives with relational significance. He named *Thirteen Reasons Why* as particularly memorable because:

> . . . like how the bullies made her feel bad . . . and like I'm just to the point where other students they say, like they be asking about what to read, and I ask

have they read this one in a while. They said, "No," and I said, "You should read it," but like, I think it's a good book.

He also took the trouble to "read like a couple of chapters to my mom of *Thirteen Reasons Why*." Similarly, he reported sharing with his father the book *Playground*, also a book about bullying.

Consider a different example. It took a long time for Simon to become engaged with the books. His engagement began when he overheard a group of peers discussing *Walking on Glass*, a book in which a young person is dealing with the suicide attempt of his mother, who is now on life support. He joined the group conversation and then read the book. As it turns out, his grandmother—although she had not attempted suicide—had been on life support, causing his family to make difficult decisions about her future. There is no way that a teacher could anticipate that connection. Neither is it likely that a required reading of, say, *Lord of the Flies* would have begun his engaged reading or offered him a tool with which to address his concern.

They Won't Be Ready for College Reading Expectations

Some adults worry that college-bound students won't be well versed in classic literature—which they assume is germane to academic competence—or to be able to read the difficult books they'll be assigned in college. On the first worry, Kathleen Yancey has suggested that there is no expectation that students will have read particular books and that maybe the place where knowledge of classics is most valuable is in the admissions essay, but not beyond.[12] She points out too that *postsecondary institution* does not mean one thing (e.g., 2-year community college, liberal arts college, state land-grant university, for-profit online), and so such a list of standards does not exist, given the variability of requirements and academic cultures. Plus, English literature classes are among myriad options for what students choose to take in college/university versus the relatively narrow collection of subjects available in high school.

The more likely context for large-scale common reading in a university is in campus-wide "Big Read" programs (often inspired by the National Endowment for the Arts [NEA] Big Read program) or freshman-year common reads. A quick search of books selected at various universities during the past 5 years includes not classics, but contemporary pieces dealing with social, cultural, and relational dilemmas (often focused on experiences of young adulthood in diverse contexts), books sharing more properties with the young adult books our students read than with Shakespeare or Beowulf: *Parkland: Birth of a Movement*, by Dave Cullen; *Educated*, by Tara Westover; *Evicted: Poverty and Profit in the American City*, by Matthew Desmond; *The Book of Unknown Americans*, by Cristina Henriquez; *Just Mercy*, by Bryan Stephenson; and *Becoming*, by Michelle Obama.

What students entering college need is general experience with reading critically and reading longer pieces of texts—something students in our work were becoming adept at. Students also need lots of experiences reading on their own. Easily done. But what makes students feel more confident about their preparation for life after high school? America's Promise Alliance surveyed teens to see what gave them a sense of being prepared for life after high school.[13] Students who found their classes engaging and challenging were five times more likely to feel prepared than those who did not. Students with strong connections to their peers and teachers, and those who had opportunities to learn about social issues, including race and racism, were twice as likely to feel prepared. All signs were that the students we interviewed and observed in 8th grade were on the right track. Pity about high school though.

Ambivalence

Often, critics of the approach represented in this book experience some ambivalence. For example, David Denby qualifies his argument that "Enjoyment is the goal and reward that trumps all others" with "But to get to that moment the ability to read *seriously* at all must be created" [italics added].[14] He praises the 10th-grade teachers he writes about for finding students

> . . . where they were as 15-year-olds, which did not mean underestimating them. Anything but. American teenagers are preoccupied with justice. . . . They also want to find some purpose in life . . . they want a way of being. . . . Basic ethical and philosophical questions of right and wrong, acting and doing, belief and skepticism, acquiescence and critical thinking fascinate them, and nothing is more effective than reading literature for churning up such questions. . . . Conversations that uncover the moral issues lodged in narrative have a good chance of meaning something special to 15-year-olds."[15]

All of this is consistent with what we have described, and yet, unable to shake his *Great Books* roots, he proclaims in the book's subtitle "*Twenty-Four Books That Can Change Lives.*"

Even those who advocate requiring "The Great Books" and "rigorous" curricula have to concede there are problems with the status quo, which is some version of assigning and working through the standard canon—perhaps not great or rigorous enough books, but in the same frame. Has this resulted in large numbers of engaged readers? David Denby observes, "Whether white, black, Asian, or Latino, American students rarely arrive at college as habitual readers"—and he's talking about undergraduates at Columbia—well-heeled students from well-funded schools.[16] Shouldn't that give us pause? They also don't necessarily come morally prepared.

PARENTS' (AND THUS TEACHERS') CONCERNS

They Shouldn't Be Reading Disturbing Books

The books 13-and 14-year-old students were drawn to included, among other topics, stories of death, drug addiction, gang-related violence, race, and sexual situations, including sexual exploitation of teens by adults. This alone is guaranteed to make some parents and teachers nervous. Heck, we had our own reservations, so we'll explore this concern in more depth. The concerns fall into three categories. First, will reading about these matters make students want to take drugs, have sex, join gangs, and so forth? The students found this concern, frankly, laughable. The effect was the opposite. If you still have this concern, you might reread Chapters 6 and 7. As Addie sagely observed in Chapter 6: "I mean, it's better to experience something tragic through a book and then be able to come out from it and know better things about it than to experience it yourself and to deal with all the pain and grief."

A second concern category might be whether these topics are too much for 12- to 14-year-olds. We saw no evidence of risk to students, partly because students could select their own texts and reject those they found problematic. As a rule, adolescent readers will quickly abandon books containing content they are not yet ready to explore. Also, students who chose to read "disturbing" texts attended centrally to the moral complexities of the narratives more than any graphic details. Besides, there is nothing in the books that is not portrayed more graphically on regular network TV programming. Furthermore, students made it clear that they were already confronting many of these matters or at least saw them in their immediate future.

Often, as adults, we make judgments about books based on entirely different meanings than those of the young adults who read them. Gay learned this lesson around the book *Identical*, a book that deals with incest and other issues that make adults, including us, nervous for young adults. The book was not in the school library, but students had discovered it by following favorite authors. They approached Gay, as a frequent source of books, to purchase it for them. Without completing her reading of the book, Gay rebuffed their request, judging the content too mature for them, a position she explained. But engaged readers will find a way to read what they need to read. Pooling their resources, they purchased *Identical*. In an end-of-year interview with Gay, Talia turned the tables on her, asking, "Why didn't you want to buy us *Identical*?" Before Gay could answer, and because Talia already knew Gay's initial misgivings, she explained:

> At the end, it was [the main character's] boyfriend that stood by her, even when it seemed like she was crazy. That's how a friend should be. When we got

to middle school, people who used to be friends weren't anymore. Everybody starts judging each other by what's on the outside. Don't you think we need books like that so we can talk about it?

Talia's comments suggest that, at least in part, she was drawn to the intricate relational dynamics among the characters and linked them to her own social world. Although the complexity of the characters' lives might not have paralleled Talia's life (but might for some of her peers), becoming intertwined with them allowed her to empathize and perhaps see others outside of the narrative differently. We cannot really know the meanings young adult readers make with books except through such conversations, and we cannot have such conversations unless the young adults feel sufficiently safe and motivated to bring us into their conversation. As we have pointed out earlier, students routinely roped their parents into conversations about what they were reading. In one of our studies, nearly half of the students, unprompted, mentioned family members in relation to their reading.[17]

Clearly the subject matter and language contained in the books did not prevent students from sharing their reading with parents and other caregivers. They reported being remarkably forthright about their reading, primarily because they wanted to persuade family members to read and talk about the books with them. Desiree convinced her mother to read *Identical*—a book that includes instances of incest and dissociative identity disorder—but they had to share the one copy borrowed from school. She explained, "[Mom] walks at the track or whatever, and she reads as she walks." Patrick was even more proactive at getting others' perspectives on *Identical*. When he finished reading it, he announced, "I'll probably give it to my mom to read it, and she'll probably give it to her mom to read, and then I'm going to tell Facebook to read it."

As we've explained elsewhere in the book, parents were the beneficiaries of the students choosing "disturbing" books. Students' heightened awareness made them re-evaluate their own relationships, particularly those with their parents. Yasir, for example, said he reconsidered how he treats others and clarified, "I'm not talking about just my friends," adding "I'm talking about my parents, too." He confessed to wanting to "hang with them more often," saying the books made him realize, "They're not always going to be with you and stuff." As Shelly observed in Chapter 6, after reading *Living Dead Girl*, she was more aware of the potential danger she could face in her own life and she realized that she had misjudged her parents as overprotective.

Throughout the book, we've shown how students connected these books to positive shifts in their relationships, intellectual development, academic and social identities, emotional regulation, moral dispositions, and agency. Our conversations with parents indicated they noticed these same types of growth, and they too attributed changes to students' reading and to the types of books they selected. Parents described their teens as "more mature," "more confident," and "more enjoyable to be around."

More specifically, though, parents made clear to us that the complex situations their children encountered in the texts they were drawn to were important sites for personal development. In sum, parents saw student access to "disturbing" books in the context in which they experienced it, not as potentially destructive, but instead as productive and meaningful, not just for their children's literacy development but for their development as healthy, happy people.

Classroom Practices and Mature, Realistic Texts

Eighth-grade reading gave parents a point of comparison for how they viewed their children's literacy instruction. Violet was quite blunt about her daughter's experiences with school reading up to that point: "I think that had Riley had one more year of mediocrity, unfortunately—I hate to call it that—we would have had to seek some serious intervention for her." Another parent, Tessa, was nervous about what might happen to her daughter Heidi as she moved out of the engagement-focused context:

> I'm really worried about her going to the high school with English. It's my biggest concern. I've actually considered substitute teaching [at the high school] a whole lot this fall! And I'm worried that will go over into the other classes, too, if she struggles. And I'm worried that Heidi will go back to that old way of doing just enough to get by. This year she has done so well. She's excelled in all of her classes.

Parents were adamant in their support of the 8th-grade teachers' decision to prioritize engagement in reading, along with the accompanying decision to introduce books that pushed the boundaries into classroom communities. They referred to these teachers as "amazing" and "inspiring" and described feelings of gratitude for the growth they had observed. As one parent put it, "They just make it come to life for those kids."

We have observed in other contexts that most problems with content are encountered when students are required to read particular texts. In the rare cases when parents of the 8th-graders we knew had questions about the appropriateness of texts, teachers were able to have productive conversations about students' options and student decision-making for the present and future. We know teachers who send letters home at the beginning of the year explaining the range of books available to students and extending an invitation to parents to recommend parameters for students' choices or to discuss particular choices at any point in the year.

Second, when introducing new books, the teachers made it a policy to speak about tough issues matter-of-factly. Sensationalizing realistic details might make books seem more appealing on the surface, but the goal would be, instead, to help students approach the issues with sensitivity. Similarly, they capitalized on opportunities to help students view sensitive subjects from new perspectives. For example, a group of students were sidetracked by a scene in which the narrator of the memoir *The Burn Journals* became embarrassed because he experienced an erection during a nurse's routine examination. Hearing the students make comments such as "That's nasty," their teacher offered: "Well, it's a human experience that all guys have to endure. So, I appreciate the author's courage to be able to say it. That actually helps some of the guys." This simple but powerful observation changed not only the direction of that conversation but also the ways that students would think through similar encounters with texts in the future.

And yet. . . . Is it scary when young adults read disturbing books? Yes, but we hope we've shown that the foundation for those fears is misplaced. And yet, teachers who wish to teach this way face serious philosophical headwinds not only from those who worry about the books young adults will choose to read—the very books responsible for the positive transformations—but also from those who insist that society will fall apart if young people aren't all required to read the same classic texts. In a recent opinion piece in the *Washington Post*, Cornel West and Jeremy Tate argued that education should be about "the maturation and cultivation of spiritually intact and morally equipped human beings."[18] They urge us to "restore true education, mobilizing all of the intellectual and moral resources we can to create human beings of courage, vision and civic virtue," to make education about "living more intensely, more critically, more compassionately" and about "learning to attend to the things that matter and turning our attention away from what is superficial." They propose that students need to "confront the fact that human existence is not easily divided into good and evil, but filled with complexity, nuance and ambiguity."

We are fully on board with those goals. Fully on board. In fact, we think those goals are a good description of our 8th graders' experience. Surprisingly, however, West and Tate, like many others, go on to claim, without evidence, that the only way to accomplish these ends is to require students to read "the classics" and that not to do so is "a sign of spiritual decay, moral decline and deep intellectual narrowness running amok." We are not convinced.

NOTES

1. Enriquez (2006).
2. Lemov et al. (2016).
3. Lemov et al. (2016, p. 53).
4. Denby (2016, p. 236); Lemov et al. (2016, p. 17).

5. Bauerlein & Stotsky (2005).

6. Northrop et al. (2019).

7. Bahrampour & Mellnik (2021).

8. Glaus (2014).

9. Ainley et al. (2002).

10. Lemov et al. (2016).

11. Denby (2016, p. 230).

12. Yancey (2009).

13. https://americaspromise.org/wp-content/uploads/pdf/gradnation-062321.pdf

14. Denby (2016, p. 232).

15. Denby (2016, p. 232).

16. Denby (1997, p. 459).

17. Ivey & Johnston (2013).

18. West & Tate (2021). Their article was in reference to undergraduates, but the arguments differ little from those of Bauerlein and Stotsky and many others.

CHAPTER 14

The Alchemy of Young Adults' Engagements Among Books

While skills like reading . . . certainly have cognitive aspects, the reason why we engage in them, the importance we assign to them, the anxiety we feel around them, and the learning that we do about them, are driven by the neurological systems for emotion, social processing and self.

—Mary Helen Immordino-Yang[1]

The complexities and risks of adolescence are reflected in the statistics that we shared in previous chapters on loneliness, anxiety, depression, suicide, drug and alcohol abuse, and risky sex—not to mention the lack of reading. The students we studied suggest it need not be that way, which they attribute to their engaged reading and its conversations. They claim they are more likely to avoid drugs, gangs, and risky sex. They report being happier, enjoying school, and having positive relationships with peers—even those very different from them—and with their teachers and family. They claim expanded understanding of their own and others' emotions along with their ability and propensity to imagine the thoughts and feelings of others. Consequently, they argue, they had more positive relationships, more close friendships, and more meaningful lives—all factors negatively related to stress, anxiety, and depressive symptoms.[2] They claim this came from their sense of autonomy and their personally meaningful and intensely socially engaging reading.

EVIDENCE

We think, collectively, these young adults make compelling arguments, but their voices don't stand alone. Their claims are entirely consistent with other empirical research showing benefits of school engagement. When students are engaged, they are more available to learn and they are more successful in the short and long term.[3] Engagement and teacher–student relationships are strongly related, particularly in high school, and positive student–teacher relationships are positively related to achievement.[4] Students who are not engaged are more likely to drop out and experience academic failure, are less likely to engage in civic behaviors or helping others, and are more likely to demonstrate antisocial behavior.[5] And the effects of disengagement are not just temporary. They negatively impact the entire trajectory of subsequent school years into adulthood.[6]

Engagement carries even more benefits when it involves narrative texts. As the students claimed, it expands mind reading, the heart of their socioemotional intelligence.[7] Their socioemotional intelligence is linked to prosocial behavior, which tends to be reciprocal. When someone helps us, we tend to want to return the favor, which builds positive relationships that provide the support needed when facing challenges.[8] When adolescents encounter difficulties, as they do, they need a strong social support network. A well-developed socioemotional intelligence both motivates individuals to help others and equips them with the skills to do so.[9]

More emotionally intelligent youngsters are less likely to have unauthorized school absences, be expelled, or engage in problematic behavior such as bullying.[10] They have better physical, social, and psychological well-being and better social interactions.[11] This web of positive outcomes doesn't stop there, either. Students with strong emotional intelligence also experience more positive emotions both because of their expanded social support and the buzz they get from their increased helping behavior.[12] The expanded positive emotions lead to a stronger sense of well-being and greater academic motivation, while expanding the range of physical and intellectual resources that allow flourishing in difficult, stressful circumstances.[13]

The students in our study reported even more benefits that are backed by other research, such as being less judgmental and less likely to stereotype. Happiness, which they also reported, decreases the tendency to stereotype, even when the emotions are below conscious awareness.[14] Collectively, this complex psychosocial network adds up to what some researchers refer to as a positive classroom emotional climate, which supports achievement, a relationship that holds across genders and grade levels and, to bring us full circle, is mediated by engagement.[15]

Most of this is also true for teachers, increasing their resilience and decreasing burnout.[16] When schools are more focused on students' social–emotional learning, teachers have a stronger sense of well-being.[17] From our observations, it also provides for teachers a greater sense of meaning in their work, which in turn is related to their students' feelings of being cared for.[18] And when students feel that their teachers care for them, they have better self-esteem and well-being and are more likely to be engaged.

In his book *Permission to Feel*, Marc Brackett proposes five emotional skills supported by his and his colleagues' successful intervention research: Recognizing our own and others' emotions from speech, face, and body language; understanding and naming feelings in all their subtleties; identifying their likely source and implications; expressing feelings contextually appropriately such that we elicit empathy from listeners; and strategically managing our own and others' feelings.[19] These skills closely match the transformations reported by the students in our study.

THE WORK OF CONVERSATIONS

It became clear from our student interviews that, unlike high school, the reading in 8th grade had served functions not recognized in current curriculum planning. In 8th grade, these young people were not working on their reading, but on something more meaningful—their lives and relationships. Trust evolved from, and made possible, otherwise difficult conversations. Students could talk about sensitive, meaningful issues through the characters without admitting that it was their own selves and relationships they were working on. There was an unspoken trust stemming from the recognition that they were all sharing vulnerabilities and were not alone. It was as if in 8th grade, they were actually living reflective lives, actively processing rich, positive, personal, and social experiences—making their lives meaningful. In high school they returned to solitary sleep walking. When everyone had to read the same, classic, personally and culturally irrelevant book (which most didn't like, perhaps on principle), the conversations disappeared and, with them, the relationships, the source of enthusiasm and information, and even the memory of the book.

The 8th-grade reading conversations enabled the development of the close friendships that provided emotional support, the necessary sense of belonging and self-worth, and a safe space for validating and exploring identities. Those friendships also predict academic motivation and achievement.[20] But this is not the experience of most adolescents. According to the National Assessment of Educational Progress, 40% of 8th-grade students report "never or hardly ever" talking with anyone about their books.[21] Less than 10% do so daily. Sherry Turkle, in her book *Reclaiming Conversation*, laments the loss of conversation, particularly among youth. She quotes a dean of a middle school who bemoans that: "Students don't seem to be making friendships as before. They make acquaintances, but their connections seem superficial."[22] Turkle ascribes the problem to technology, which has offered:

> the illusion of companionship without the demands of friendship and then, as the programs got really good, the illusion of friendship without the demands of intimacy. Because face-to-face people ask for things that computers never do. . . . Real people demand responses to what they are feeling. And not just any response.[23]

Relational and emotional work in ELA

Though our focus is not on the perils of technology, we are confident that Turkle is right about the significance of conversations. Importantly, she asks, "What is the work of conversations?"[24] It's a good question for teachers of the English language arts (ELA). The relational and emotional work of conversations, though dependent on language, is rarely placed at the heart of ELA curricula.

Perhaps this oversight is due to our tendency to treat ELA as merely a matter of content to be learned—books and strategies for comprehending them. The books students read have been the focus of a great deal of angst and argument, as if the particular book or books are the crucial element. *Canon* We "teach" *Catcher in the Rye* or *The Great Gatsby* as if the qualities of that book are nowhere else to be found, as if reading it will increase the students' reading skills, expand their intellectual reach and cultural literacy like no other book, whether or not the book engages them. This is the delusional thinking upon which Spark Notes and others have created profitable business models. By the same token, some books are viewed as toxic, blamed for perverting and dumbing down students' minds. We are currently enduring another round of book bannings. But reading banned books has no effect on school achievement and it is not linked to violent or nonviolent crime.[25] On the other hand, it *is* linked to increased civic behavior. Besides, the more choice reading adolescents do, the higher their achievement; this is not the case for required school reading.[26] Perhaps it's better to view books centrally as opportunities for conversations— conversations that expand students' social, emotional, moral, and intellectual development.

THE WORK OF ELA TEACHERS AND THEIR BOOKS

Perhaps we should ask why we have young adults read literature. Many writers have taken up this question in expansive terms. In the previous chapter, we quoted Cornel West and Jeremy Tate's hopes for education to be about:

> the maturation and cultivation of spiritually intact and morally equipped human beings . . . human beings of courage, vision and civic virtue . . . [who live] more intensely, more critically, more compassionately . . . [and who] confront the fact that human existence is not easily divided into good and evil, but filled with complexity, nuance and ambiguity.[27]

Lofty goals that are not usually listed in state ELA standards. Yet the students we interviewed suggest that these developments are certainly within the reach of their ELA experience. Missing from those descriptors, of course, are the relational and emotional resources and competencies accomplished by the books and conversations that provide the foundation for much of the rest of adolescents' social–emotional and moral development.

If these hopes are important, not just academics waxing lyrical about classics, and they aren't in the ELA curriculum, where are they? Twenty-nine states have some form of social–emotional learning (SEL) standards.[28] Sometimes they receive a nod in a preamble and then disappear in the weeds of subject matter standards. Sometimes we encounter parts of them in the physical education standards. That's right, *physical* education. For example, New York's physical education standard 4 is: "Exhibits responsible personal and social behavior that respects self and others."[29] North Carolina's health and physical education standards for grades 6–8 include a small section on "interpersonal communication and relationships."[30] While avoiding the emotional (except in the case of the negative consequences of early sexual activity), these attend to verbal and nonverbal communication and caring for and respecting others, along with the complexities and signs of sexual harassment, bullying, and abuse.

Researchers agree on the importance of SEL. Even the National Conference of State Legislatures does.[31] But where to put it? Research on SEL generally presents it as an intervention in school life, with lessons added into the curriculum. But effective interventions, such as those advocated by the Collaborative for Academic, Social and Emotional Learning (CASEL) and by Marc Brackett and his colleagues, encourage integration of SEL across the curriculum and invest considerable effort in teacher professional development. Our chapters on the subtleties of teaching practices emphatically reinforce that. Some of the conversations we documented, such as those around culture and race, might easily be seen as social studies content. Certainly, consistency across the school day in what is often referred to as "classroom management" or "discipline" is also important, but by now it should be clear that focusing on engagement and attending closely to SEL not only make discipline less of a concern but also reframe what it might mean. Nonetheless, to avoid becoming an afterthought for which nobody takes responsibility, SEL also needs a home, and here's our pitch.

SEL centrally involves language. As a simple example, Deaf children born to hearing parents are, on average, delayed relative to their hearing peers in most aspects of their socioemotional development.[32] Deaf children born to Deaf parents show no such delays because they are born into a language they can use, Sign Language. It is language that allows us to make sense of our own and others' emotional-relational lives, to learn with and from each other, to build relationships and prevent and solve relational problems. This is why the obvious home for SEL is the ELA class, particularly if it approaches reading in the manner we have described, because the books the students choose quite naturally produce conversations about the complexities of social–emotional life. As parents found, even sensitive conversations can be approached through characters, offering participants plausible deniability much the same as "I have this friend who has this problem. . . ." The books at once offer the opportunity to reflect on the significance of language chosen by authors and characters and on our own language choices, while expanding our linguistic options for making sense of and managing our feelings and relationships. Exactly how these conversations arise naturally in physical education class is a mystery.

THE SOCIALNESS OF READING

Engaged reading, as these students described it, was socially saturated. Readers formed dialogic relationships with characters, authors, each other, teachers, and family members as they solved reading problems along with the social and emotional problems of characters and their own lives. They deliberately recruited alternative perspectives, if not to resolve their uncertainties, then to understand them more fully. This process guaranteed ongoing reflection through multiple continued conversations (and relationships) long after the book had passed into others' hands, conversations that were again provoked by seeing someone else reading the book. The readers, the text, the community, and the relationships among them were changed in the process.[33] Although students could choose what and how to read and respond to their reading, they experienced more meaningful shared experiences than we have seen in classes requiring all students to read the same texts specifically to produce that shared knowledge and experience.

This socialness generates community building, and we can't address the individual's development without addressing the community of which the individual is a member. There is little doubt that students need a sense of community relatedness for healthy development and well-being or that their sense of competence and identity are constructed within the context of their community.[34] But the community is constructed by its members as they solve joint problems and share and expand meanings. In the process, they build the trust, caring, and respect that make the community possible, particularly for those on the margins. Students in our study deliberately and incidentally made others feel cared for and valued as they pursued personally meaningful knowledge, listening intently to each other. They surprised themselves by, in their own interests, engaging with students who might otherwise have been marginalized, dispensing with stereotyping, while normalizing caring, respectful relationships.

Although these interactions began with self-interested engagement, students' actions and comments suggest that the community served more than that. Students came to believe they had a responsibility to contribute positively to their community. A CASEL study surveyed students in high schools either strongly supportive of SEL development or not. Students in the strong

SEL schools reported being over twice as likely to volunteer regularly in their community and 25% were more likely to participate in public service for their community or country, including full-time military service.[35] Barbara Thayer-Bacon suggested that in order for democratic communities to flourish:[36]

> . . . they need to be caring and just, to be inclusive and affirming, and to be balanced and harmonious as well as allow for dissonance and discord, striving to meet the needs of the individual and the group . . . democratic classrooms need shared interests and free interaction, the opportunity to be together and learn how to communicate with each other . . . time to develop relationships with each other and feel a sense of responsibility to the community . . . the opportunity to find successful ways to contribute to the community. . . . People who feel cared for want to contribute to a community and feel a responsibility to do so.

This is consistent with the experience and actions of the students we studied.

WHAT DO WE WANT?

We are tempted to conclude, as Addie put it in Chapter 5, "This is your keys to the kingdom. Like, I don't know why you would ever not! There it is!" Our goals are more modest. Our hope is that these students' and teachers' experiences will provoke useful conversations about literacy; literature; and young people's academic, social, emotional, and moral development and teaching that promotes it. As we see it, schooling is about apprenticing new generations into humanity, helping them acquire the accumulating tools of civilization in ways that will help them sustain and develop humanity into the future. Whether we prioritize young people's academic, physical, psychological, social, or economic well-being, their social–emotional development is critical. Beyond that, our increasingly polarized democratic society might not survive if our citizens are socially and emotionally ill-prepared to productively engage with one another.

We can arrange classrooms so that young adults will choose to be fully engaged in their reading and in conversation with peers, teachers, and parents, with all the social, emotional, moral, and general well-being benefits that confers. But we might have to stop insisting that all students read the same personally and culturally irrelevant books and holding them accountable for doing so with projects and comprehension questions. We might have to stop insisting that reading is silent and solo and only happens when in contact with the page. We might have to stop thinking that it's the adults' meaning of a particular book that matters rather than the young adult's development and the qualities of the learning community.

Are we afraid to give students power?

Paradoxically, the books and freedoms responsible for these students' development are ones that frighten many adults. We should at least ask: What do we want and need from students' middle and high school reading experience? What do they want and need? The students we interviewed were quite clear about what they wanted and found they needed—once they had experienced it. But is it what the adults in their lives want for them, or are we too afraid?

NOTES

1. Immordino-Yang (2011, p. 101).
2. Li et al. (2019).
3. Skinner et al. (2008); Reyes et al. (2012).
4. Roorda et al. (2011).
5. Wang & Fredricks (2014).
6. Orthner et al. (2013).
7. Bal & Veltkamp (2013); Djikic (2013b); Mar & Oatley (2008).
8. Lopes et al. (2011); Kong et al. (2012); Koydemir et al. (2013); Mavroveli et al. (2008).
9. Kaltwasser et al. (2017).
10. Poulou (2014); Petrides et al. (2004); Mavroveli & Sánchez-Ruiz (2011).
11. Andrei et al. (2014); Jellesma et al. (2011).
12. Zhao et al. (2020); Martin-Raugh et al. (2016).
13. Emadpoor et al. (2016); Fredrickson (2001).
14. Ric (2004). Negative emotions, particularly sadness, have the reverse effect.
15. Reyes et al. (2012).
16. Gloria et al. (2013).
17. Hamilton & Doss (2020).
18. Lavy & Naama-Ghanayim (2020).
19. Brackett (2019).
20. Parker et al. (1995); Altermatt & Pomerantz (2003); Buhrmester (1990).
21. National Assessment of Educational Progress (NAEP) Reading Assessment data for years 2002, 2003, 2005, 2007, 2009, 2011, 2013, and 2015. https://www.nationsreportcard.gov/ndecore/landing
22. Turkle (2016, p. 5).
23. Turkle (2016, p. 7)
24. Turkle (2016, p. 8)
25. Ferguson (2014).
26. Ferguson (2014).
27. West & Tate (2021).
28. Positive Action Staff (2020).
29. NYSED (n.d.).
30. https://www.dpi.nc.gov/documents/cte/curriculum/healthfulliving/new-standards/healthful-living/health-education-essential/open
31. https://www.ncsl.org/state-legislatures-news/details/whole-child-education-gets-high-marks-in-creating-healthy-learning-environments

32. Peterson & Siegal (2000).
33. Rosenblatt (1978).
34. Reis et al. (2000).
35. Civic with Hart Research Associates et al. (2018).
36. Thayer-Bacon (1996, p. 301).

The Study

If you are interested in the details of our research methods, we urge you to consult two original studies[1] on which much of the information in this book is based. For the sake of brevity, we offer here a collective overview of the studies and the data.

Over a period of 4 years, one or both of us were immersed in the classrooms of the four 8th-grade English teachers who, from the start, were interested in improving their reading instruction. The school is located in a working-class community in the Mid-Atlantic United States. At that time, 45% of students at the school were eligible for free/reduce-priced lunch, and students represented the following ethnicities: 68% Caucasian, 27% African American, and 5% Hispanic.

During the first and second years of our association with these teachers, Gay collaborated with them to identify, starting with existing principles from research, the changes necessary for every student to become engaged in reading, all with the aim of improving student reading competence, which according to standardized test scores, fell below the state average. Discontinuing all assigned reading, providing the students with choices from a wide array of high-interest young adult literature, setting aside ample time to read during class, and removing assignments connected to reading resulted in massive shifts in students' willingness to read and in their volume of reading. Unexpectedly, though, students reported shifts in how they thought about their own lives, their well-being, and relationships connected to their reading.

During years 3 and 4, Gay and Peter explicitly studied these previously unanticipated social, emotional, and intellectual consequences of reading with the help of a total of 258 students, along with their teachers. We interviewed the students and their teachers across the school year and observed the classrooms at least twice each week over the 2-year period, frequently audio- and video-recording classroom practices, book engagements, and discussions. Our interviews centered on how students had become engaged in reading (who or what persuaded them) and how that compared to previous years, whether or not and with whom they talked about their reading, and whether they or others had changed as readers during 8th grade. We asked the students if they or others had changed as people and if their families' perceptions of them had changed, but without explicitly linking these possibilities to reading in our questioning. Our interviews with teachers focused on the changes they had made in their instruction, how they saw the changes affecting students (and which students), their personal and professional identities, and their relationships with students and each other. We also interviewed a small number of parents during the summer following one academic year to understand their perceptions of change in their adolescents.

Two years later we conducted follow-up interviews with 26 of the students, then in either 10th or 11th grade. We were interested in understanding how students perceived their 8th- grade reading experiences from a distance and also to what extent the reading practices they assumed in 8th grade had persisted into high school.

NOTE

1. Ivey & Johnston (2013); Ivey & Johnston (2015).

Young Adult Books and Other Trade Books Mentioned

A child called it. Pelzer, D. (1995). Health Communications.
A man named Dave. Pelzer, D. (1999). Dutton.
A stolen life: A memoir. Dugard, J. (2012). Simon & Schuster.
Beautiful. Reed, A. (2009). Simon & Schuster.
Becoming. Obama, M. (2018). Crown.
Before I fall. Oliver, L. (2010). HarperCollins.
Bittersweet. Ockler, S. (2012). Simon & Schuster.
Blood on my hands. Strasser, T. (2010). Egmont.
Blue rage, black redemption: A memoir. Williams, S. T. (2004). Simon & Schuster.
Breathing underwater. Flinn, A. (2001). Harper Teen.
Chasing Brooklyn. Schroeder, L. (2010). Simon Pulse.
Crank. Hopkins, E. (2004). Margaret K. McElderry Books.
Crossing lines. Volponi, P. (2011). Viking.
Destroying Avalon. McCaffrey, K. (2006). Fremantle Press.
Divergent. Roth, V. (2014). Harper Collins.
Drama High: The fight. Divine, L. (2006). K-Teen/Dafina.
Educated: A memoir. Westover, T. (2018). Random House.
Episodes: My life as I see it. Ginsberg, B. (2009). Roaring Brook Press.
Esperanza rising. Ryan, P. M. (2000). Scholastic.
Estrella's Quinceañera. Alegria, M. (2006). Simon & Schuster.
Evermore. Noel, A. (2009). St. Martin's Griffin.
Evicted: Poverty and profit in the American city. Desmond, M. (2016). Crown.
Far from you. Schroeder, L. (2009). Simon & Schuster.
Friday night lights. Bissinger, H. G. (1990). Addison-Wesley.
Glass. Hopkins, E. (2007). Margaret K. McElderry.
Glimpse. Williams, C. L. (2010). Simon & Schuster.
Go ask Alice. Anonymous. (1971). Simon Pulse.
Good behavior. Henry, N. L. (2010). Bloomsbury.
Gym candy. Deuker, C. (2007). Houghton-Mifflin.
Harry Potter and the sorcerer's stone. Rowling, J. K. (1998). Scholastic.

Hate list. Brown, J. (2009). Little, Brown.

Homeboyz. Sitomer, A. L. (2007). Hyperion.

Hunger games. Collins, S. (2008). Scholastic.

I am Nujood, age 10 and divorced. Ali, N. (2010). Penguin Random House.

Identical. Hopkins, E. (2008). Margaret K. McElderry.

If I stay. Forman, G. (2010). Penguin.

In ecstasy. McCaffrey, K. (2009). Annick Press.

Jumping off swings. Knowles, J. (2009). Candlewick.

Just mercy. Stevenson, B. (2014). Random House.

Keeping you a secret. Peters, J. A. (2003). Little, Brown.

Leverage. Cohen, J. C. (2012). Penguin.

Linger. Stiefvater, M. (2010). Scholastic.

Living dead girl. Scott, E. (2008). Simon Pulse.

Love and leftovers. Tregay, S. (2012). Harper Collins.

Marine sniper: 93 confirmed kills. Henderson, C. W. (1986). Stein and Day.

My bloody life: The making of a Latin king. Sanchez, R. (2000). Chicago Review Press.

Not simple. Ono, N. (2010). Viz Media

November blues. Draper, S. (2007). Atheneum.

Paranoid park. Nelson, B. (2006). Viking.

Parkland: Birth of a movement. Cullen, D. (2019). Harper.

Perfect chemistry. Elkeles, S. (2008). Walker.

Playground. 50 Cent. (2011). Razorbill.

Pointe. Colbert, B. (2014). Penguin.

Prime choice. Perry-Moore, S. (2007). Kensington.

Push. Sapphire. (1996). Alfred A. Knopf.

Rucker Park setup. Volponi, P. (2007). Viking.

Rules of attraction. Elkeles, S. (2010). Walker.

Rules of survival. Werlin, N. (2006). Dial.

Shiver. Stiefvater, M. (2009). Scholastic.

Shooting star. McKissack, F. (2009). Atheneum.

Smile for the camera. James, K. (2010). Simon & Schuster.

Snitch. Van Diepen, A. (2009). Simon Pulse.

Sold. McCormick, P. (2006). Hyperion.

Some girls are. Summers, C. (2009). St. Martin's Press.

Something like hope. Goodman, S. (2011). Delacorte.

Soul surfer: A true story of faith, family, and fighting to get back on the board. Hamilton, B., Bundschuh, R., & Berk, S. (2004). MTV Books.

Stolen. Christopher, L. (2010). The Chicken House.

Ten things we did: (and probably shouldn't have). Mlynowski, S. (2011). HarperTeen.

The absolutely true diary of a part-time Indian. Alexie, S. (2007).
   Little Brown.
The beckoners. Mac, C. (2004). Orca.
The book of bright ideas. Kring, S. (2006). Delta.
The book thief. Zusak, M. (2007). Alfred A. Knopf.
The bully. Langan, P. (2002). Townsend Press.
The burn journals. Runyan, B. (2004). Knopf Doubleday
The catastrophic history of you and me. Rothenberg, J. (2012). Dial.
The day before. Schroeder, L. (2012). Simon Pulse.
The hunger games. Collins, S. (2008). Scholastic.
The last shot. Frey, D. (1994). Touchstone.
The lost boy. Pelzer, D. (1997). Health Communications.
The outsiders. Hinton, S. E. (1967) Viking.
The rivalry: Mystery at the Army-Navy game. Feinstein, J. (2010). Knopf.
The rose that grew from concrete. Shakur, T. (1999). MTV Books.
The secret story of Sonia Rodriguez. Sitomer, A. (2008). Hyperion
The sky is everywhere. Nelson, J. (2010). Dial Books.
Thirteen reasons why. Asher, J. (2007). Penguin Random House.
Twilight. Meyer, S. (2005). Little Brown.
Twisted. Anderson, L. H. (2007). Viking.
Tyrell. Booth, C. (2007). Scholastic.
Unwind. Shusterman, N. (2007). Simon and Shuster.
Walking on glass. Fullerton, A. (2007). Harper Teen.
War of the blood in my veins. Morris, D. J. (2008). Scribner.
What happened to Cass McBride? Giles, G. (2007). Little, Brown.
Where she went. Forman, G. (2011). Penguin.
Wintergirls. Anderson, L. H. (2010). Viking.
You against me. Downham, J. (2011). David Fickling Books.
Yummy: The last days of a southside shorty. Neri, D., & Duburke,
   R. (2010). Lee.

Some Other Books in Circulation But Not Referred to in the Book

All American boys. Reynolds, J., & Kiely, B. (2015). Atheneum.
Because I am furniture. Chaltas, T. (2009). Viking.
Black and white. Volponi, P. (2005). Viking Juvenile.
Boot camp. Strasser, T. (2007). Simon & Shuster.
Burned. Hopkins, E. (2006). Margaret K. McElderry.
Cashay. McMullan, M. (2009). Houghton Mifflin.
Delirium. Oliver, L. (2011). HarperCollins.
Dirty little secrets. Omololu, C. J. (2010). Walker.
Evolution, me and other freaks of nature. Brande, R. (2007). Knopf.
Forged by fire. Draper, S. M. (1997). Simon and Schuster.
Give a boy a gun. Strasser, T. (2000). Simon & Shuster.

I heart you, you haunt me. Schroeder, L. (2008). Simon Pulse.
If I grow up. Strasser, T. (2009). Simon and Schuster
Kinda like brothers. Booth, C. (2014). Scholastic.
Lockdown. Meyers, W. D. (2011). Harper Collins
Orbiting Jupiter. Schmidt, G. D. (2015). Clarion.
Quad. Watson, C. (2007). Razorbill.
Response. Volponi, P. (2009). Penguin.
Scars. Rainfield, C. (2010). Westside Books.
Something like hope. Goodman, S. (2010). Delacorte.
Street pharm. Van Diepen (2006). Simon Pulse.
Why I fight. Oaks, J. A. (2009). Atheneum.
Wish you were dead. Strasser, T. (2009). Egmont.

References

Adrián, J. E., Clemente, R. A., & Villanueva, L. (2007). Mothers' use of cognitive state verbs in picture-book reading and the development of children's understanding of mind: A longitudinal study. *Child Development, 78*(4), 1052–1067. https://doi.org/10.1111/j.1467-8624.2007.01052.x

Agnoli, S., Mancini, G., Andrei, F., & Trombini, E. (2019). The relationship between trait emotional intelligence, cognition, and emotional awareness: An interpretative model. *Frontiers in Psychology, 10*(1711). https://doi.org/10.3389/fpsyg.2019.01711

Ainley, M., Hillman, K., & Hidi, S. (2002). Gender and interest processes in response to literary texts: situational and individual interest. *Learning & Instruction, 12*(4), 411. https://doi.org/10.1016/S0959-4752(01)00008-1

Algoe, S. B., Haidt, J., & Gable, S. L. (2008, June). Beyond reciprocity: Gratitude and relationships in everyday life. *Emotion, 8*(3), 425–429.

Altermatt, E. R., & Pomerantz, E. M. (2003). The development of competence-related and motivational beliefs: An investigation of similarity and influence among friends. *Journal of Educational Psychology, 95*, 111–123.

American Library Association. (n.d.). Banned book FAQ. https://www.ala.org/advocacy/bbooks/banned-books-qa

Andrei, F., Mancini, G., Baldaro, B., Trombini, E., & Agnoli, S. (2014). A systematic review on the predictive utility of the trait emotional intelligence questionnaire (TEIQue). *Applied Psychology Bulletin, 271*, 2–29.

Armsden, G. C., & Greenberg, M. T. (1987). The inventory of parent and peer attachment: Individual differences and their relationship to psychological well-being in adolescence. *Journal of Youth and Adolescence, 16*(5), 427–454. https://doi.org/10.1007/BF02202939

Armstrong, A. R., Galligan, R. F., & Critchley, C. R. (2011). Emotional intelligence and psychological resilience to negative life events. *Personality & Individual Differences, 51*(3), 331–336. https://doi.org/10.1016/j.paid.2011.03.025

Asher, S. R., & Paquette, J. A. (2003). Loneliness and peer relations in childhood. *Current Directions in Psychological Science, 12*(3), 75–78. https://doi.org/10.1111/1467-8721.01233

Azmitia, M., & Montgomery, R. (1993). Friendship, transactive dialogues, and the development of scientific reasoning. *Social Development, 2*(3), 202–221.

Bahrampour, T., & Mellnik, T. (2021, August 12). Census data shows widening diversity; number of White people falls for first time. *The Washington Post.* https://www.washingtonpost.com/dc-md-va/2021/08/12/census-data-race-ethnicity-neighborhoods/

Bal, P. M., & Veltkamp, M. (2013). How does fiction reading influence empathy? An experimental investigation on the role of emotional transportation. *PLoS ONE, 8*(1), e55341. https://doi.org/10.1371/journal.pone.0055341

Balmer, B. R., Sippola, J., & Beehler, S. (2021). Processes and outcomes of a communalization of trauma approach: Vets & Friends community-based support groups. *Journal of Community Psychology,* 1. https://doi.org/10.1002/jcop.22516

Barrett, L. F. (2017). The theory of constructed emotion: an active inference account of interoception and categorization. *Social Cognitive & Affective Neuroscience, 12*(1), 1–23. https://doi.org/10.1093/scan/nsw154

Barriga, A. Q., Morrison, E. M., Liau, A. K., & Gibbs, J. C. (2001). Moral cognition: Explaining the gender difference in antisocial behavior. *Merrill-Palmer Quarterly, 47,* 532–562. https://doi.org/10.1353/mpq.2001.0020

Bauminger, N., Finzi-Dottan, R., Chason, S., & Har-Even, D. (2008). Intimacy in adolescent friendship: The roles of attachment, coherence, and self-disclosure. *Journal of Social & Personal Relationships, 25*(3), 409–428. https://doi.org/10.1177/0265407508090866

Bauerlein, M., & Stotsky, S. (2005, January 25). Why Johnny won't read. *The Washington Post.* https://www.washingtonpost.com/wp-dyn/articles/A33956-2005Jan24.html

Boele, S., Van der Graaff, J., de Wied, M., Van der Valk, I. E., Crocetti, E., & Branje, S. (2019). Linking parent–child and peer relationship quality to empathy in adolescence: A multilevel meta-analysis. *Journal of Youth & Adolescence, 48*(6), 1033–1055. https://doi.org/10.1007/s10964-019-00993-5

Bonanno, R. A., & Hymel, S. (2013). Cyber bullying and internalizing difficulties: Above and beyond the impact of traditional forms of bullying. *Journal of Youth and Adolescence, 42*(5), 685–697. https://doi.org/ 10.1007/s10964-013-9937-1

Bono, G., & Froh, J. J. (2009). Gratitude in school: Benefits to students and schools. In R. Gilman, E. S. Huebner, & M. Furlong (Eds.), *Handbook of positive psychology in schools* (pp. 77–88). Routledge.

Bowlby, J. (1969). *Attachment and loss* (Vol. 1). Basic Books.

Brackett, M. (2019). *Permission to feel: Unlocking the power of emotions to help our kids, ourselves, and our society thrive.* Celadon Books.

Brumariu, L. E., & Kerns, K. A. (2010). Mother–child attachment patterns and different types of anxiety symptoms: Is there specificity of relations? *Child Psychiatry & Human Development, 41*(6), 663–674. https://doi.org/10.1007/s10578-010-0195-0

Buhrmester, D. (1990). Intimacy of friendship, interpersonal competence and adjustment during preadolescence and adolescence. *Child Development, 61*(4), 1101–1111.

Burge, D., Hammen, C., Davila, J., Daley, S. E., Paley, B., Lindberg, N., Herzberg, D., & Rudolph, K. D. (1997). The relationship between attachment cognitions and psychological adjustment in late adolescent women. *Development and psychopathology, 9*(1), 151–167. https://doi.org/10.1017/s0954579497001119

Burns, A. B., Brown, J. S., Sachs-Ericsson, N., Ashby Plant, E., Thomas Curtis, J., Fredrickson, B. L., & Joiner, T. E. (2008). Upward spirals of positive emotion and coping: Replication, extension, and initial exploration of neurochemical substrates. *Personality & Individual Differences, 44*(2), 360–370. https://doi.org/10.1016/j.paid.2007.08.015

Cacioppo, J. T., Hawkley, L. C., Norman, G. J., & Berntson, G. G. (2011). Social isolation. *Annals of the New York Academy of Sciences, 1231*(1), 17–22. https://doi.org/10.1111/j.1749-6632.2011.06028.x

Call, K. T., & Mortimer, J. T. (2001). *Arena of comfort in adolescence: A study of adjustment in context.* Lawrence Erlbaum.

Centers for Disease Control and Prevention. (n.d.). *Mental health.* U.S. Department of Health and Human Services. https://www.cdc.gov/healthyyouth/mental-health/index.htm

Cerniglia, L., Bartolomeo, L., Capobianco, M., Lo Russo, S. L. M., Festucci, F., Tambelli, R., Adriani, W., & Cimino, S. (2019). Intersections and divergences between empathizing and mentalizing: Development, recent advancements by neuroimaging and the future of animal modelling. *Frontiers in Behavioral Neuroscience, 13,* 212.

Chiu, C., Dweck, C. S., Tong, J. Y., & Fu, J. H. (1997). Implicit theories and conceptions of morality. *Journal of Personality and Social Psychology, 3,* 923–940.

Chung, T., Creswell, K. G., Bachrach, R., Clark, D. B., & Martin, C. S. (2018). Adolescent binge drinking developmental context and opportunities for prevention. *Alcohol Research: Current Reviews, 39*(1). https://www.ncbi.nlm.nih.gov/pmc/articles/PMC6104966/pdf/arcr-39-1-e1_a01.pdf

Civic with Hart Research Associates, DePaoli, J. L., Atwell, M. N., Bridgeland, J. M., & Shriver, T. P. (2018). *Respected: Perspectives of youth on high school and social and emotional learning.* CASEL. https://casel.s3.us-east-2.amazonaws.com/CASEL-Resources-Respected.pdf

Clark, K. (2021, September 16). Lake Travis ISD pulls, will review book deemed sexually explicit. KXAN. https://www.kxan.com/news/education/lake-travis-isd-pulls-will-review-book-deemed-sexually-explicit/

Cohn, M. A., Fredrickson, B. L., Brown, S. L., Mikels, J. A., & Conway, A. M. (2009). Happiness unpacked: Positive emotions increase life satisfaction by building resilience. *Emotion, 9*(3), 361–368.

Comer, J. (2001). Foreword. In J. Cohen (Ed.), *Caring classrooms/intelligent schools: The social emotional education of young children* (pp. ix–x). Teachers College Press.

Cooper, M. L., Shaver, P. R., & Collins, N. L. (1998). Attachment styles, emotion regulation, and adjustment in adolescence. *Journal of Personality & Social Psychology, 74*(5), 1380–1397. https://doi.org/10.1037/0022-3514.74.5.1380

Csikszentmihalyi, M., Larson, R., & Prescott, S. (1977). The ecology of adolescent activity and experience. *Journal of Youth and Adolescence, 6,* 281–294. http://dx.doi.org/10.1007/BF02138940

Curtin, S. C., & Heron, M. (2019, October). *Death rates due to suicide and homicide among persons aged 10–24: United States, 2000–2017.* Centers for Disease Control and Prevention, U.S. Department of Health and Human Services. https://www.cdc.gov/nchs/data/databriefs/db352-h.pdf

Damon, W., Colby, A., & King, P. E. (2018). They do care: An interview with William Damon and Anne Colby on moral development. *Journal of Moral Education, 47*(4), 383–396. https://doi.org/10.1080/03057240.2018.1494972

Darnon, C., Muller, D., Schrager, S. M., Pannuzzo, N., & Butera, F. (2006). Mastery and performance goals predict epistemic and relational conflict regulation. *Journal of Educational Psychology, 98*(4), 766–776. https://doi.org/10.1037/0022-0663.98.4.766

De Grada, E., & Kruglanski, A. W. (1999). Motivated cognition and group interaction: Need for closure affects the contents and processes. *Journal of Experimental Social Psychology, 35*(4), 346.

de Luca, C., & Olefsky, J. M. (2006). Stressed out about obesity and insulin resistance. *Nature Medicine, 12*(1), 41–42. https://doi.org/10.1038/nm0106-41

Denby, D. (1997). *Great books: My adventures with Homer, Rousseau, Woolf, and other indestructible writers of the Western World*. Touchstone.

Denby, D. (2016). *Lit up: One reporter, three schools, twenty-four books that can change lives*. Henry Holt.

Diebel, T., Woodcock, C., Cooper, C., & Brignell, C. (2016). Establishing the effectiveness of a gratitude diary intervention on children's sense of school belonging. *Educational & Child Psychology, 33*(2), 117–129. https://psycnet.apa.org/record/2016-40016-009

Djikic, M., Oatley, K., & Moldoveanu, M. C. (2013a). Opening the closed mind: The effect of exposure to literature on the need for closure. *Creativity Research Journal, 25*(2), 149–154. https://doi.org/10.1080/10400419.2013.783735

Djikic, M., Oatley, K., & Moldoveanu, M. C. (2013b). Reading other minds: Effects of literature on empathy. *Scientific Study of Literature, 3*(1), 28–47. https://doi.org/10.1075/ssol.3.1.06dji

Djikic, M., Oatley, K., Zoeterman, S., & Peterson, J. B. (2009a). Defenseless against art? Impact of reading fiction on emotion in avoidantly attached individuals. *Journal of Research in Personality, 43*(1), 14–17. https://doi.org/10.1016/j.jrp.2008.09.003

Djikic, M., Oatley, K., Zoeterman, S., & Peterson, J. B. (2009b). On being moved by art: How reading fiction transforms the self. *Creativity Research Journal, 21*(1), 24–29.

Dong, T., Anderson, R. C., Lin, T. J., & Wu, X. (2009). Concurrent student-managed discussions in a large class. *International Journal of Educational Research, 48*, 352–367. https://doi.org/10. 1016/j.ijer.2010.03.005

Dopp, A., & Cain, A. (2012). The role of peer relationships in parental bereavement during childhood and adolescence. *Death Studies, 36*(1), 41–60. https://doi.org/10.1080/07481187.2011.573175

Dore, R. A., Amendum, S. J., Golinkoff, R. M., & Hirsh-Pasek, K. (2018). Theory of mind: A hidden factor in reading comprehension? *Educational Psychology Review, 30*(3), 1067–1089. https://doi.org/10.1007/s10648-018-9443-9

Dweck, C. S. (2000). *Self-theories: Their role in motivation, personality, and development*. Psychology Press.

Dweck, C. S. (2006). *Mindset: The new psychology of success*. Random House.

Eisenberg, N., Hofer, C., Sulik, M. J., & Liew, J. (2014). The development of prosocial moral reasoning and a prosocial orientation in young adulthood: Concurrent and longitudinal correlates. *Developmental Psychology, 50*(1), 58–70. http://dx.doi.org/10.1037/a0032990

Eisenberg, N., Shell, R., Pasternack, J., Lennon, R., Beller, R., & Mathy, R. M. (1987). Prosocial development in middle childhood: A longitudinal study. *Developmental Psychology, 23*, 712–718. http://doi.org/10.1037/0012-1649.23.5.712

Emadpoor, L., Lavasani, M., & Shahcheraghi, S. (2016). Relationship between perceived social support and psychological well-being among students based on mediating role of academic motivation. *International Journal of Mental Health & Addiction, 14*(3), 284–290. https://doi.org/10.1007/s11469-015-9608-4

Emmons, R. A., & McCullough, M. E. (2003). Counting blessings versus burdens: An experimental investigation of gratitude and subjective well-being in daily life. *Journal of Personality & Social Psychology, 84*(2), 377–389. https://doi.org/10.1037/0022-3514.84.2.377

Enriquez, G. (2006). The reader speaks out: Adolescent reflections about controversial young adult literature. *ALAN Review*, Winter 2006, 16–23.

Epley, N., & Schroeder, J. (2014). Mistakenly seeking solitude. *Journal of Experimental Psychology: General, 143*(5), 1980–1999. https://doi.org/https://doi.org/10.1037/a0037323

Erikson, E. H. (1963). *Childhood and society* (2nd ed.). Norton.

Ethier, K. A., Kann, L., & McManus, T. (2018, January 18). Sexual intercourse among high school students—29 states and United States overall, 2005–2015. *Morbidity and Mortality Weekly Report (MMWR), 66*(5152), 1393–1397. Accessed May 6, 2021 from https://www.cdc.gov/mmwr/volumes/66/wr/mm665152a1.htm

Ferguson, C. J. (2014). Is reading "banned" books associated with behavior problems in young readers? The influence of controversial young adult books on the psychological well-being of adolescents. *Psychology of Aesthetics, Creativity & the Arts, 8*(3), 354–362. https://doi.org/10.1037/a0035601

Fivush, R. (2019). Integration and differentiation of self through reminiscing and narrative. *Social Development, 28*(4), 835–839. https://doi.org/10.1111/sode.12399

Flvush, R. (2021, January 30). Exchanging stories builds respect. *Psychology Today.* https://www.psychologytoday.com/us/blog/the-stories-our-lives/202101/exchanging-stories-builds-respect

Fong, K., Mullin, J. B., & Mar, R. A. (2015). How exposure to literary genres relates to attitudes toward gender roles and sexual behavior. *Psychology of Aesthetics, Creativity & the Arts, 9*(3), 274–285. https://doi.org/10.1037/a0038864

Fousiani, K., Dimitropoulou, P., Michaelides, M. P., & Van Petegem, S. (2016). Perceived parenting and adolescent cyber-bullying: Examining the intervening role of autonomy and relatedness need satisfaction, empathic concern and recognition of humanness. *Journal of Child & Family Studies, 25*(7), 2120–2129.

Fredrickson, B. L. (2001). The role of positive emotions in positive psychology: The broaden-and-build theory of positive emotions. *American Psychologist, 56*(3), 218–226. http://dx.doi.org/10.1037/0003-066X.56.3.218

Frias, A., Watkins, P. C., Webber, A. C., & Froh, J. J. (2011). Death and gratitude: Death reflection enhances gratitude. *Journal of Positive Psychology, 6*(2), 154–162. https://doi.org/10.1080/17439760.2011.558848

Friedman, J., & Johnson, N. F. (2022, September 19). Banned in the USA: The growing movement to censor books in schools. *PEN America.* https://pen.org/report/banned-usa-growing-movement-to-censor-books-in-schools/

Fulmer, S. M., D'Mello, S. K., Strain, A., & Graesser, A. C. (2015). Interest-based text preference moderates the effect of text difficulty on engagement and learning. *Contemporary Educational Psychology, 41*, 98–110. https://doi.org/10.1016/j.cedpsych.2014.12.005

Fulmer, S. M., & Frijters, J. C. (2011). Motivation during an excessively challenging reading task: The buffering role of relative topic interest. *Journal of Experimental Education, 79*(2), 185–208. https://doi.org/10.1080/00220973.2010.481503

Furman, W., & Rose, A. (2015). Friendships, romantic relationships, and other dyadic peer relationships in childhood and adolescence: A unified relational perspective. In R. Lerner (Ed.), *Handbook of child psychology and developmental science* (pp. 1–43). Wiley.

Furrow, D., Moore, C., Davidge, J., & Chiasson, L. (1992). Mental terms in mothers' and children's speech: Similarities and relationships. *Journal of Child Language, 19*, 617–631.

Galinsky, A. D., & Moskowitz, G. B. (2000). Perspective-taking: Decreasing stereotype expression, stereotype accessibility, and in-group favoritism. *Journal of Personality & Social Psychology, 78*, 708–724. https://doi.org/10.1037//0022-3514.78.4.708

Giles, G. (2006). *What happened to Cass McBride?* Little, Brown & Company.

Gilligan, C. (1982). *In a different voice: Psychological theory and women's development.* Harvard University Press.

Glaus, M. (2014). Text complexity and young adult literature: Establishing its place. *Journal of Adolescent & Adult Literacy, 57*(5), 406–417.

Gloria, C., Faulk, K., & Steinhardt, M. (2013). Positive affectivity predicts successful and unsuccessful adaptation to stress. *Motivation & Emotion, 37*(1), 185–193. https://doi.org/10.1007/s11031-012-9291-8

Gloria, C. T., & Steinhardt, M. A. (2016). Relationships among positive emotions, coping, resilience and mental health. *Stress & Health: Journal of the International Society for the Investigation of Stress, 32*(2), 145–156. https://doi.org/10.1002/smi.2589

Goossens, L. (2018). Loneliness in adolescence: Insights from Cacioppo's Evolutionary Model. *Child Development Perspectives, 12*(4), 230–234. https://doi.org/10.1111/cdep.12291

Graham, S., Munniksma, A., & Juvonen, J. (2014). Psychosocial benefits of cross-ethnic friendships in urban middle schools. *Child Development, 85*(2), 469–483. https://doi.org/10.1111/cdev.12159

Grizzard, K. (2021, December 11). Controversy circulates over books: School board asked to look at titles after parent complains books are not appropriate. *Reflector.* https://www.reflector.com/news/local/controversy-circulates-over-books-school-board-asked-to-look-at-titles-after-parent-complains-books/article_54e4d129-8158-5884-9791-96f314eb3573.html

Guajardo, N. R., & Cartwright, K. B. (2016). The contribution of theory of mind, counterfactual reasoning, and executive function to pre-readers' language comprehension and later reading awareness and comprehension in elementary school. *Journal of Experimental Child Psychology, 144*, 27–45. https://doi.org/10.1016/j.jecp.2015.11.004

Guthrie, J. T., & Humenick, N. M. (2004). Motivating students to read: Evidence for classroom practices that increase reading motivation and achievement. In P. McCardle & V. Chhabra (Eds.), *The voice of evidence in reading research* (pp. 329–354). Paul H. Brookes.

Guthrie, J. T., Wigfield, A., & You, W. (2012). Instructional Contexts for Engagement and Achievement in Reading. In S. Christensen, C. Wylie, & A. Reschly (Eds.), *Handbook of Research on Student Engagement* (pp. 675–694). Springer.

Haidt, J. (2013). *The righteous mind: Why good people are divided by politics and religion.* Vintage Books.

Hall-Lande, J. A., Eisenberg, M. E., Christenson, S. L., & Neumark-Sztainer, D. (2007). Social isolation, psychological health, and protective factors in adolescence. *Adolescence, 42*(166), 265–286.

Hamilton, L. S., & Doss, C. J. (2020). *Supports for social and emotional learning in American schools and classrooms: Findings from the American teacher panel.* Rand Corporation. https://www.rand.org/pubs/research_reports/RRA397 -1.html

Hardy, S. (2006). Identity, reasoning, and emotion: An empirical comparison of three sources of moral motivation. *Motivation & Emotion, 30*(3), 205–213. https://doi.org/10.1007/s11031-006-9034-9

Hardy, S. A., Francis, S. W., Zamboanga, B. L., Kim, S. Y., Anderson, S. G., & Forthun, L. F. (2013). The roles of identity formation and moral identity in college student mental health, health-risk behaviors, and psychological well-being. *Journal of Clinical Psychology, 69*(4), 364–382. https://doi.org/10.1002 /jclp.21913

Hardy, S. A., Walker, L., J., Olsen, J. A., Woodbury, R. D., & Hickman, J. R. (2014). Moral identity as moral ideal self: Links to adolescent outcomes. *Developmental Psychology, 50*(1), 45–57.

Hawkley, L. C., & Cacioppo, J. T. (2010). Loneliness matters: A theoretical and empirical review of consequences and mechanisms. *Annals of Behavioral Medicine, 40,* 218–227. https://doi.org/10.1007/s12160-010-9210-8

Hidi, S. (2001). Interest, reading, and learning: Theoretical and practical considerations. *Educational Psychology Review, 13*(3), 191–209.

Hill, P. L., & Allemand, M. (2011). Gratitude, forgivingness, and wellbeing in adulthood: Tests of moderation and incremental prediction. *The Journal of Positive Psychology, 6*(5), 397–407.

Holbrook, S. (2017, January 4). I can't answer these Texas standardized test questions about my own poems. *Huffpost.* https://www.huffpost.com/entry /standardized-tests-are-so-bad-i-cant-answer-these_b_586d5517e4b0c3539e 80c341

Howard, M. S., & Medway, F. J. (2004). Adolescents' attachment and coping with stress. *Psychology in the Schools, 41*(3), 391–402. https://doi.org/10.1002 /pits.10167

Immordino-Yang, M. H., Darling-Hammond, L., & Krone, C. R. (2019). Nurturing nature: How brain development is inherently social and emotional, and what this means for education. *Educational Psychologist, 54*(3), 185–204. https:// doi.org/10.1080/00461520.2019.1633924

Immordino-Yang, M. H., & Gotlieb, R. (2017). Embodied brains, social minds, cultural meaning: Integrating neuroscientific and educational research on social-affective development. *American Educational Research Journal, 54*(1_suppl), 344S–367S. https://doi.org/10.3102/0002831216669780

Isen, A. M. (1999). Positive affect. In T. Dalgleish & M. Power (Eds.), *The handbook of cognition and emotion* (pp. 521–539). Wiley.

Isen, A. M. (2000). Some perspectives on positive affect and self-regulation. *Psychological Inquiry, 11*, 184–187.

Ivey, G., & Broaddus, K. (2001). "Just plain reading": A survey of what makes students want to read in middle school classrooms. *Reading Research Quarterly, 36*(4), 350. https://doi.org/10.1598/RRQ.36.4.2

Ivey, G., & Johnston, P. H. (2013). Engagement with young adult literature: Outcomes and processes. *Reading Research Quarterly, 48*(3), 255–275.

Ivey, G., & Johnston, P. H. (2015). Engaged reading as a collaborative, transformative practice. *Journal of Literacy Research, 47*(3), 297–327.

Jellesma, F. C., Rieffe, C., Meerum Terwogt, M., & Westenberg, P. M. (2011). Children's sense of coherence and trait emotional intelligence: A longitudinal study exploring the development of somatic complaints. *Psychology & Health, 26*(3), 307–320. https://doi.org/10.1080/08870440903411021

Jerrim, J., & Moss, G. (2019). The link between fiction and teenagers' reading skills: International evidence from the OECD PISA study. *British Educational Research Journal, 45*, 181–200.

Ji, L., Pan, B., Zhang, W., Zhang, L., Chen, L., & Deater-Deckard, K. (2019). Bidirectional Associations between Peer Relations and Attention Problems from 9 to 16 Years. *Journal of Abnormal Child Psychology, 47*(3), 381–392. https://doi.org/10.1007/s10802-018-0440-8

Johnson, D. W., & Johnson, R. T. (1981a). Building friendships between handicapped and nonhandicapped students: Effects of cooperative and individualistic instruction. *American Educational Research Journal, 18*, 415–424.

Johnson, D. W., & Johnson, R. T. (1981b). Effects of cooperative and individualistic learning experiences on interethnic interaction. *Journal of Educational Psychology, 73*, 454–459.

Johnson, D. W., & Johnson, R. T. (2009). An educational psychology success story: Social interdependence theory and cooperative learning. *Educational Researcher, 38*, 365–379.

Johnson, K., Waugh, C., & Fredrickson, B. (2010). Smile to see the forest: Facially expressed positive emotions broaden cognition. *Cognition & Emotion, 24*(2), 299–321. https://doi.org/10.1080/02699930903384667

Johnston, L. D., Miech, R. A., O'Malley, P. M., Bachman, J. G., Schulenberg, J. E., & Patrick, M. E. (2018). *Monitoring the future national survey results on drug use: 1975–2017: Overview, key findings on adolescent drug use.* Institute for Social Research, The University of Michigan. http://www.monitoringthefuture.org/pubs/monographs/mtf-overview2017.pdf

Jones, M. G., & Gerig, T. M. (1994). Silent sixth-grade students: Characteristics, achievement, and teacher expectations. *The Elementary School Journal, 95*(2), 169–182.

Jood, K., Redfors, P., Rosengren, A., Blomstrand, C., & Jern, C. (2009). Self-perceived psychological stress and ischemic stroke: A case-control study. *BMC Medicine, 7*, 53–60. https://doi.org/10.1186/1741-7015-7-53

Joseph, D. L., & Newman, D. A. (2010). Emotional intelligence: An integrative meta-analysis and cascading model. *Journal of Applied Psychology, 95*(1), 54–78. http://dx.doi.org/10.1037/a0017286

Joshanloo, M., Sirgy, M. J., & Park, J. (2018). Directionality of the relationship between social well-being and subjective well-being: Evidence from a 20-year longitudinal study. *Quality of Life Research, 27*(8), 2137–2145. https://doi.org/10.1007/s11136-018-1865-9

Jost, J. T., Kruglanski, A. W., & Simon, L. (1999). Effects of epistemic motivation on conservatism, intolerance and other system-justifying attitudes. In L. I. Thompson, J. M. Levine, & D. M. Messick (Eds.), *Shared cognition in organizations: The management of knowledge* (pp. 91–116). Erlbaum.

Judi's House. (n.d.). Childhood Bereavement Estimation Model (CBEM). https://judishouse.org/research-tools/cbem/

Kaltiala-Heino, R., & Fröjd, S. (2011). Correlation between bullying and clinical depression in adolescent patients. *Adolescent Health, Medicine and Therapeutics, 2*, 37–44.

Kaltwasser, L., Hildebrandt, A., Wilhelm, O., & Sommer, W. (2017). On the relationship of emotional abilities and prosocial behavior. *Evolution and Human Behavior, 38*(3), 298–308. https://doi.org/10.1016/j.evolhumbehav.2016.10.011

Kemeny, M. E., & Schedlowski, M. (2007). Understanding the interaction between psychosocial stress and immune-related diseases: A stepwise progression. *Brain, Behavior & Immunity, 21*(8), 1009–1018. https://doi.org/10.1016/j.bbi.2007.07.010

Kohlberg, L. (1981). *Essays on moral development (Vol. 1): The philosophy of moral development.* Harper & Row.

Kong, F., Zhao, J., & You, X. (2012). Social support mediates the impact of emotional intelligence on mental distress and life satisfaction in Chinese young adults. *Personality & Individual Differences, 53*(4), 513–517. https://doi.org/10.1016/j.paid.2012.04.021

Konrath, S. H., O'Brien, E. H., & Hsing, C. (2011). Changes in dispositional empathy in American college students over time: A meta-analysis. *Personality & Social Psychology Review, 15*(2), 180–198. https://doi.org/10.1177/1088868310377395

Koydemir, S., Şimşek, Ö., Schütz, A., & Tipandjan, A. (2013). Differences in how trait emotional intelligence predicts life satisfaction: The role of affect balance versus social support in India and Germany. *Journal of Happiness Studies, 14*(1), 51–66. https://doi.org/10.1007/s10902-011-9315-1

Kruglanski, A. W., Pierro, A., Mannetti, L., & De Grada, E. (2006). Groups as epistemic providers: Need for closure and the unfolding of group-centrism. *Psychological Review, 113*(1), 84–100. https://doi.org/10.1037/0033-295X.113.1.84

Kruglanski, A. W., & Webster, D. M. (1991). Group members' reactions to opinion deviates and conformists at varying degrees of proximity to decision deadline and of environmental noise. *Journal of Personality and Social Psychology, 61*, 212–225.

Kruglanski, A. W., Webster, D. M., & Klein, A. (1993). Motivated resistance and openness to persuasion in the presence or absence of prior information. *Journal of Personality & Social Psychology, 65*(5), 861–876.

Kubin, E., Puryear, C., Schein, C., & Gray, K. (2021). Personal experiences bridge moral and political divides better than fact. *Proceedings of the National Academy of Sciences of the United States of America, 118*(6), 1–9. https://doi.org/10.1073/pnas.2008389118

Kuiken, D., Miall, D. S., & Sikora, S. (2004). Forms of self-implication in literary reading. *Poetics Today, 25*(2), 171–203.

Kwok, S. Y. C. L., & Fang, S. (2021). A cross-lagged panel study examining the reciprocal relationships between positive emotions, meaning, strengths use and study engagement in primary school students. *Journal of Happiness Studies, 22*(3), 1033–1053. https://doi.org/10.1007/s10902-020-00262-4

Landstedt, E., Hammarström, A., & Winefield, H. (2015). How well do parental and peer relationships in adolescence predict health in adulthood? *Scandinavian Journal of Public Health, 43*(5), 460–468. https://doi.org/10.1177/1403494815576360

Large majorities of voters oppose book bans and have confidence in libraries [Press Release]. (2022, March 24). American Library Association. http://www.ala.org/news/press-releases/2022/03/large-majorities-voters-oppose-book-bans-and-have-confidence-libraries

Larson, R. W., Richards, M. H., Moneta, G., Holmbeck, G., & Duckett, E. (1996). Changes in adolescents' daily interactions with their families from ages 10 to 18: Disengagement and transformation. *Developmental Psychology, 32*, 744–754. https://doi.org/10.1037/0012-1649.32.4.744

Latawiec, B. M., Anderson, R. C., Shufeng, M., & Kim, N.-J. (2016). Influence of collaborative reasoning discussions on metadiscourse in children's essays. *Text & Talk, 36*, 23–46. https://doi.org/10.1515/text-2016-0002

Laursen, B., & Hartl, A. C. (2013). Understanding loneliness during adolescence: Developmental changes that increase the risk of perceived social isolation. *Journal of Adolescence, 36*, 1261–1268. https://doi.org/10.1016/j.adolescence.2013.06.003

Lavy, S., & Naama-Ghanayim, E. (2020). Why care about caring? Linking teachers' caring and sense of meaning at work with students' self-esteem, well-being, and school engagement. *Teaching & Teacher Education, 91*. https://doi.org/10.1016/j.tate.2020.103046

Lebrun-Harris, L. A., Sherman, L. J., Limber, S. P., Miller, B. D., & Edgerton, E. A. (2019). Bullying victimization and perpetration among U.S. children and adolescents: 2016 National Survey of Children's Health. *Journal of Child & Family Studies, 28*(9), 2543–2557. https://doi.org/10.1007/s10826-018-1170-9

Lecce, S., Bianco, F., & Hughes, C. (2021). Reading minds and reading texts: Evidence for independent and specific associations. *Cognitive Development, 57*. https://doi.org/10.1016/j.cogdev.2021.101010

Lemov, D., Driggs, C., & Woolway, E. (2016). *Reading reconsidered: A practical guide to rigorous literacy instruction.* Jossey-Bass.

Levy, S. R., & Dweck, C. S. (1998). Trait- versus process-focused social judgment. *Social Cognition, 16*(1), 151–172. https://doi.org/10.1521/soco.1998.16.1.151

Li, D. K. (2010). Texas school district pulls books by critically acclaimed Black author amid critical race theory claims. *NBCnews.com.* https://www.nbcnews.com/news/us-news/texas-school-district-pulls-books-acclaimed-children-s-author-n1280956

Li, P. F. J., Wong, Y. J., & Chao, R. C. L. (2019). Happiness and meaning in life: Unique, differential, and indirect associations with mental health. *Counselling Psychology Quarterly, 32*(3/4), 396–414. https://doi.org/10.1080/09515070.2019.1604493

Lili, T., Luyang, P., Huebner, E. S., Minmin, D., Lundy, T. J., & Scherer, R. (2016). Gratitude and adolescents' subjective well-being in school: The multiple mediating roles of basic psychological needs satisfaction at school. *Frontiers in Psychology*, 1–8. https://doi.org/10.3389/fpsyg.2016.01409

Lin, C.-C. (2015). Impact of gratitude on resource development and emotional well-being. *Social Behavior & Personality*, 43(3), 493–504. https://doi.org/10.2224/sbp.2015.43.3.493

Lin, T. J., Anderson, R. C., Hummel, J. E., Jadallah, M., Miller, B. W., Nguyen-Jahiel, K., Morris, J. A., Kuo, L.-J., Kim, I.-H., Wu, X., & Dong, T. (2012). Children's use of analogy during collaborative reasoning. *Child Development*, 83, 1429–1443. https://doi.org/10.1111/j.1467-8624.2012.01784.x

Lindquist, K. A., MacCormack, J. K., & Shablack, H. (2015). The role of language in emotion: predictions from psychological constructionism. *Frontiers in Psychology*, 6, 1–17.

Liu, Y., Wang, Z., & Lü, W. (2013). Resilience and affect balance as mediators between trait emotional intelligence and life satisfaction. *Personality and Individual Differences*, 54(7), 850–855. https://doi.org/10.1016/j.paid.2012.12.010

Lopes, P. N., Nezlek, J. B., Extremera, N., Hertel, J., Fernández-Berrocal, P., Schütz, A., & Salovey, P. (2011). Emotion regulation and the quality of social interaction: Does the ability to evaluate emotional situations and identify effective responses matter? *Journal of Personality*, 79(2), 429–467. https://doi.org/10.1111/j.1467-6494.2010.00689.x

Ma, S., Anderson, R. C., Lin, T.-J., Zhang, J., Morris, J. A., Nguyen-Jahiel, K., Miller, B. W., Jadallah, M., Scott, T., Sun, J., Grabow, K., Latawiec, B. M., & Yi, S. (2017a). Instructional influences on English language learners' storytelling. *Learning & Instruction*, 49, 64–80. https://doi.org/10.1016/j.learninstruc.2016.12.004

Ma, S., Zhang, J., Anderson, R. C., Morris, J., Nguyen-Jahiel, K. T., Miller, B., Jadallah, M., Sun, J., Lin, T.-J., Scott, T., Hsu, Y.-L., Zhang, X., Latawiec, B., & Grabow, K. (2017b). Children's productive use of academic vocabulary. *Discourse Processes*, 54, 40–61. https://doi.org/10.1080/0163853X.2016.1166889

Ma, M., Kibler, J. L., & Sly, K. (2013). Gratitude is associated with greater levels of protective factors and lower levels of risks in African American adolescents. *Journal of Adolescence*, 36(5), 983–991. https://doi.org/10.1016/j.adolescence.2013.07.012

MacEvoy, J. P., Weeks, M. S., & Asher, S. R. (2011). Loneliness. In B. B. Brown & M. J. Prinstein (Eds.), *Encyclopedia of adolescence* (Vol. 2, pp. 178–187). Academic Press.

Maes, M., Danneel, S., den Noortgate, W. V., Nelemans, S. A., Fernández-Castilla, B., Goossens, L., & Vanhalst, J. (2019). Loneliness and social anxiety across childhood and adolescence: Multilevel meta-analyses of cross-sectional and longitudinal associations. *Developmental Psychology*, 55(7), 1548–1565. https://doi.org/10.1037/dev0000719

Mar, R. A., & Oatley, K. (2008). The function of fiction is the abstraction and simulation of social experience. *Perspectives on Psychological Science*, 3(3), 173–192. https://doi.org/10.1111/j.1745-6924.2008.00073.x

Mar, R. A., Oatley, K., Hirsh, J., dela Paz, J., & Peterson, J. B. (2006). Bookworms versus nerds: Exposure to fiction versus non-fiction, divergent associations with social ability, and the simulation of fictional social worlds. *Journal of Research in Personality, 40*(5), 694–712. https://doi.org/10.1016/j.jrp.2005.08.002

Marion, D., Laursen, B., Zettergren, P., & Bergman, L. (2013). Predicting life satisfaction during middle adulthood from peer relationships during mid-adolescence. *Journal of Youth & Adolescence, 42*(8), 1299–1307. https://doi.org/10.1007/s10964-013-9969-6

Martin-Raugh, M. P., Kell, H. J., & Motowidlo, S. J. (2016). Prosocial knowledge mediates effects of agreeableness and emotional intelligence on prosocial behavior. *Personality & Individual Differences, 90*, 41–49. https://doi.org/10.1016/j.paid.2015.10.024

Masi, C. M., Chen, H.-Y., Hawkley, L. C., & Cacioppo, J. T. (2011). A meta-analysis of interventions to reduce loneliness. *Personality & Social Psychology Review, 15*(3), 219–266. https://doi.org/10.1177/1088868310377394

Mauss, I. B., Savino, N. S., Anderson, C. L., Weisbuch, M., Tamir, M., & Laudenslager, M. L. (2012). The pursuit of happiness can be lonely. *Emotion, 12*(5), 908–912. https://doi.org/10.1037/a0025299

Mavroveli, S., Petrides, K. V., Rieffe, C., & Bakker, F. (2007). Trait emotional intelligence, psychological well-being and peer-rated social competence in adolescence. *British Journal of Developmental Psychology, 25*(2), 263–275. https://doi.org/10.1348/026151006X118577

Mavroveli, S., Petrides, K. V., Sangareau, Y., & Furnham, A. (2009). Exploring the relationships between trait emotional intelligence and objective socio-emotional outcomes in childhood. *British Journal of Educational Psychology, 79*, 259–272. https://doi.org/10.1348/000709908X368848

Mavroveli, S., Petrides, K. V., Shove, C., & Whitehead, A. (2008). Investigation of the construct of trait emotional intelligence in children. *European Child & Adolescent Psychiatry, 17*(8), 516–526. https://doi.org/10.1007/s00787-008-0696-6

Mavroveli, S., & Sánchez-Ruiz, M. J. (2011). Trait emotional intelligence influences on academic achievement and school behavior. *British Journal of Educational Psychology, 81*(1), 112–134. https://doi.org/10.1348/2044-8279.002009

McCullough, K., & Simon, S. R. (2011). Feeling heard: A support group for siblings of children with developmental disabilities. *Social Work with Groups, 34*(3–4), 320–329. https://doi.org/10.1080/01609513.2011.558819

Mercer, N., Dawes, L., Wegerif, R., & Sams, C. (2004). Reasoning as a scientist: Ways of helping children to use language to learn science. *British Educational Research Journal, 30*, 359–377.

Mercer, N., & Sams, C. (2008). Teaching children how to use language to solve maths problems. *Language and Education, 20*, 507–528.

Mercer, N., Wegerif, R., & Dawes, L. (1999). Children's talk and the development of reasoning in the classroom. *British Educational Research Journal, 25*, 95–111.

Miller, B. W., Anderson, R. C., Morris, J., Lin, T. J., Jadallah, M., & Sun, J. (2014). The effects of reading to prepare for argumentative discussion on cognitive engagement and conceptual growth. *Learning & Instruction, 33*, 67–80. https://doi.org/10.1016/j.learninstruc.2014.04.003

Moeller, J., Brackett, M. A., Ivcevic, Z., & White, A. E. (2020). High school students' feelings: Discoveries from a large national survey and an experience sampling study. *Learning & Instruction, 66*. https://doi.org/10.1016/j.learninstruc.2019.101301

Mohr, P., Howells, K., Gerace, A., Day, A., & Wharton, M. (2007). The role of perspective taking in anger arousal. *Personality & Individual Differences, 43*(3), 507–517. https://doi.org/10.1016/j.paid.2006.12.019

Molden, D. C., & Dweck, C. S. (2006). Finding "meaning" in psychology. *American Psychologist, 61*(3), 192–203. https://doi.org/ 10.1037/0003-066X.61.3.192

Murdoch, D., English, A. R., Hintz, A., & Tyson, K. (2020). Feeling heard: Inclusive education, transformative learning, and productive struggle. *Educational Theory, 70*(5), 653–679. https://doi.org/10.1111/edth.12449

Myers, M., Laurent, S., & Hodges, S. (2014). Perspective taking instructions and self-other overlap: Different motives for helping. *Motivation & Emotion, 38*(2), 224–234. https://doi.org/10.1007/s11031-013-9377-y

Natanson, H. (2022, September 19). School book bans and challenges, at record highs, are rising again. *The Washington Post.* https://www.washingtonpost.com /education/2022/09/19/school-book-bans-challenges-record-highs-are-rising-again/

National Alliance for Children's Grief. (n.d.). National poll of bereaved children & teenagers. https://nacg.org/national-poll-of-bereaved-children-teenagers/

National Assessment of Educational Progress (NAEP) Reading Assessment data for years 2002, 2003, 2005, 2007, 2009, 2011, 2013, and 2015. https://www .nationsreportcard.gov/ndecore/landing.

National Center for Drug Abuse Statistics. (n.d.). *Drug use among youth: Facts & statistics.* https://drugabusestatistics.org/teen-drug-use/

National Center for Health Statistics. (2016). *Health, United States, 2015: With special feature on racial and ethnic health disparities.* National Center for Health Statistics. https://www.cdc.gov/nchs/data/hus/hus15.pdf

National Institute of Mental Health. (n.d.). *Any anxiety disorders.* U.S. Department of Health and Human Services, National Institutes of Health. https://www .nimh.nih.gov/health/statistics/any-anxiety-disorder

National Research Council. (2003). *Engaging schools: Fostering high school students' motivation to learn.* National Academies Press.

Nicholls, J. G. (1989). *The competitive ethos and democratic education.* Harvard University Press.

Niven, K., Holman, D., & Totterdell, P. (2012). How to win friendship and trust by influencing people's feelings: An investigation of interpersonal affect regulation and the quality of relationships. *Human Relations, 65*(6), 777–805. https://doi .org/10.1177/0018726712439909

Northrop, L., Borsheim-Black, C., & Kelly, S. (2019). Matching students to books: The cultural content of eighth-grade literature assignments. *Elementary School Journal, 120*(2), 243–271. https://doi.org/10.1086/705797

NYSED. (n.d.). *Physical Education Learning Standards.* New York State Education Department. http://www.nysed.gov/curriculum-instruction/physical-education -learning-standards

Nystrand, M., Gamoran, A., Kachur, R., & Prendergast, C. (1997). *Opening dialogue: Understanding the dynamics of language and learning in the English classroom.* Teachers College Press.

Organisation for Economic Co-operation and Development. (2011). *PISA 2009 results: Students on line, Vol. 6, Digital technologies and performance.* OECD. https://www.oecd-ilibrary.org/education/pisa-2009-results-students-on -line_9789264112995-en

Ornaghi, V., & Grazzani, I. (2013). The relationship between emotional-state language and emotion understanding: A study with school-age children. *Cognition & Emotion, 27*(2), 356–366.

Orthner, D., Jones-Sanpei, H., Akos, P., & Rose, R. (2013). Improving middle school student engagement through career-relevant instruction in the core curriculum. *Journal of Educational Research, 106*(1), 27–38. https://doi.org/10.1080/0022 0671.2012.658454

Osborne, J., & Chin, C. (2010). The role of discourse in learning science. In K. Littleton & C. Howe (Eds.), *Educational dialogues: Understanding and promoting productive interaction.* Routledge.

Osterman, K. F. (2000). Students' need for belonging in the school community. *Review of Educational Research, 70*(3), 323. https://doi.org/10.3102 /003465543070003323

Parker, J. G., & Asher, S. R. (1987). Peer relations and later personal adjustment: Are low-accepted children at risk? *Psychological Bulletin, 102*(3), 357–389.

Parker, J., Rubin, K. H., Price, J. M., & DeRosier, M. E. (1995). Peer relationships, child development, and adjustment: A developmental psychopathology perspective. In D. Cicchetti, & D. J. Cohen (Eds.), *Developmental psychopathology, Vol. 2, Risk, disorder and adaptation* (pp. 96–161). Wiley.

Pasupathi, M., & Wainryb, C. (2019). When I hurt others, and when I get hurt: Integrating victim and perpetrator experiences of harm into a sense of moral agency. *Social Development, 28*(4), 820–834. https://doi.org/10.1111/sode.12334

Peterson, C. C., & Siegal, M. (2000). Insights into theory of mind from deafness and autism. *Mind & Language, 15*(1), 123. https://doi.org/10.1111/1468-0017.00126

Petrides, K. V., Frederickson, N., & Furnham, A. (2004). The role of trait emotional intelligence in academic performance and deviant behavior at school. *Personality and Individual Differences, 36*(2), 277–293. https://doi.org/https:// doi.org/10.1016/S0191-8869(03)00084-9

Pfeifer, J. H., & Berkman, E. T. (2018). The development of self and identity in adolescence: Neural evidence and implications for a value-based choice perspective on motivated behavior. *Child Development Perspectives, 12,* 158–164. http:// dx.doi.org/10.1111/cdep.12279

Phillips, W. S., Baron-Cohen, S., & Rutter, M. (1998). Can children with autism understand intentions? *British Journal of Developmental Psychology, 16,* 337–348.

Pierro, A., Mannetti, L., De Grada, E., Livi, S., & Kruglanski, A. W. (2003). Autocracy bias in informal groups under need for closure. *Personality and Social Psychology Bulletin, 29,* 405–417.

Pineda, D. (2020, November 12). In Burbank schools, a book-banning debate over how to teach antiracism. *Los Angeles Times.* https://www.latimes.com/ entertainment-arts/books/story/2020-11-12/burbank-unified-challenges-books -including-to-kill-a-mockingbird

Positive Action Staff. (2020, August 7). Social-emotional learning (SEL) standards in all 50 states. *Positive Action.* https://www.positiveaction.net/blog/sel-standards

Poulou, M. S. (2014). How are trait emotional intelligence and social skills related to emotional and behavioural difficulties in adolescents? *Educational Psychology, 34*(3), 354–366. https://doi.org/10.1080/01443410.2013.785062

Pratt, M. W., Arnold, M. L., & Lawford, H. (2009). Growing towards care: A narrative approach to prosocial moral identity and generativity of personality in emerging adulthood. In D. Narvaez & D. K. Lapsley (Eds.), *Personality, identity, and character: Explorations in moral psychology* (pp. 295–315). Cambridge University Press. https://doi.org/10.1017/CBO9780511627125.014

Pratt, M. W., Hunsberger, B., Pancer, S. M., & Alisat, S. (2003). A longitudinal analysis of personal values socialization: Correlates of a moral self-ideal in late adolescence. *Social Development, 12*(4), 563–585. https://doi.org/10.1111/1467-9507.00249

Pronk, J., Olthof, T., Aleva, E. A., Meulen, M., Vermande, M. M., & Goossens, F. A. (2020). Longitudinal associations between adolescents' bullying-related indirect defending, outsider behavior, and peer-group status. *Journal of Research on Adolescence, 30*, 87–99. https://doi.org/10.1111/jora.12450

Qualter, P., Vanhalst, J., Harris, R., Van Roekel, E., Lodder, G., Bangee, M., Maes, M., & Verhagen, M. (2015). Loneliness across the life span. *Perspectives on Psychological Science, 10*, 250–264.

Ragelienė, T. K. (2016). Links of adolescents identity development and relationship with peers: A systematic literature review. *Journal of the Canadian Academy of Child and Adolescent Psychiatry, 25*, 97–105. https://www.ncbi.nlm.nih.gov/pmc/articles/PMC4879949/

Raja, S. N., McGee, R., & Stanton, W. R. (1992). Perceived attachments to parents and peers and psychological well-being in adolescence. *Journal of Youth and Adolescence, 21*(4), 471–485. https://doi.org/10.1007/BF01537898

Recchia, H. E., Wainryb, C., Bourne, S., & Pasupathi, M. (2014). The construction of moral agency in mother–child conversations about helping and hurting across childhood and adolescence. *Developmental Psychology, 50*(1), 34–44.

Reis, H. T., Sheldon, K. M., Gable, S. L., Roscoe, J., & Ryan, R. M. (2000). Daily well-being: The role of autonomy, competence, and relatedness. *Personality & Social Psychology Bulletin, 26*(4), 419–435. https://doi.org/10.1177/0146167200266002

Reyes, M. R., Brackett, M. A., Rivers, S. E., White, M., & Salovey, P. (2012). Classroom emotional climate, student engagement, and academic achievement. *Journal of Educational Psychology, 104*(3), 700–712. http://dx.doi.org/10.1037/a0027268

Ribeiro, J. D., Franklin, J. C., Fox, K. R., Bentley, K. H., Kleiman, E.M., Chang, B. P., & Nock, M. K. (2016). Self-injurious thoughts and behaviors as risk factors for future suicide ideation, attempts, and death: A meta-analysis of longitudinal studies. *Clinical Psychology Review, 46*, 225–236.

Ric, F. (2004). Effects of the activation of affective information on stereotyping: When sadness increases stereotype use. *Personality & Social Psychology Bulletin, 30*(10), 1310–1321. https://doi.org/10.1177/0146167204264661

Rieffe, C., & Rooij, M. (2012). The longitudinal relationship between emotion awareness and internalising symptoms during late childhood. *European Child & Adolescent Psychiatry, 21*(6), 349–356. https://doi.org/10.1007/s00787-012-0267-8

Roach, A. (2018). Supportive peer relationships and mental health in adolescence: An integrative review. *Issues in Mental Health Nursing, 39*(9), 723–737. https://doi.org/10.1080/01612840.2018.1496498

Roekel, E., Goossens, L., Verhagen, M., Wouters, S., Engels, R. C. M. E., & Scholte, R. H. J. (2014). Loneliness, affect, and adolescents' appraisals of company: An experience sampling method study. *Journal of Research on Adolescence, 24*(2), 350–363. https://doi.org/10.1111/jora.12061

Rojas-Drummond, S., Mazon, N., Littleton, K., & Velez, M. (2014). Developing reading comprehension through collaborative learning. *Journal of Research in Reading, 37*, 138–158. https://doi.org/10.1111/j.1467-9817.2011.01526.x

Roorda, D. L., Koomen, H. M. Y., Spilt, J. L., & Oort, F. J. (2011). The influence of affective teacher–student relationships on students' school engagement and achievement: A meta-analytic approach. *Review of Educational Research, 81*(4), 493–529. https://doi.org/10.3102/0034654311421793

Rosenblatt, L. (1978). *The reader, the text, the poem: The transactional theory of the literary work.* Southern Illinois University Press.

Ryan, R. M., & Deci, E. L. (2000). Self-determination theory and the facilitation of intrinsic motivation, social development, and well-being. *American Psychologist, 55*, 68–78.

Saltzstein, H. D., & Takagi, Y. (2019). Some critical issues in the study of moral development. *International Journal of Developmental Science, 13*(1/2), 21–24. https://doi.org/10.3233/DEV-170244

Sandler, I. N., Wolchik, S., & Ayers, T. (2008). Resilience rather than recovery: A contextual framework on adaptation following bereavement. *Death Studies, 32*, 59–73.

Sarrionandia, A., Ramos-Díaz, E., & Fernández-Lasarte, O. (2018). Resilience as a mediator of emotional intelligence and perceived stress: A cross-country study. *Frontiers in Psychology, 9*(2653). https://doi.org/10.3389/fpsyg.2018.02653

Schaeffer, K. (2021, November 12). Among many U.S. children, reading for fun has become less common, federal data shows. *Pew Research Center.* https://www.pewresearch.org/short-reads/2021/11/12/among-many-u-s-children-reading-for-fun-has-become-less-common-federal-data-shows/

Schneider, T. R., Lyons, J. B., & Khazon, S. (2013). Emotional intelligence and resilience. *Personality & Individual Differences, 55*(8), 909–914. https://doi.org/10.1016/j.paid.2013.07.460

Seligman, M. E. P., Steen, T. A., Park, N., & Peterson, C. (2005). Positive psychology progress. *American Psychologist, 60*(5), 410–421.

Shah, J. Y., Kruglanski, A. W., & Thompson, E. P. (1998). Membership has its (epistemic) rewards: Need for closure effects on in-group bias. *Journal of Personality and Social Psychology Bulletin, 75*, 383–393.

Share, D. L. (1999). Phonological recoding and orthographic learning: A direct test of the self-teaching hypothesis. *Journal of Experimental Child Psychology, 72*(2), 95. https://doi.org/10.1006/jecp.1998.2481

Sharp, C. (2008). Theory of mind and conduct problems in children: Deficits in reading the "emotions of the eyes." *Cognition & Emotion, 22*(6), 1149–1158. https://doi.org/10.1080/02699930701667586

Shukla, M., Rasmussen, E. C., & Nestor, P. G. (2019). Emotion and decision-making: Induced mood influences IGT scores and deck selection strategies. *Journal of Clinical & Experimental Neuropsychology, 41*(4), 341–352. https://doi.org/10.1080/13803395.2018.1562049

Sims Bishop, R. (1990). Mirrors, windows, and sliding glass doors. *Perspectives on Psychological Science, 1*(3), ix–xi.

Skinner, E., Furrer, C., Marchand, G., & Kindermann, T. (2008). Engagement and disaffection in the classroom: Part of a larger motivational dynamic? *Journal of Educational Psychology, 100*(4), 765–781. https://doi.org/10.1037/a0012840

Sodian, B., Hulsken, C., & Thoermer, C. (2003). The self and action in theory of mind research. *Consciousness & Cognition, 12*(4), 777. https://doi.org/10.1016/S1053-8100(03)00082-5

Solomon, D., & Watson, M. (1996). Creating classrooms that students experience as communities. *American Journal of Community Psychology, 24*(6), 719. https://doi.org/10.1007/BF02511032

Somerville, L. H. (2013). Special issue on the teenage brain: Sensitivity to social evaluation. *Current Directions in Psychological Science, 22*, 121–127. http://dx.doi.org/10.1177/0963721413476512

Sparks, A. M., Fessler, D. M. T., & Holbrook, C. (2019). Elevation, an emotion for prosocial contagion, is experienced more strongly by those with greater expectations of the cooperativeness of others. *PLoS ONE, 14*(12), 1–29. https://doi.org/10.1371/journal.pone.0226071

Stanovich, K. E. (1992). Are we overselling literacy? In C. Temple & P. Collins (Eds.), *Stories and readers: New perspectives on literature in the classroom* (pp. 209–231). Christopher Gordon Publishers.

Stefanou, C. R., Perencevich, K. C., DiCintio, M., & Turner, J. C. (2004). Supporting autonomy in the classroom: Ways teachers encourage decision making and ownership. *Educational Psychologist, 39*(2), 97–110. https://doi.org/10.1207/s15326985ep3902_2

Steinhardt, M. A., Smith Jaggars, S. E., Faulk, K. E., & Gloria, C. T. (2011). Chronic work stress and depressive symptoms: Assessing the mediating role of teacher burnout. *Stress & Health: Journal of the International Society for the Investigation of Stress, 27*(5), 420–429. https://doi.org/10.1002/smi.1394

Stewart, W. F., Ricci, J. A., Chee, E., Hahn, S. R., & Morganstein, D. (2003a). Cost of lost productive work time among US workers with depression. *JAMA: Journal of the American Medical Association, 289*(23), 3135. https://doi.org/10.1001/jama.289.23.3135

Stewart, W. F., Ricci, J. A., Chee, E., & Morganstein, D. (2003b). Lost productive work time costs from health conditions in the United States: Results from the American productivity audit. *Journal of Occupational & Environmental Medicine, 45*(12), 1234–1246. https://doi.org/ 10.1097/01.jom.0000099999.27348.78

Stifter, C., Augustine, M., & Dollar, J. (2020). The role of positive emotions in child development: A developmental treatment of the broaden and build theory. *Journal of Positive Psychology, 15*(1), 89–94. https://doi.org/10.1080/17439760.2019.1695877

Sugarman, J., & Martin, J. (2011). Theorizing relational agency. *Journal of Constructivist Psychology, 24*(4), 283–289. https://doi.org/10.1080/10720537.2011.593455

Sun, J., Anderson, R. C., Perry, M., & Lin, T.-J. (2017). Emergent leadership in children's cooperative problem solving groups. *Cognition & Instruction, 35*, 212–235. https://doi.org/10.1080/07370008.2017.1313615

Taubman–Ben-Ari, O., Eherenfreund-Hager, A., & Findler, L. (2011). Mortality salience and positive affect influence adolescents' attitudes toward peers with physical disabilities: Terror management and broaden and build theories. *Death Studies, 35*(1), 1–21. https://doi.org/ 10.1080/07481187.2010.501012

TeacherVision. (n.d.). Character Traits List & Examples. https://www.teachervision.com/writing/character-traits-list-examples

Thaler, R. H., & Sunstein, C. R. (2008). *Nudge: Improving decisions about health, wealth, and happiness.* Yale University Press.

Thayer-Bacon, B. J. (1996). Relational qualities between selves and communities. *Journal for a Just & Caring Education, 2*(3), 283–303.

Tian, L., Du, M., & Huebner, E. (2015). The effect of gratitude on elementary school students' subjective well-being in schools: The mediating role of prosocial behavior. *Social Indicators Research, 122*(3), 887–904. https://doi.org/10.1007/s11205-014-0712-9

Todd, A. R., & Galinsky, A. D. (2014). Perspective-taking as a strategy for improving intergroup relations: Evidence, mechanisms, and qualifications. *Social & Personality Psychology Compass, 8,* 374–387. https://doi.org/10.1111/spc3.12116

Trickey, S., & Topping, K. J. (2004). "Philosophy for children": A systematic review. *Research Papers in Education, 19,* 365–380.

Trickey, S., & Topping, K. J. (2006). Collaborative philosophical enquiry for school children. *School Psychology International, 27,* 599–614.

Turkle, S. (2016). *Reclaiming conversation: The power of talk in a digital age.* Penguin.

Turner, R. H., & Killian, L. (1957). *Collective behavior.* Prentice Hall.

Umberson, D., & Montez, J. K. (2010). Social relationships and health: A flashpoint for health policy. *Journal of Health and Social Behavior, 51*(Suppl), S54–S66. http://dx.doi.org/10.1177/0022146510383501

Urada, D. I., & Miller, N. (2000). The impact of positive mood and category importance on crossed categorization effects. *Journal of Personality & Social Psychology, 78*(3), 417–433. https://doi.org/10.1037/0022-3514.78.3.417

Valenzuela, J. P., Gómez Vera, G., & Sotomayor, C. (2015). The role of reading engagement in improving national achievement: An analysis of Chile's 2000–2009 PISA results. *International Journal of Educational Development, 40,* 28–39. https://doi.org/10.1016/j.ijedudev.2014.11.011

van den Bos, E., de Rooij, M., Miers, A. C., Bokhorst, C. L., & Westenberg, P. M. (2014). Adolescents' increasing stress response to social evaluation: Pubertal effects on cortisol and alpha-amylase during public speaking. *Child Development, 85,* 220–236. http://dx.doi.org/10.1111/cdev.12118

Vlasova, H. (2023, March 22). What percent of high school graduates go to college? (Facts & Figures). *Admissionsly.* https://admissionsly.com/percentage-who-go-to-college/

Vuorinen, K., Hietajärvi, L., & Uusitalo, L. (2021). Students' usage of strengths and general happiness are connected via school-related factors. *Scandinavian Journal of Educational Research, 65*(5), 851–863.

Wang, M. T., & Fredricks, J. A. (2014). The reciprocal links between school engagement, youth problem behaviors, and school dropout during adolescence. *Child Development, 85*(2), 722–737. https://doi.org/10.1111/cdev.12138

Ward. A. (2021, January 21). Economic sociology with Anna Gifty Opoku-Agyeman and Steven Levitt [Ologies Podcast]. https://static1.squarespace.com/static/5998d8226f4ca3396027aae2/t/606f311cb8eef00cbea9d43a/1617899804607/Ologies+-+Economic+Sociology.pdf

Wegerif, R. (2005). Reason and creativity in classroom dialogues. *Language & Education: An International Journal, 19,* 223–237.

Wentzel, K. R. (1998). Social relationships and motivation in middle school: The role of parents, teachers, and peers. *Journal of Educational Psychology, 90*(2), 202–209.

West, C., & Tate, J. (2021, April 19). Howard University's removal of classics is a spiritual catastrophe. *The Washington Post.* https://www.washingtonpost.com /opinions/2021/04/19/cornel-west-howard-classics/

White, R. E., & Carlson, S. M. (2016). What would Batman do? Self-distancing improves executive function in young children. *Developmental Science, 19*(3), 419–426. https://doi.org/10.1111/desc.12314

Wolchik, S. A., Ma, Y., Tein, J., Sandler, I. N., & Ayers, T. S. (2008). Parentally bereaved children's grief: Self-system beliefs as mediators of the relations between grief and stressors and caregiver–child relationship quality. *Death Studies, 32,* 597–620.

Wood, A. M., Joseph, S., & Maltby, J. (2008). Gratitude uniquely predicts satisfaction with life: Incremental validity above the domains and facets of the five factor model. *Personality and Individual Differences, 45*(1), 49–54. https://doi .org/10.1016/j.paid.2008.02.019

Worden, J. W., & Silverman, P. R. (1996). Parental death and the adjustment of school-age children. *Omega: The Journal of Death and Dying, 33,* 91–102.

Wortham, S. (2004). The interdependence of social identification and learning. *American Educational Research Journal, 41,* 715–750.

Wortham, S. (2005). *Learning identity: The joint emergence of social identification and academic learning.* Cambridge University Press.

Worthy, J., Consalvo, A. L., Bogard, T., & Russell, K. W. (2012). Fostering academic and social growth in a primary literacy workshop classroom: "Restorying" students with negative reputations. *Elementary School Journal, 112*(4), 568–589.

Xiaoying, W., Anderson, R. C., Kim, N.-J., & Miller, B. (2013). Enhancing motivation and engagement through collaborative discussion. *Journal of Educational Psychology, 105,* 622–632. https://doi.org/10.1037/a0032792

Xin, Z., Anderson, R. C., Ting, D., Kim, N.-J., Yuan, L., Tzu-Jung, L., & Miller, B. (2013). Children's moral reasoning: Influence of culture and collaborative discussion. *Journal of Cognition & Culture, 13,* 503–522. https://doi .org/10.1163/15685373-12342106

Xu, J., Eggum-Wilkens, N. D., & Bradley, R. H. (2020). Children's friendship quality trajectories from middle childhood to early adolescence and prediction from sex. *Journal of Social & Personal Relationships, 37*(6), 1843–1851. https://doi .org/10.1177/0265407520910784

Yancey, K. B. (2009). The literacy demands of entering the university. In L. Christenbury, R. Bomer, & P. Smagorinksy (Eds.), *Handbook of adolescent literacy research* (pp. 256–270). Guilford Press.

Yeager, D. S., Fong, C. J., Lee, H. Y., & Espelage, D. L. (2015). Declines in efficacy of anti-bullying programs among older adolescents: Theory and a three-level meta-analysis. *Journal of Applied Developmental Psychology, 37,* 36–51. https://doi.org/10.1016/j.appdev.2014.11.005

Zalusky, S. (2022, April). *State of America's libraries.* American Library Association. https://www.ala.org/news/sites/ala.org.news/files/content/state-of-americas -libraries-special-report-pandemic-year-two.pdf

Zhao, J.-L., Cai, D., Yang, C.-Y., Shields, J., Xu, Z.-N., & Wang, C.-Y. (2020). Trait emotional intelligence and young adolescents' positive and negative affect: The mediating roles of personal resilience, social support, and prosocial behavior. *Child & Youth Care Forum, 49*(3), 431–448. https://doi.org/10.1007/s10566-019-09536-2

Index

Note: Page numbers followed by *n* and number represent end note and note number respectively.

About the Authors

Gay Ivey is the William E. Moran Distinguished Professor in Literacy at the University of North Carolina at Greensboro. She studies the contexts that support reading engagement among children and young adults and the positive consequences of that engagement for their literacy and lives. She has published many scholarly books and articles. She is a past president of the Literacy Research Association, recipient of the P. David Pearson Scholarly Influence Award, and a member of the Reading Hall of Fame.

Peter Johnston is professor emeritus at the University at Albany. His research explores relationships among children's engagement; their literate, social, and emotional development; and classroom talk. He has published many scholarly articles and books. Recognition for his work includes the Albert J. Harris Award from the International Literacy Association, the State University of New York Chancellor's Award for Excellence in Research, the Literacy Research Association's Oscar Causey Award for outstanding contributions to reading research, and the P. David Pearson Scholarly Influence Award. He is a member of the Reading Hall of Fame.